EAST ASIAN HISTORICAL MONOGRAPHS

General Editor: WANG GUNGWU

ADMINISTRATION IN THE FEDERATED MALAY STATES 1896-1920

Federation of Malaya and Singapore

ADMINISTRATION IN THE FEDERATED MALAY STATES 1896-1920

JAGJIT SINGH SIDHU

KUALA LUMPUR
OXFORD UNIVERSITY PRESS
OXFORD NEW YORK MELBOURNE
1980

Oxford University Press
OXFORD LONDON GLASGOW
NEW YORK TORONTO MELBOURNE WELLINGTON
KUALA LUMPUR SINGAPORE JAKARTA HONG KONG TOKYO
DELHI BOMBAY CALCUTTA MADRAS KARACHI
NAIROBI DAR ES SALAAM CAPE TOWN

● *Oxford University Press 1980*

ISBN 0 19 580432 5

*Printed by P. K. Ghosh at Eastend Printers,
3 Dr Suresh Sarkar Road, Calcutta 700 014
Published by Oxford University Press, 3 Jalan 13/3,
Petaling Jaya, Selangor, Malaysia*

To my Father

CONTENTS

ABBREVIATIONS

ADO	Assistant District Officer
CO	Colonial Office
CS	Chief Secretary
Col. Sec.	Colonial Secretary
Coll. & Mag.	Collector and Magistrate
DO	District Officer
FMJ	Federation Museums Journal
FMS	Federated Malay States
Govt.	Government
HC	High Commissioner
JIA	*Journal of the Indian Archipelago and Eastern Asia*
JMBRAS	*Journal of the Royal Asiatic Society, Malayan Branch*
JSBRAS	*Journal of the Royal Asiatic Society, Straits Branch*
JSEAH	*Journal of Southeast Asian History*
MAS	Malay Administrative Service
MCS	Malayan Civil Service
MJTG	*Malayan Journal of Tropical Geography*
OAG	Officer Administering the Government
PMS	*Papers on Malay Subjects*
PWD	Public Works Department
RG	Resident-General
RGO	Resident-General's Office
Rs.	Rupees
SGR	Selangor Government Records
SS	Straits Settlements
Sec.	Secretary

PREFACE

THE writing of Malaysian history has for decades been dominated almost exclusively by a group of men who were, directly or indirectly, members of the Malayan Civil Service. This was because they came fresh to an area where there was no historical tradition in the established sense. To the pre-twentieth century Malay history was not an art or a science but an entertainment. As such the emphasis was not on accuracy, completeness, or organized narrative but on the ability to interest and to infuse colour and fantasy into an otherwise drab description. Most of the early histories were unwritten, having been handed down from generation to generation by an oral tradition and could not be expected to be accurate or reliable. The earliest written history is the *Sejarah Melayu* or Malay Annals compiled in the fifteenth or sixteenth century. Of this and other Malay chronicles in general Wilkinson has said:

> We can easily criticise the various Malay histories and prove that their chronology is unreliable and that many of their legends are only echoes from Indian and Persian literature, but we need not, on that account, discard Malay chronicles as altogether worthless. *The Sejarah Melayu* has the merits and failings of all anecdotal history; it may often sacrifice truth to the point of a story or the interest of a pedigree, it adorns many anecdotes with unreliable details as to private interviews and secret conversations that could never have transpired, but it must be true to the ideas and to the spirit of its age. It gives us a very lifelike picture of the times. It tells us tales of the tyranny and profligacy of the old Malay Kings, of the corruption of the Court, of the bribery of the officials, of murders and judicial trials, of feuds, vendettas, intrigues and elopements, and of the attitude of the people to all these episodes. We may not be specially interested in the fate of 'Tun Mi Hairy Caterpillar' and other gentlemen of that sort,[1] but we are deeply concerned in the setting of the tales—the details that come out incidentally about etiquette, about houses and clothing, about judicial procedure, and about the government of the country. Such matters are of very real importance to the scientific historian who cares more about the condition of the people than about the biographies of individual Kings.[2]

More specifically, the *Sejarah Melayu* is a splendid account of the power and extent of the Malaccan Empire, the details of which are, to some extent, confirmed by Tomé Pires.[3] As a historical source its importance cannot be denied and represents the best contemporary description of the then society of Malacca.

The *Hikayat Merong Maha Wangsa*, more commonly known as the Kedah Annals, is not as significant, and according to Winstedt:

> Were it not for a colophon giving a list of Kedah Rulers, a preface copied from later recensions of the 'Malay Annals' and the borrowing of the Arabic title of those Chronicles, the Hikayat Merong (or Marong) Mahawangsa would never have been styled the 'Kedah Annals' or accepted as serious history.[4]

Of the later Malay histories the *Misa Melayu*[5] and the *Tuhfat-al-Nafis*[6] are the most important.[7] The former, written by Raja Chulan, is an interesting account of events in Perak during the late eighteenth century, especially in the reign of Sultan Iskandar (1750–64). It contains information on relations between Perak and the Dutch authorities in the Straits of Malacca, the Bugis in Selangor, and a long poem describing a trip around the coast of Perak by Sultan Iskandar. The *Tuhfat-al-Nafis* by Raja Ali Haji of Riau was begun in 1865 and although it contains brief accounts of the early history of Singapore, Malacca, and Johor based on oral traditions, it is mainly concerned with Riau and South Malayan history from the end of the seventeenth century until the early 1860s. There is, however, some information on Selangor, the Dutch, English, and Bugis, and there are a number of interesting genealogical trees. It differs from the other Malay chronicles in that it was written with a sense of awareness of sources which are not always accepted uncritically.

The early British accounts of Malaya were rather restricted in that they were concerned primarily with affairs in the Straits Settlements. The Malay States were important only in so far as they affected the well-being and the security of the Colony. The writings of Anderson, Begbie, Crawfurd, Low, Newbold, and Raffles fall largely into this category.[8] With the introduction of the Residential System, and more direct involvement of British officials in the affairs of the Malay States, greater attention was focused on the Peninsula itself. The works of Wilkinson and Winstedt cover a whole series of issues ranging from language, history, economics, culture, arts and crafts, law, and religion. The latter has indeed been referred to as the greatest of the 'colonial' scholars of Malaya whose interest in Malay affairs was both comprehensive and penetrating.[9] Of the writings concerned with the establishment and growth of British rule in nineteenth-century Malaya Swettenham's contributions are the most relevant. In his book *British Malaya*[10] he attempts to explain the rationale behind the British decision to intervene and describes in detail the conditions that prevailed in the Peninsula, the features of the country, and the character of the people. The evolution of an administrative system and the workings of the Residential System culminating in the signing of the Federation Agreement is discussed in full. The account is invaluable in the sense that it was written by an official intimately involved in all the major decisions taken during the period. On the other hand, because Swettenham himself was in many instances the architect of British policy in the Protected Malay States, the book tends to glorify uncritically the amount of progress made and is therefore highly subjective. But so long as this latter point is borne in mind Swettenham's contributions to the store of historical knowledge should not be minimized. There has been a tendency with some historians to dismiss the contributions of British administrators as being inaccurate, biased, and therefore needing radical reinterpretation[11] but although some shift of emphasis might be in order it would be imprudent to relegate these works to the realm of fiction.

Professionally trained historians only turned their attention to Malayan issues in the twentieth century. Initially, between 1920 and about 1950, the bulk of their work concentrated on the history of the country during the nineteenth century. There were two significant reasons for this, firstly, that this was the period when British activities in the Peninsula gained momentum, and, secondly, because the mass of the research materials, aided no doubt by the Colonial Office fifty-year rule, related to that period. The first important contribution in this category is L. A. Mills' work, *British Malaya*,[12] which records in detail the administrative growth and the development of the Straits Settlements, and discusses relations between the British authorities and the Peninsular States in the decades before intervention. The succeeding events are taken up by C. N. Parkinson in his book on British intervention[13] which looks at the phenomenon from the standpoint of the British Empire as a whole. According to him, the developments in the Malayan region were only part of a broader pattern of Imperialistic activity which have to be viewed in the context of securing a safe British maritime route between Europe and Asia. As a naval historian it was perhaps only natural for Parkinson to lay special emphasis on the importance of sea power. A somewhat different interpretation of the same subject is advanced by Professor C. D. Cowan.[14] His book is concerned with the origins of British political control within the framework of policy as formulated by the Colonial Office in London, and the reactions of the authorities in the Straits Settlements. Particular attention is drawn to the reluctance

of the decision makers in England to get involved in greater territorial responsibilities at the instigation of Straits Chinese or British
speculators; but Cowan also points out that in circumstances where
local disorders threatened British supremacy in the area Whitehall
was prepared to assume wider obligations. The book also discusses
the tendency among some officials, like the Governor, Andrew
Clarke (November 1873 – May 1875), to embark on vigorous and
independent action on their own initiative, only afterwards reporting
the matter to the Colonial Office. Finally, the beginnings and the
early development of the Residential system are considered and
analysed.

The evolution of the Residential System from intervention to the
Federation Agreement has been treated by E. Sadka.[15] The shaping
of imperial policy and strategy, and the part played by local administrators in the matter of intervention, are thoroughly investigated.
The author considers the development of the governmental system,
communications, the formulation of immigration, labour, and land
policies. The study contains an interesting discussion of the manner
in which the Secretary of State, the Governor of the Straits Settlements, and the Residents exercised authority in the Protected Malay
States that were, nominally at least, under advice. The extent to
which Malay Rulers, chiefs, and other indigenous authorities affected
the process of decision making is examined in detail, and an analysis
is given of economic policies and their effect on economic development and social change.

A Malaysian trained in Australia, Chai Hon Chan, attempts in
his book[16] to do something more than merely describe the political
and economic aspects of British Colonial policy by drawing together
subjects like labour and education, medical research, the rubber
industry, tin mining, the development of communications, currency,
immigration policies, and constitutional reforms.

The political and economic history of the nineteenth-century
Malay States where British interest was most pronounced has been
adequately studied. A recent work by another Malaysian historian,
Khoo Kay Kim,[17] adds considerably to the body of literature already
published on the nineteenth century. It differs from its predecessors
in that it concentrates on Malayan events and personalities and
endeavours to view developments in the Peninsula from a local
standpoint. The emphasis is placed on Malay politics and how these
were influenced by the rapidly changing economic circumstances,
and on the role of Chinese merchants and miners in the ensuing

events. The activities of Straits Settlements British commercial interests, and the interaction between European and Chinese financiers on the one hand, and the Malay ruling *élite* on the other, and the changes thus brought about, are also well reviewed.

Twentieth-century Malayan history, however, has been less fortunate. The paucity of historical writing on the period before the outbreak of the Second World War in 1941 is both striking and disappointing. The best study on the four decades is a book which was first published as long ago as 1937.[18] The American author, Rupert Emerson, caused a stir at that time because of his radical interpretation of British colonial policy. The work was vehemently criticized by retired British Civil Servants like Swettenham and Peel[19] who alleged that the study was prejudiced against Imperialism and lacked judgement and perspective. Emerson contends that colonialism, as manifested in the Malay States, had concentrated on the development of Imperial trade and capitalist interests and had ignored the welfare of the Malays. In many ways these views were ahead of their times but the validity of Emerson's conclusions can be measured by the fact that they have been widely accepted by contemporary Malay opinion.[20] In the context of Federated Malay States history, the greatest value of the book lies in its discussion of 'Decentralisation' between 1920 and 1933. At the time when the controversy about decentralization reached its peak in 1932 it was fortunate that Emerson was visiting Malaya, as he was able to collect material which might otherwise have been difficult to obtain, especially oral information. In the circumstances it was hardly surprising that the major part of the section in the book on the Federation concerns itself with decentralization, and it skims over the first twenty years of the twentieth century.

It is, therefore, with the intention of filling this obvious gap that this book has been written. It is an attempt to offer a detailed study of British administrative methods from the Treaty of Federation, 1896, until the arrival of Sir Laurence Guillemard as Governor and High Commissioner in 1920, and to discuss how these developments affected the Malay aristocracy and, more importantly, the Malay masses in the States that made up the Federation. The period is significant, not only because it has never been satisfactorily studied, but also because of the important changes and innovations that occurred in those years. In writing the book every effort has been made to be as objective as possible and if some of the conclusions are considered to be unfair to the Colonial authorities they represent the sincere opinion of the author after a detailed study of the facts. Of course the approach to the subject has, doubtless, been influenced by the fact that the author is a Malaysian national, but he has always tried to keep any subjective bias to the background, and, as far as possible, to support his conclusions by the presentation of the available evidence.

In the completion of this study I am most grateful to the generosity of the Universiti Sains Malaysia which awarded me a Senior Staff Research Fellowship and granted me two years' leave of absence. In particular I owe a debt to the University's first Vice-Chancellor, Tan Sri Datuk Hamzah Sendut, for his personal encouragement and constant sympathy. Much of the research was undertaken in London and would not have been possible but for the helpfulness and co-operation of the staff at the Public Record Office, the British Museum, and the School of Oriental and African Studies Library. There are a number of other individuals to whom I should always be grateful but it would be impossible for me to name all of them. Professors Wang Gungwu, K. G. Tregonning, and Eunice Thio were largely responsible for introducing me to the subject of Malaysian history and for spurring me on. To Dr. J. S. Bastin and Professor C. D. Cowan who contributed constructive criticism, comment and sound advice through the various stages of the draft I owe a special and lasting debt. For all the errors and shortcomings in the book the blame, however, is solely mine.

1. Tun Mi Ulat Bulu: a nickname for one of the nobles at the Court of Sultan Mahmud Shah of Malacca.

2. R. J. Wilkinson, 'Literature: History', *PMS* I, 1907, pp. 33–4.

3. Zainal Abidin bin Abdul Wahid, 'Glimpses of the Malaccan Empire—I', in Zainal Abidin bin Abdul Wahid (ed.), *Glimpses of Malaysian History*, Kuala Lumpur, 1970, p. 18.

4. R. O. Winstedt, 'A History of Malay Literature', *JMBRAS*, Vol. XXII, Part 3 (1939); rev. ed., *JMBRAS*, Vol. XXXI, June 1958, p. 110.

5. Raja Chulan bin Raja Hamid, *Misa Melayu* (ed.) R. O. Winstedt, Singapore, 1919.

6. Raja Ali al-Haji Riau, *Tuhfat al-Nafis*, Singapore, 1965.

7. For a more complete list of Malay Sources, see J. C. Bottoms, 'Malay Sources', in K. G. Tregonning (ed.), *Malaysian Historical Sources*, Singapore, 1962, pp. 36–62.

8. J. Anderson, *Political and Commercial Considerations relative to the Malayan Peninsula and the British Settlements in the Straits of Malacca*, Prince of Wales Island, 1824; facsimile reprint *JMBRAS*, Vol. XXXV, No. 4, 1962;

P. J. Begbie, *The Malayan Peninsula* . . ., Madras, 1834; reprinted Kuala Lumpur, 1967; J. Crawfurd, *Journal of an Embassy from the Governor General of India to the Courts of Siam and Cochin China* . . ., London, 1828; reprinted Kuala Lumpur, 1967; J. Low, 'An Account of the Origin and Progress of the British Colonies in the Straits of Malacca', *JIA*, Vol. III, 1849; J. Low, 'On the Ancient Connections between Kedah and Siam', *JIA*, Vol. V, 1851; T. J. Newbold, *Political and Statistical Account of the British Settlements in the Straits of Malacca*, London, 1839; reprinted Kuala Lumpur, 1971, 2 vols.; Lady Raffles, *Memoir of the Life and Public Services of Sir Thomas Stamford Raffles* . . ., London, 1830.

9. J. S. Bastin, 'Problems of Personality in the Reinterpretation of Modern Malayan History', in *Malayan and Indonesian Studies* (eds.) J. S. Bastin and R. Roolvink, Oxford, 1964.

10. F. A. Swettenham, *British Malaya*, London, 1906; rev. ed. London, 1948.

11. The controversy was triggered by an article by K. G. Tregonning, 'A New Approach to Malayan History', *The Straits Times*, 21 and 24 November 1958. The argument was later joined by J. S. Bastin, *The Study of Modern Southeast Asian History*, An Inaugural Lecture delivered on 14 December 1959 at the University of Malaya, Kuala Lumpur, 1959; D. P. Singhal, 'Some Comments on Western Element in Modern Southeast Asian History', *JSEAH*, Vol. 1, No. 2, 1960, pp. 118–23; J. W. R. Smail, 'On the Possibility of an autonomous history of Modern Southeast Asia', *JSEAH*, Vol. 2, No. 2, 1961, pp. 72–102; G. I. T. Machin, 'Colonial Post Mortem: a survey of the historical controversy', *JSEAH*, Vol. 3, No. 2, 1962, pp. 129–38; Bastin, *Malayan and Indonesian Studies*; Zainal Abidin bin Abdul Wahid, 'Some Aspects of Malay History', *Journal of the Historical Society, University of Malaya*, Vol. IV, 1965–6; R. Bonney, 'Towards a Malaysian History', *Journal of the Historical Society, University of Malaya*, Vol. IV, 1965–6; Khoo Kay Kim, 'J. W. W. Birch, A Victorian Moralist in Perak's Augean Stables', *Journal of the Historical Society, University of Malaya*, Vol. IV, 1965–6; J. de V. Allen, 'J. W. W. Birch and the Writing of Malaysian History', *Journal of the Historical Society, University of Malaya*, Vol. V, 1966–7; Syed Hussein Alatas, 'Theoretical Aspects of Southeast Asian History', *Journal of the Historical Society, University of Singapore*, 1968–9.

12. L. A. Mills, 'A History of British Malaya, 1824–1867', *JMBRAS*, Vol. III, Part 2, 1925; reprinted *JMBRAS*, Vol. XXXIII, Part 3, 1960; edited as a book with an Introduction by D. K. Bassett and bibliography by C. M. Turnbull, Kuala Lumpur, 1966.

13. C. N. Parkinson, *British Intervention in Malaya, 1867–1877*, Singapore, 1960.

14. C. D. Cowan, *Nineteenth Century Malaya*, London, 1961.

15. E. Sadka, *The Protected Malay States, 1874–1895*, Kuala Lumpur, 1968; reprinted Kuala Lumpur, 1970.

16. Chai Hon Chan, *The Development of British Malaya 1896–1909*, Kuala Lumpur, 1964; reprinted Kuala Lumpur, 1967.

17. Khoo Kay Kim, *The Western Malay States 1850–1873*, Kuala Lumpur, 1972.

18. R. Emerson, *Malaysia: A Study in Direct and Indirect Rule*, London, 1937, reprinted Kuala Lumpur, 1964.

19. Sir William Peel was a former Chief Secretary to the Government of the FMS.

20. See J. S. Bastin's Introduction to Emerson, *Malaysia*, 1964 edition.

B

I

THE SETTING

The Malay Peninsula, later called British Malaya, and known today as West Malaysia, stretches from latitude 1°20′ N to latitude 6°40′ N and from longitude 99°35′ E to longitude 104°20′ E and is linked to mainland Asia in the north by the Kra Isthmus. The country occupies an area of 50,886 square miles and is dominated by a mountainous core of eight roughly parallel ranges aligned from north to south. Unlike its northern neighbours Burma, Thailand, and Indo-China, West Malaysia does not have any large or extensive plains and whatever flat land there is lies between the mountainous centre and the coast on either side of the Peninsula. These coastal plains occur mostly on the west and average some twenty miles in width, reaching their maximum in the lower reaches of the Perak and Bernam Rivers where the alluvium extends forty miles inland.[1] It is with the three west-coast states of Perak, Selangor, and Negri Sembilan, and the east-coast state of Pahang that this study is primarily concerned.[2]

During the nineteenth century in the period before direct political intervention by Great Britain, the population pattern of the peninsula was a fairly simple one. Wandering groups of aborigines, whose economies were centred on hunting, the gathering of forest produce, and on shifting padi cultivation, lived in the coastal swamps and on the jungle-covered slopes. It is difficult to fix with any degree of accuracy the number of aborigines, but Newbold, writing in the 1830s, estimated that there were 9,000 spread over the country.[3] Apart from the aborigines the other major population group was the Malays whose distribution followed an arrangement dictated by the physical features of the land. Heavy and uniform tropical rainfall over the centuries has given rise to a multiplicity of rivers and streams flowing east and west from the central mountains into the South China Sea and the Straits of Malacca; these waterways are narrow and swift in their upper reaches, and slow and meandering in the broader flat plains, and although neither the Pahang nor the Perak Rivers are navigable for large vessels, small craft use them freely. Malay settlements were drawn to these rivers in the lowlands and the coastal areas partly because they represented the easiest lines of movement and partly because wet padi cultivation, the basis of Malay agriculture, required the presence of flat, irrigable land near convenient sources of water. The sea and rivers were also natural sources of fish, and the rivers served as bathing and washing places in addition to providing water for drinking and cooking. These considerations therefore attracted the Malays to sites near the sea and the rivers, and the majority settled in the riverine, deltaic, and estuarine areas. The mouths of rivers were particularly favoured as they reflected strategic locations which commanded all movement along the coast and rivers.[4] The Malay economy was largely a subsistence one founded on padi, with fishing as the main supplement.[5] There was no pressure on land and the economy possessed a flexibility which solved increases in the population by bringing more land under cultivation.[6]

In its traditional form the largest Malay political unit was the State. This consisted, typically, of the basin of a large river or of a group of adjacent rivers, encompassing an area stretching from the coast inland to the central watershed. Normally, the capital of the State was built on a spot where the principal river met the sea and which allowed the Ruler not only to control movement in and out of the territory and defend it against hostile enemy attacks, but also effectively impose export and import taxes.[7] The Ruler was the most powerful and significant personality within the State and was variously referred to as *Yang-di-Pertuan*, Raja, or Sultan. He did not, however, embody an exceptional concentration of administrative authority because there were a number of district chiefs who could, and often did, challenge his supremacy. In practice the Sultan controlled a royal district which he administered in much the same way as a district chief supervised his district. What made the Ruler superior was that he symbolized and preserved the unity of the States as a whole, and although there often existed forces of conflict and disintegration, considerations of trade, defence, and the need for law and order emphasized this wider role as well as the office of the Sultanate. In the day-to-day business of government the Sultan relied on the advice of an informal body of counsellors who were either of royal or non-royal descent and whose functions varied from administrative and military to ceremonial.[8]

Outside the confines of the royal district the crucial political personage was the district chief. Although appointed in the first instance by the Sultan, he exercised total control over his district and its population. He collected his own taxes and dominated the area by virtue of his own strength rather than that of the Sultan. His followers included volunteers and mercenaries, debt bondsmen, and women in bondage. The males formed the bodyguard and the fighting force which kept the district secure and followed the chief on his journeys. The women performed domestic functions and acted as the mistresses and potential wives of the entourage.[9]

If the Sultan was the apex of the political system then the masses or *raiat* were its base. The Malay social structure was an intrinsic part of the political edifice and divided the population into those who ruled—and therefore constituted the privileged and élite minority—and those whose very survival was contingent on their ability and willingness to serve their masters. This system of values which underlined the subservience of the masses to the aristocracy also extended to the economic sphere. The source of all economic initiative and leadership was the ruling clique, which formed the entrepreneurial class and predetermined exports, imports, and investments. It was the impelling force in Malay society and commanded the development of the social system until it was undermined and replaced by a British-type administration.[10]

The absolute ideal of the position of the Malay rulers was, of course, embodied in the Malacca Sultanate (*c.* 1400–1511) to which during the ensuing centuries the Malays frequently looked back. The establishment of the Malaccan Empire marked the culmination of a process which had begun with the growth of a number of city states in the region of the Isthmus of Kra.[11] The commercial prosperity and strategic position of Malacca[12] attracted the attention of the Portuguese who captured it in 1511 in an effort to establish a monopoly of the valuable spice trade.[13] Contrary to their expectations traders and merchants at first deserted and avoided Malacca and founded alternative trading centres in the northern Malay Peninsula and Sumatra. By the time they began drifting back the Portuguese were a spent power, and in 1641, another European mercantile giant, Holland, captured Malacca and hoped to restore its past grandeur and, by doing so, create for itself a monopolistic trading position in the Straits of Malacca. The Dutch were determined to secure control of the tin and spice trade and eliminate all other competition. For the next one hundred and fifty years or so they tried to impose their supremacy along the coasts of Malaya, while the interior of the country became a battle ground for invaders from Thailand, Aceh, and Menangkabau, each group attempting to snatch and control as much territory as it could lay its hands on.[14]

The first British settlement in the Malayan area was at Penang, founded by Francis Light in 1786. It was meant to be an entrepôt as well as a maritime base and its rapid development dealt a virtual death blow to the Dutch in Malacca and along the coast. British forces attacked and captured Malacca in 1795 and stayed there till 1818 when the settlement was returned to the Dutch. The Anglo-Dutch Treaty of 1824, however, resulted in the town and environs becoming permanently British. Meanwhile in 1819 Sir Stamford Raffles acquired the island of Singapore for the East India Company and the three British Settlements together with Province Wellesley, obtained by cession from the Sultan of Kedah in 1800, and the Dindings, which came under British control in 1826, amalgamated to form the Straits Settlements. In 1858 the Company handed over jurisdiction of the Colony to the India Office, but later, in 1867, due largely to local British agitation, the Colonial Office was persuaded to assume direct administrative responsibility over the area.[15]

Throughout the first half of the nineteenth century the British in the Straits Settlements showed little interest in what was happening in the Malay States. They were more concerned with the commercial and strategic importance of their possessions *vis-à-vis* the India–China trade. There was also the reluctance to take on extra-territorial obligations which could turn out to be uneconomic and might arouse the interest of other European colonial powers in imperialist ventures.[16] This general policy, however, was not strictly adhered to by British administrators on the spot who, in their desire to remove trade barriers erected by Malay and other European monopolies, actively interfered in the affairs of the Peninsula. For example, the actions of indigenous rulers to exercise what they regarded as their traditional rights to levy taxes on trading vessels, were referred to as acts of piracy and the British navy was often used to prevent this.[17] Also, local government officials in the Straits Settlements found it advisable to counteract the possibility of Thailand extending her political influence and suzerainty further south of Kedah, Kelantan, and Trengganu. This they did by concluding a number of agreements which excluded Thailand from meddling in the affairs of those Malay States south of the Kedah–Kelantan boundary, prevented the Malay States from interfering in each other's affairs, and virtually invested in the British authorities the power to conduct the foreign affairs of the States.[18]

After 1867 a new, more positive British attitude towards the Malay States began to emerge. The prime advocates of this changed stance were the Governor of the Straits Settlements, Sir Harry St. George Ord (April 1867 – September 1873),[19] and his second in command, Lieutenant-Colonel A. E. H. Anson.[20] The disturbed conditions in some of the Malay States, especially Selangor and Perak, and a change in the thinking of influential Colonial Office administrators, provided added encouragement to the proponents of a forward policy in the Malay States.[21] The Pangkor Engagement of 20 January 1874, concluded between the chiefs of Perak and the representatives of the British Government, marked the culmination of the new mood and the beginning of a fresh British initiative in the Peninsula. By May 1875 British Residents were appointed to Perak, Selangor, and Sungei Ujong, and the process was extended to Pahang in 1877–8 and the remainder of Negri Sembilan[22] between 1883 and 1887.[23]

A major reason for the external challenge to established Malay traditional systems was probably the accumulation of trading capital in the Straits Settlements from the second quarter of the nineteenth century onwards. The capital, both European and Chinese, was in the hands of individuals like W. H. Read, J. G. Davidson, Tan Kim Cheng, and W. T. Lewis,[24] and companies like Paterson, Simons and Company, the Tanjong Pagar Dock Company, and the Eastern Asia Telegraph Company who were anxious to discover new, convenient and profitable outlets for financial investment.[25] The Malay States were particularly attractive because they possessed a number of products, such as tin, sought after by both Europe and the surrounding Asian countries. At the beginning, the increased trade and commerce was welcomed by the ruling Malay élite who stood to reap significant financial rewards as a consequence of the authority they exercised over their economies. But as competition increased among Straits merchants as well as among the Malay ruling class itself, tensions began to develop and political conflict resulted. From the 1850s onwards the problem was compounded when a new element of discord was introduced in the form of a substantially increasing Chinese population.[26] In spite of these problems, Straits capital continued to flow into the Malayan hinterland and speculators anxious to safeguard their investments sought more active support from the British Government, tried to establish better relations with influential Malay chiefs, and were willing to do all they could to guarantee the supremacy of such chiefs.[27]

Although political considerations played an important part in the final decision to intervene, the prospects of large-scale economic development within the Malay States featured large in the British plans. British economic policies were geared to the long-term aims of establishing a large number of successful agricultural enterprises, and modernizing the tin mining industry by the injection of highly capitalized European companies with up-to-date equipment and improved techniques. The methods used to achieve these goals included a variety of liberal policies, supplemented by the rapid development of public works, and the establishment of an efficient communications system. The implementation of more detailed economic measures was left in the hands of individual British Residents who, because of their relative isolation, had wide powers and could act as they pleased.[28] Capitalists were encouraged to invest, concessions of land were freely given out, Government revenues paid for the construction of public works and railways, and cash loans were made available at low rates of interest. Much emphasis was placed on agriculture because the British were anxious to establish an alternative to tin, the supply of which, it was feared, would soon be exhausted.[29]

The exploitation of the economy was, however, handicapped by the existence of a small Malay population unwilling to desert its traditional habitat or abandon its customary occupations. The government tried to solve the serious labour problem by adopting an open immigration policy designed to attract workers from the over-populated land masses of China and India. As a general rule the rate of Chinese immigration depended very much on the state of the Malayan economy and the consequent demand for labour.[30] Mention has already been made of the size of the Chinese population in the Malay States before 1874, but it needs to be realized that during much of that period the Chinese had come in spite of the opposition and hostility of the Chinese government to emigration. The first change in this official attitude took place in 1860 when the Anglo-Chinese Convention permitted Chinese citizens to negotiate labour contracts in British territories as soon as regulations between the two governments had been agreed upon. In 1866 a Draft Convention attended by representatives from Britain, France, and China drew up these regulations which, as it turned out, were acceptable only to the Chinese. Britain and France rejected them on the grounds that emigration could only take place under official Chinese supervision and any unauthorized acts carried the death sentence.[31] Those emigrants leaving at their own expense and initiative were free to do what they pleased, but those indebted for their passages had to enter into contracts in China which spelt out in detail the place and length of employment; hours per day and days per year to be worked, wages, food, lodging, and medical facilities to be provided; and the amount of money which the emigrant proposed to remit monthly to China.[32]

When the Straits Settlements were separated from India in 1867, the subject of Chinese immigration began to attract more and more official concern. By that time serious abuses had come to light so far as the mechanics of this movement was concerned and several newly arrived labourers were known to have disappeared without trace.[33] A petition was sent to the Government in 1873 which alleged the kidnapping of *sin-khehs*, or new arrivals, asked for legislation to outlaw such acts, and requested the setting up of depots where immigrants could be temporarily lodged. An immigration law was enacted in 1873 but was opposed by the business community and was not implemented. In 1876 a Commission appointed to investigate the situation concluded that the system was satisfactory in the case of immigrants in the Straits Settlements, but its other recommendations resulted in the enactment of two laws in 1877, the Chinese Immigrants Ordinance and the Crimping Ordinance. The first Ordinance established a Chinese Protectorate to supervise the landing of Chinese immigrants, the conclusion of labour contracts, and keep a check on secret society activities.[34] The Crimping Ordinance dealt with the abuse of kidnapping labourers for service in the Dutch Settlements, and prohibited, in the absence of a licence from the Protector, the signing of contracts for service outside the Colony.[35] Further laws were passed in 1880, 1882, and 1883 which tried to strengthen British control over Chinese immigration but these Bills remained dead letters and were not effectively enforced.[36]

The process of Chinese immigration consisted of *sin-khehs* being recruited in South China by Chinese recruiters who made a small profit from the business.[37] Most of the newcomers eventually found their way to the tin mines of the Malay States, there being a considerable amount of movement from one mining area to another. In 1879 most of the Perak mines were located in Larut and were worked, theoretically, on the 'truck system' whereby 90 per cent of the tin produced went to the labourers and the remainder to the mine owners who also supplied the labourers with food and stores at mining prices which were normally about twice as much as the market rates. In practice, when the time came for settlement, and this was an annual affair at Chinese New Year, more often than not the labourers found themselves in debt to the mine owners and were obliged to work for another year, and still another if they did not get out of debt. The punishment for absconding was flogging but since communications were difficult, escape from a mining site was generally impossible and never easy. Conditions of living were primitive, working hours long, and amusements few and far between. With the discovery, however, of tin in Kinta and the resulting demand for labour, Larut mining employees ran away in their hundreds to take up employment in the new, if smaller, mines under different Chinese employers. As new roads and bridle tracks increased in number, absconding became an easier proposition and labour conditions, as a result, improved. A Secretary for Chinese Affairs, later called Protector, was appointed in Perak in 1883 and in Selangor in 1890, who introduced, in the interests of Chinese capitalists, a registration system.[38]

The Chinese also dominated nineteenth-century agricultural enterprises in Malaya and this was particularly so in Perak where the influx of Chinese sugar planters into Krian began in 1877. They were encouraged by the policies of the British Resident, Hugh Low,[39] and his hard-working District Officer in Krian, Noel Dennison. Till 1881 the pioneer sugar planters were given land rent-free and they concentrated their activities along the Krian River above Parit Buntar, along the Kurau River, and at Bagan Tiang. In 1881 twelve Chinese owned sugar estates covering over 10,000 acres operated in Krian and this monopoly was preserved until 1883. The first successful European sugar enterprise was the Gula Estate launched by W. V. Drummond of Shanghai and administered by the Perak Sugar Cultivation Company Limited. No other European ventures met with any success until the 1890s.[40] In 1891 Perak had four European owned estates, three of which grew coffee and one sugar cane. The British presence in Selangor was more imposing, and involved the planting of Liberian coffee. The first of the coffee plantations was the Weld Hill Estate in Kuala Lumpur, started in 1881 and occupying an area of 194 acres. By 1893 European-owned estates numbered seventy-two, occupied an area of 10,835 acres, and employed eighty-eight Malays, forty-eight Chinese, and four hundred and sixty-five Indians.[41] The majority of the planters had come from Ceylon where their coffee estates had been ruined by leaf disease.[42]

Although the flow of British capital into Malaya was slow in arriving Chinese financial enterprises and Chinese labourers were quick to take advantage of the stable conditions ensured by British protection. This trend became more pronounced as more and more jungle was cleared, roads constructed, mines expanded, and plantations established. The majority of the Chinese immigrants arrived penniless and came from inferior social backgrounds. Their main ambition was to earn and save as much money as possible and then return to their homeland. The British attitude to this was, from the beginning, one of removing all restrictions on immigration and they regarded the Chinese 'fitted by their character and predilections to act as the working bees of the hive'.[43] The whole aspect of the Chinese influx seemed to be governed by the natural law of the survival of the fittest. Chinese participation in Malaya was an outstanding success and the newcomers were able to thrive and prosper in complete freedom. The urgent need for labour assured for them a warm welcome from the British who allowed the Chinese to enjoy their new-found wealth without in any way being harassed.[44]

Under British rule tin production in the Malay States continued to expand and in 1898 a sharp increase in the price of the metal triggered off a new boom and, with it, an unprecedented demand for Chinese labour. Various measures were suggested with a view to maintaining an adequate supply, including the introduction of immigrants by means of steamers, specially chartered for the purpose, plying direct between China and ports in the Federated Malay States; assisting immigration by arranging with steamship companies in China for cheap deck passages from Singapore to Port Dickson, Klang, and Telok Anson; the granting of Government loans to employers of Chinese labour to assist them in importing *sin-khehs*; and paying importers of Chinese labour a cash bonus per head of arrivals.[45] Nothing concrete resulted from these proposals, and in December 1899 arrangements were made by Frank Swettenham, the Resident-General, and some Chinese merchants in Singapore to form a steamship company to trade with Chinese ports and to import Chinese immigrants direct from China to the Federated Malay States. The only hitch was the prejudice and suspicion of the Chinese government authorities.[46] The British Consul in Canton, B. C. George-Scott, considered the plan but could not recommend it for fear that it would reopen the whole question of emigration to the Straits Settlements, a traffic which, from the Chinese point of view, was replete with abuses.[47] In spite of these problems the Chinese population of the Federation increased by 257,629 in the ten years 1891 to 1901.[48]

The failure of Government-initiated or sponsored schemes to attract Chinese labour did not deter G. T. Hare, the Secretary for Chinese Affairs, from proposing, in August 1902, the introduction of Chinese agricultural colonies into the country. With the Colonial Office's approval, arrangements were made in March 1903 to assist Dr. H. L. E. Luehring of the American Episcopalian Mission to obtain Chinese agricultural families and settle them in Sitiawan, Perak.[49] Luehring left Singapore in May of that year and, as a result of his mission in Foochow, returned with 363 immigrants composed of 236 males, 72 females, and 55 children.[50] Although these colonists possessed little ready cash they soon began to prosper. On their arrival they occupied seven large communal houses constructed for them by the Government. With fifty or more people to one house some sickness and numerous quarrels were inevitable, but within a year most of the inhabitants built houses on their own land and moved out of the communal blocks. The concession occupied 2,700 acres of land covered with jungle. This was surveyed into lots of about three acres each and distributed to the colonists. Some of the land was high and dry so that the men could build and begin planting, but the rest was swampy and under two or three feet of water. The Government planned to cut drains through the swamps and it was hoped that padi could eventually be grown there. The high land was suitable for *gutta percha*, coconuts, and a little plant called *nilam* from the leaves of which a very expensive scent was manufactured.[51] The people were very industrious, constructed a good-sized smithy, a large vermicelli factory, made agricultural tools, and kept pigs, poultry, and cattle.[52] In January 1904 they even opened a Chinese school with twenty-two pupils on its roll and obtained a teacher from Foochow, Ling Ding Jug.[53]

Government participation in the mechanics of Chinese immigration, however, remained minimal. The main official organization concerned with Chinese affairs was the Chinese Protectorate which, in Malaya, occupied a unique position. The Protectorate consisted of Chinese-speaking officers of the Civil Service who dealt with problems such as the suppression of secret societies and the protection of Chinese immigrants, and was the channel of communication between the Government and the Chinese community.[54] In the first decade of the twentieth century the problem most widely discussed was the importation of indentured Chinese labour. The trend was towards the declining popularity of this category of labour, reflected by the fact that whereas 7,462 such workers had arrived in 1900 the figure for 1909 was only 864. Chinese mining employers were against the system because improved communications resulted in increased absconding, with the result that by 1910 the indentured labourer had virtually disappeared.[55] The only area where this type of labour remained significant were the sugar plantations in Krian and those European coffee and rubber estates which relied on Chinese labour contractors. The form of contract signed by the *sin-kheh* was set out in the Labour Enactment of 1904 and applied to all who were in receipt of advances from employers. These workers had to toil for 300 days and do overtime whenever required to do so. They could free themselves from their contracts by paying their employers all advances together with $2 for each month that remained uncompleted. One reason for the decrease in the number of contracts signed at the Protectorate was that employers did not find themselves forced to turn to the law to ensure that agreements were honoured. By 1910 mining employers preferred to recruit direct from China by sending agents with funds to fetch a batch of friends and relatives to work for their employers until such time as the money expended on passages had been paid off.[56] The success of rubber and the adverse effect this had on sugar further reduced the number of indentured labourers in Malaya.[57] The death knell for indentured labour was finally sounded by the Labour Code of 1912 which made labour contracts illegal on 1 July 1914. Meanwhile the flow of Chinese labour continued and those employed on rubber estates in the Federation increased from 21,439 in 1912 to 40,866 in 1920.[58]

A characteristic of Chinese labour was that it was most reluctant to work for non-Chinese employers. This, combined with their disinclination to engage in low-paid jobs, left significant gaps in the labour market, and it was with a view to plugging these that the immigration of Indians was considered. The fact that the subcontinent of India was under British rule gave the whole operation a more contrived look than was the case with Chinese immigration. Indian labour was meant to be purely migratory, designed to meet the immediate requirements and return to India after a few years. The South Indians, considered most suitable for the role, were needed for European agricultural estates and for the construction of Government-financed projects and public works.[59] Until 1885 these labourers were recruited on a system of indenture governed by the

India Act V of 1877.[60] The results, from the European planters' point of view, were highly unsatisfactory. They expressed a lack of faith in the whole enterprise, pressed for the right to recruit freely, unhampered by agreements, and claimed that the shortage of suitable labour had resulted in the abandonment of coffee estates that had been forced to rely on Malay labour.[61] The pressure exerted by the planting fraternity led to the repeal of the 1877 Act by the Government of India, and from 1885 onwards Indian immigration to Malaya was regulated by the Straits Settlements Government under the Indian Immigration Ordinance of 1884.[62] The provisions of the new legislation enabled the Straits Immigration Agent to register and grant licences to recruiters sent to India to obtain South Indian workers on three-year contracts. The labourers were enlisted on agreed wages and transported to the Malay States at the expense of individual employers. At the end of their period of indenture they could either settle on the estates as 'free' labourers or return home to India. The effects of this modification in the law failed to produce the desired results and Malaya remained desperately short of labour. Early in 1891 Selangor planters alleged that labour employed on Government projects had been lured from their estates and that wages paid by the administration and its contractors were constantly increasing. The accusation was strenuously denied but this did not detract from the fact that the flow of South Indian labour had scarcely risen from the bare trickle it had always been.[63] Several factors were responsible for this and among them was the substandard nature of advertisement in Indian villages regarding information about, and conditions in, the Protected Malay States. There was also the heavy and steady drain on Indian villages to the tea and coffee estates in India, and to other better-known countries. The prevalence of the truck system, where the peasant found himself perpetually in debt to the headman or *jamindar*, was another drawback and as the lessee of the land on which he lived and worked, the peasant found it very difficult to pack up and go to a foreign country, even if he wanted to. The system of recruitment used by agents involved in indentured emigration was also responsible for the marked lack of enthusiasm among potential recruits. Sixteen rupees per head were paid as commission to recruiters for every labourer brought to the Immigration Depot at Nagapatam, and passed fit by the Medical Officer there. Since the amount was paid without any reference to the money actually spent by the agents, and this was sometimes negligible, the recruiters were naturally opposed to free labour operations where stringent accounts of expenditure would be required. The agents also had a monopoly and the majority were individuals who, so long as they obtained the recruits, cared little for the methods that they employed and, as a result, commanded neither the respect nor the confidence of the villagers.[64]

The European planters were thus placed in a most awkward situation. They had to import labour from South India because recruiting in Malaya was generally impossible and always unsatisfactory. To obtain this labour they either had to apply to the Indian Immigration Agent or send their own agents to India. The chief complaints of the planters were the wretched physique of the workers that arrived, the heavy initial recruiting expenses, the dissatisfaction of the labourers themselves about the way in which the system functioned, the uncertainty of the supply, and the constant annoyance caused by the interference of the Immigration Department. Indeed the most damning evidence that the system was unsatisfactory originated from the Immigration Agent himself who, in his annual report for 1893, stated that it was an unmitigated failure. The effects on the coffee estates, especially in Selangor, were that their progress was seriously impaired and fell far short of expectations. Although new estates were opened from time to time rapid extension failed to take place.[65]

So far as the number of South Indian immigrants was concerned the figures increased after the Immigration Ordinance of 1884,[66] but the rate declined again after 1889. The high mortality level among Indians in the Malay States caused much concern in India and it was to allay those fears that European planters in Malaya urged the establishment of an official commission to look into the state of labour. The Labour Commission of 1890, composed entirely of Europeans, recommended that the Government should place recruitment in India on a proper basis and that labour conditions should be improved and made comparable with those existing in countries popular with Indian emigrants. Planters welcomed the report, but the administration pleaded financial stringency so far as the first of the recommendations was concerned and, although an ordinance to improve indentured labour conditions was passed in 1892, the opposition of the planters prevented its implementation.[67]

The planters continued to exert pressure on the Government to participate directly in the importation of Indian labour and a commission set up in 1896 endorsed the recommendations of the 1890 Commission. A Bill was introduced by the Straits Settlements

Legislative Council in 1897 to improve the terms and conditions of Indian labour but again the bitter reaction of European sugar planters, who believed that the enactment would practically ruin the indentured labour system, resulted in the non-enforcement of the law. Further argument and discussion followed and finally in 1899 some of the restrictions were removed from the importation of 'free' labour, contracts of indentured labourers were reduced to two years and their wages increased, and arrangements were made to station an agent at Nagapatam to grant assisted passages to intending emigrants.[68]

The Ceylon system of *Kangany* recruitment, considered impracticable in 1890 and difficult in 1894, had by 1898 become more and more popular. The main difference between such labour and the indentured system was that in the case of the former no contracts were signed and the workers were at liberty to leave their employers at any time.[69] Despite these improvements the supply of labour could not keep pace with the demand and the situation was exacerbated when an increasing amount of land began to be devoted to rubber. The problem attained crisis dimensions and the administration was pressurized to seek new methods of encouraging Indian immigration. In June 1901, T. H. Hill[70] was appointed Superintendent of Immigration and Protector of Labour. His duties were to advise the Government and other employers of Indian labour on recruitment in India. The appointment itself was a strange one because Hill was the owner of extensive private plantations which he was unwilling to surrender. In any case an official deputation led by Hill went to India in 1902 to investigate ways of promoting emigration to the Federation. On its return the deputation recommended the appointment of a Government official to be stationed in India or, alternatively, to designate a European company in India, to supervise the activities of professional recruiters. At the same time employers were urged to get together and channel their labour requirements to the Government agent or recruiting firm so as to reduce the competition for labour as well as improve wages and conditions in Malaya.[71]

The Government chose to appoint a private firm to supervise recruiting and the company began operating early in 1903. New legislation was also introduced in 1904 to increase wages and improve conditions for indentured labourers.[72] None of these measures, however, made any difference to the rate of Indian immigration. Indentured labourers in Malaya continued to desert their employers, *kangany* labourers were persistently paid their wages late to discourage them from absconding, and it was clear that substantial improvements were vital if the desired increase was to become a reality. In 1906 the Resident-General, W. T. Taylor,[73] visited India and on his return recommended the appointment of an Emigration Agent in India, the formation of an Immigration Committee of two officials and two unofficials under the chairmanship of the Superintendent of Indian Immigrants, and the enactment of a law requiring all immigrant labour to be imported under the Committee's direct supervision.[74] Taylor's recommendations were accepted and implemented in 1907. At the first meeting of the Immigration Committee an unofficial member, J. Turner,[75] stated that what was needed was a scheme for introducing labour on a massive scale, the cost of which would be borne by all employers of imported labour. The Committee favoured a poll tax being levied to meet the cost, and its ideas were incorporated into the Tamil Immigration Fund Enactment which came into force in early 1908. It marked the turning point in the history of Indian immigration into Malaya. The new arrangements began functioning smoothly in 1910 when details of the proposals became common knowledge in India.[76] The number of *kangany* licences increased from 1,225 in 1908 to 6,278 in 1910 and 10,145 in 1912. By then the system was firmly established and was a resounding success. The Indian population in the Federation increased from 115,000 in 1907 to 220,000 in 1913.[77] The system of indentured labour was abolished in June 1910 but existing contracts were allowed to run their course.

In the wider context of the politics of the Federated Malay States, Indian immigration was seen as a phenomenon not entirely connected with economic considerations. This aspect of the subject was most eloquently expressed by the Governor, Sir Frederick Weld (1880–7),[78] who believed that an Indian element in Malaya was necessary because 'it was advisable in a country like this, the preponderance of any one Eastern nationality should not be excessive and because the Indians are a peaceable and easily governed race'.[79] More specifically Weld was 'anxious for political reasons that the great preponderance of the Chinese over any other races in these Settlements, and to a less marked degree in some of the Native States under our administration, should be counterbalanced, as much as possible, by the influx of Indian and other nationalities'.[80] This idea, which some may construe as coming close to the doctrine of 'divide and rule', might not have been a totally new concept and had indeed been employed in other areas of British domination.[81] In the circumstances of the Malay States, however, it assumed added significance due to the state of development of the Malay population. To begin with, the Malays in the Federated Malay States were few in number, possessed easy-going attitudes, and were extremely reluctant to move out of their traditional rural environment. The few village vernacular schools established by the administration did not prove popular and parents had to be coerced into sending their children to be educated. The Malays were unable to equate the relevance of education for children who would grow up to be farmers and fishermen.[82] For the adults, the mining and planting enterprises held no particular attractions and the prospects of crowded living accommodation, hard and monotonous work, stringent supervision, and low wages kept them firmly rooted to their customary setting.[83] Accordingly, British immigration policies represented a conscious effort to create a plural society in Malaya and resulted in the indigenous population being subjected to a situation where their very survival in the economic, political, and social spheres was seriously jeopardized. Throughout the early years of British rule the only tangible benefits that accrued to the mass of the Malays were that debt bondage slavery was abolished and improvements from the construction of roads, railways, and bridle tracks enabled them to move more easily and thus facilitated new settlement.

A comprehensive census of the Protected Malay States, conducted in 1891, showed that the total population of 418,527 consisted of 232,172 Malays, 163,821 Chinese, and 20,177 Indians. In terms of percentages the Chinese were 39 per cent of the total, but in Perak, Selangor and Sungei Ujong they constituted a staggering 44 per cent, 62 per cent and 42 per cent respectively.[84] With the passage of years the situation became progressively worse, and in 1921 the Federation population of 1,320,000 consisted of 511,000 Malays, 495,000 Chinese and 305,000 Indians.[85] There was no doubt that so far as the indigenous population was concerned it was saddled with all the problems of having to live in a plural society.[86]

In order to cope with the political situation created by the decision to intervene in the affairs of the Malay States, the British devised an administrative framework commonly referred to as the 'Residential System', which revolved around officers known as 'Residents'. Although these officials were obviously designed to be the bulwarks of the new political order, it was strange that no document existed which clearly set out their duties. Nobody, in fact, knew exactly what these appointments involved.[87] Selected in the first instance by the Governor of the Straits Settlements, the Residents were the senior British officials in the Malay States and were expected to perform a variety of important functions ranging from the protection of British subjects and other foreign traders; the establishment of channels of communication between the States and the outside world; and the exertion of a progressive influence on the organization and policies of government. In the early years they were counsellors and advisers to Sultans in all matters other than those connected with Islam and Malay customs. But although they were expected to maintain law and order, set up sound taxation systems, develop the country's economic resources, and supervise the collection of revenue, they were not supposed to involve themselves unduly with the minor details of government and administration. It soon became apparent that, under normal circumstances, it was impossible for Residents to perform all their duties to the letter except in situations where, as was the case in Selangor, the Ruler in the person of the Viceroy, Tunku Dziauddin, and the Resident, Davidson, were good friends,[88] and the British officer was able to introduce several measures and reforms without any serious opposition from the Malay ruling class.[89] On the other hand, a good instance of the kind of conflict that could be generated when traditional Malay authority clashed head on with the new British order, was the situation in Perak[90] between Sultan Abdullah[91] and J. W. W. Birch.[92] The result there was a collision not only between two contrasting personalities but also between two completely different sets of values and concepts. The friction culminated in November 1875 when Birch was killed by a group of Malays while on a visit to Pasir Salak in Lower Perak.[93]

The assassination of the British Resident was a traumatic experience for the British authorities in Singapore and in Whitehall, and led to a thorough and detailed reappraisal of the role of Residents in the Protected Malay States. The Governor of the Straits Settlements, Sir William Jervois (May 1875–February 1877),[94] insisted that the Pangkor Engagement in its unvarnished form meant rule, not just advice, and that the disturbances in Perak served only to reinforce the argument that British intentions in the Malay States had to be stated in plain, unequivocal language. The Colonial Office, on the other hand, laid great emphasis on the fact, or perhaps the fiction, that the Sultans had voluntarily accepted British advice and therefore reiterated the point that the functions of Residents should continue to remain advisory. Despite this very vital difference of opinion it was apparent that the events in Perak had demonstrated succinctly the true state of affairs. The enhanced responsibilities and authority of the Residents gained fresh recognition and it was increasingly acknowledged that the officers were in fact answerable for the proper government of the Protected Malay States.[95] On the other hand the Malays also realized that they were in no position to resist the British power.

The evolution in the status and functions of Residents can best be illustrated by two official declarations of British policy. The first was in the form of a despatch from the Colonial Office of 1 June 1876 which stated:

> You will observe that in continuing the Residential System, Her Majesty's Government define the functions of the Resident to be the giving of influential and responsible advice to the ruler, a position the duties of which are well understood in the East.
>
> The Residents are not to interfere more frequently or to a greater extent than is necessary with the minor details of government; but their special objects should be the maintenance of peace and law, the initiation of a sound system of taxation, with the consequent development of the resources of the country, and the supervision of the collection of the revenue, so as to ensure the receipt of funds necessary to carry out the principal engagements of the Government, and to pay for the cost of the British officers and whatever establishments may be necessary to support them.[96]

In contrast to this was the minute of 19 December 1893 from the Acting Governor, W. E. Maxwell,[97] to Residents:

> The powers of the Resident are not confined to the enforcement of the few written laws which the State possesses. In special cases he may exercise in the name of the Sultan the authority which His Highness undoubtedly possesses, of passing any order or sentence which may seem to be just, subject to the instructions, special or general, of the Governor.[98]

The metamorphosis left the Residents with supreme power in the Malay States. In their everyday tasks they were assisted by a number of District Officers who, in the early years of British administration in Perak and Selangor, were known as Collectors and Magistrates. The first of them, appointed in Selangor in January 1876 and posted to Kuala Selangor, was Robert R. Bruce, a Eurasian, on an annual salary of $960. In May 1876, James Innes of the Sarawak Civil Service was sent to Klang as Collector and Magistrate on a salary of $2400 a year, and in August of the same year, another Eurasian, L. E. Neubronner, went to Bernam in a similar capacity but at $1800 an annum.[99] When Low was appointed Resident of Perak in 1877, Matang had a Collector, but soon after his arrival Collectors were posted to Krian and Kinta as well.[100] These officials collected revenue within their districts, took charge of the general administration, and presided as judges of minor offences.[101] They were directly responsible to the Residents and had to submit monthly journals containing details of every important event, accounts of interviews with Malay chiefs, and descriptions of the physical features of the country. Copies of the journals were kept in the District Offices and were intended to be a confidential record which might benefit successive officers.[102] In more general terms, District Officers were looked upon as 'god-fathers' by the Malays who relied on them to arbitrate in petty disputes and quarrels as well as to doctor their illnesses.[103]

The District Officer system, which had proved successful in India and in parts of Africa, was theoretically a good one and should have resulted in efficient government. In practice, however, district administration did not fulfil its potential and this was clearly the case in Selangor when Captain Bloomfield Douglas was Resident.[104] He made no attempt to appoint officers to the interior districts of the State and did not bother to associate Malay *datoh* and *penghulu* with the pattern of local government initiated by the British. The Resident objected even to *penghulu* being allowed to maintain their traditional rights to collect revenue, and resented every one of their constructive efforts. So although in June 1882 thirteen Malay chiefs and one Chinese headman were nominally employed by the Selangor Government at an annual cost of $17,520, they were not required to collect any portion of the revenues because Douglas had no confidence in them. He reached the purely arbitrary and unreasonable conclusion that with few exceptions local officials could not be trusted.[105] Douglas's suspicions and superior attitudes rankled with the Malay chiefs in particular, and caused much dissatisfaction because they recalled the wide revenue-collecting powers they had enjoyed prior to British intervention. The substitution of these rights by fixed wage payments aroused resentment and did not altogether endear the British system to them. Malay officials were tempted to compare the new administration most unfavourably with the greater personal opportunities that had existed under indigenous rule.[106]

The conduct and intentions of individuals like Douglas were not unnoticed in Singapore and the concern that kind of behaviour aroused was reflected in the anxiety of the Governor, Sir Frederick Weld, to review the entire system. Weld was convinced that the total energy and vigour as well as the wholehearted support of the Malay ruling class was not being adequately exploited especially in those districts where the Malays predominated.[107] The reorganization of district administration began in Selangor in September 1882 when F. A. Swettenham was appointed Resident. In view of the very important role this officer played in the history of late nineteenth and early twentieth-century Malaya, it is appropriate to digress slightly and trace briefly his early career. Born in 1854, Swettenham joined the Straits Settlements Civil Service as a cadet in 1870. Two years later he passed a difficult examination in the Malay language, and was chosen to accompany the Governor, Sir Harry Ord, on visits to Johor, Pahang, Kelantan, Petani, and Kedah. In the same year he went to Klang and Kuala Lumpur as Davidson's guest and while there was entertained by Tunku Dziauddin and Yap Ah Loy.[108] He also visited Perak on his own account. During 1873 and 1874 he was stationed in Penang where he served as Collector of Land Revenue, and Magistrate. In the months preceding the Pangkor Engagement he was sent on a number of missions to the Malay States where his good practical knowledge of the Peninsula, and the cordial relations he had established with the major Malay and Chinese personalities, stood him in good stead. In December 1874 Swettenham was appointed Assistant Resident, Selangor, but in 1876 was transferred to Singapore as Assistant Colonial Secretary for the Native States. Just prior to his appointment as Resident of Selangor he had been Assistant Colonial Secretary.[109] He therefore possessed, for an Englishman, a unique insight into Malay affairs and was able to communicate fluently with the indigenous population. The choice of Swettenham as Resident of Selangor at that particular time was also propitious because he had, for some time, recognized the advantages that could accrue if the amount of Malay participation in State governments was, somehow, increased. As far back as 1875 he had suggested the appointments of intelligent and trustworthy Malays to aid the British in trying petty cases and collecting local taxes,[110] but these initial and tentative proposals were not favourably received and were shelved. Now, with added power and with the support of Weld, the Governor, he embarked on a far-reaching programme of reform.[111] At the thirty-fifth meeting of the Selangor State Council in Jugra on 2 September 1883, twenty-five penghulu were formally appointed by the Sultan, and were armed with letter of authority laying down certain guidelines. These documents authorized the Malay officials to settle petty cases and impose fines not exceeding $5, hold court and judge cases involving not more than $10, collect revenues in their areas and despatch them to the State

Treasury, repair and maintain roads, paths, and bridges, and generally look after the well-being of their districts.[112]

Changes also took place in the conceptual aspects of the District Officer system. The experiences of the early years dictated the issue of a more comprehensive set of instructions. In the collection of revenue the District Officers were directed to maintain their books in accordance with a rigid format devised by the State Treasurer, and to submit monthly returns within the first three days of the following month. They were each given a copy of the Land Regulations so that they could decide for themselves the amount of quit rent payable by land owners in their districts. As magistrates, the District Officers were guided by the Indian Penal and Civil Codes, received detailed instructions relating to their powers of jurisdiction, and were told how to deal with cases of a particular nature. They were encouraged to become thoroughly acquainted with their districts, keep all bridges and roads in good order, supervise the activities of the *penghulu*, maintain up-to-date district maps, and induce as many people as possible to settle permanently in the State by developing resources and thus increasing prosperity.[113]

The improvements, although substantial, did not entirely rectify the situation and in 1890 it was widely recognized that many District Officers failed to comprehend fully their duties and functions. A large number of them lacked the necessary initiative and preferred to rely too heavily on the guidance and instructions of their superiors before initiating reforms that would have the effect of improving the administration. Their predisposition to disclaim all responsibility for subjects controlled by professional departments located in the State capitals,[114] and their reluctance to adhere to general orders, were further handicaps. They were also unable to get the most out of their *penghulu* and many of their diaries and monthly letters indicated that little effort was being made to interest the people in the prosperity and material advancement of the Protected States. There were many District Officers who did not themselves understand all the judicial regulations and enactments, and court procedure often left much to be desired.[115]

To streamline the situation, Maxwell drew up a regulation in 1890 which set out in clear and unambiguous language the multifarious duties of District Officers. Subject to the orders of Residents, District Officers were to be in sole executive charge of districts assigned to them. Their principal duties were to convene civil and criminal courts at the chief stations of their districts on days fixed by the Residents, act as coroners, superintend land offices, collect revenue, and manage the sub-treasuries. Their other functions included the supervision of roads, the maintenance of sanitary facilities, inspection of government hospitals, and making arrangements for vaccinations whenever the need arose. They were also expected to visit periodically vernacular schools, encourage the concept of education among the people, and, in coastal districts, to act as Harbour Masters.[116]

An important adjunct of the Residential System was the State Councils which were considered, by the British, to be the institutions that provided the constitutional framework for the Government of the Protected States. The first of the Councils, established in Perak and Selangor in 1877, aimed to reconcile all the conflicting interests within the States. They were composed of small intimate bodies of Malay chiefs, Chinese leaders, and British administrators. Their principal function was, when so consulted, to advise the Government on proposals for taxation, appointments, concessions, and the enactment and repeal of laws. They were also supposed to help in the administration of the States by approving, and then aiding to implement, measures submitted by the Government. The Perak State Council began with eight members of whom four were Malays, two Chinese, and two British, while the Council in Selangor had seven members made up of four Malays, one Chinese, and two British.[117]

At first, the State Councils were concerned largely with improving old laws, introducing new enactments, and considering petitions from people who complained about oppression and other grievances. The actual influence exerted by Councils on the course of State administrations depended very much on the personalities and attitudes of Residents and of the members. Events in Selangor reflect this clearly, for when Douglas was Resident the Council was a mere rubber stamp of the administration because the Resident was a man with a 'strong voice heard everywhere in authoritative tones'.[118] Douglas was not inclined to tolerate anyone who showed independence of character or who dared to disagree with him. He insulted many of the Malay chiefs and caused them to become estranged from the British.[119] Tunku Dziauddin demonstrated his feelings by refusing to attend State Council meetings after June 1877 and towards the end of 1878 retired to his native State of Kedah. The only person to play an active role in Council discussions and who provided the 'opposition' to Douglas was Yap Ah Loy. The Capitan China showed an avid interest for the welfare of the Chinese in Selangor, succeeded in getting the duty on tin reduced from $11.60 to $9 per *bhara*,[120] and prevented an increase in the duty on opium.[121] Generally, however, the Resident was able to do as he pleased, and persuaded the Council to act according to his wishes.[122] His flagrant abuse of power became so obvious that it earned Douglas a rebuke from Weld, the Governor, who reminded him that '. . . the Residents have been placed in the Native States as Advisers, not as Rulers and if they take upon themselves to disregard this principle they will most assuredly be held responsible if trouble springs out of their neglect of it. . . .'[123]

When Swettenham succeeded Douglas as Resident a basic shift in policy took place so far as the State Council was concerned. The new Resident, and in his absence, the Acting Resident, J. P. Rodger,[124] believed that for sound government it was essential to gain the active co-operation of the people, especially the Malays.[125] To begin with, the Sultan, Abdul Samad,[126] was brought into the Council and, although Swettenham was unable to lure him completely out of his semi-retirement at Langat, the Sultan presided over all but four State Council meetings between 1883 and 1887.[127] The presence of Abdul Samad led to fundamental changes in the working of the Council. It became the final legislative authority in Selangor and all minutes and resolutions were confirmed at the start of each meeting,[128] and not, as previously, taken to Langat for the Sultan's forced sanction, a practice which had involved much loss of time.[129] The increased efficiency enabled legislation to be enforced with the minimum of delay, an important consideration especially when it coincided, as it did, with a period of rapid economic development. Road and railway construction was placed under Council control although final authority still rested with the Governor and the Secretary of State, and it assumed responsibility over telegraphs and the issue of all kinds of licences. Malay participation in debates and discussions increased, and attendances improved.

But even under an enlightened Resident like Swettenham this sanguine state of affairs was too good to last. The growing pressure of work left him little time to explain intricate legislation, or consult members' opinions. In 1888 the Council began to lose its advisory functions and the Sultan retired as its President, not because he was indifferent but because he wanted to preserve his dignity. The Presidency of the Council thenceforth passed into the hands of the Resident.[130] When Maxwell succeeded Swettenham in June 1889 the situation deteriorated further, there being little or no discussion in the Council. The new Resident, like Douglas, disliked opposition and even refused to publish State Council Minutes in the Government Gazette.[131]

In the 1890s a further factor appeared in the development of State Councils. Clear signs emerged that the Governor was interfering more and more in Council affairs. At a meeting of the Selangor State Council in April 1893, the Resident, W. H. Treacher,[132] announced that measures due for consideration by the Council had been introduced with the concurrence of the Governor,[133] Sir Cecil Clementi Smith (1887–93).[134] In the same year the Regulation for the Control of Buffaloes was repealed by the Governor on the grounds that there was no longer a need for such a law.[135] Judicial functions were also interfered with, as in June 1894, when on Sir Cecil Smith's earlier instructions the Selangor State Council revoked a death sentence on two Bengalis.[136] Nor did the Perak State Council escape the Governor's influence. In July 1891 an Order for Brothel Registration Fees was passed which displeased Sir Cecil who indicated initially that he would not press his objections if the Council really favoured the retention of the system.[137] When, however, the Council confirmed its desire to retain the Order, a Draft Order for the Abolition of Brothel Registration Fees arrived from the Governor for confirmation.[138] The Council, of course, had no alternative but to conform to Sir Cecil's wishes.[139] From the point of view of the State Councils this tendency was very unhealthy and affected their efficiency because on questions of public health, education, and general state administration, the Councils possessed personal and intimate knowledge, whereas the information available in Singapore was limited and, usually, confined to what the Residents reported to the Governor. Thus, looking at the series of events in the pre-Federation period, the declining influence of Malay opinion, as expressed through the State Councils, and the corresponding growth in the power of the British administration, is obvious. There were, admittedly, short periods when Swettenham first went to Selangor as Resident and during Low's tenure in Perak, where the Councils seemed to be evolving into organizations with positive and constructive roles but these, unfortunately, were brief and were soon swallowed by the pace of economic development.

To sum up, British administration of the Protected Malay States created a variety of dilemmas. Politically, the Residential System established a colonial-type system of government responsible, through the Governor of the Straits Settlements, to the British Government in Whitehall. Within Malaya little attempt was made to link and co-ordinate policies and innovations introduced by different Residents at different times. The largest common factor was the Governor, but his relative isolation and remoteness from the Protected States, together with his comparative ignorance of detailed conditions on the Peninsula and his preoccupation with the Straits Settlements, left him no time to direct effectively the activities of Residents. The men on the spot, with few exceptions, acted independently and governed their states as individual units rather than as parts of a larger entity with common interests.

Economically, the hopes of encouraging large-scale European commercial enterprise, especially in the field of agriculture, were not completely realized. Until the end of the nineteenth century neither their sugar nor their coffee estates met with outstanding success. Chinese commercial enterprise was more fortunate and peaceful conditions within the Protected States allowed them to expand their economic activities. Nowhere was this more obvious than in the tin mining industry which yielded the bulk of the country's revenue.[140] By contrast, the Malays remained in their economic backwater and British economic policies ignored them completely.

On the social level, several important changes took place. British rule resulted in the growth of urban centres in each of the States which were apart and distinct from the traditional Malay royal capitals. In Perak the towns of Taiping and Ipoh grew rapidly, in Selangor, Kuala Lumpur developed, in Negri Sembilan the town of Seremban expanded, and in Pahang, Kuantan overtook Pekan as the State's largest metropolitan area.[141] The centre of gravity of the Malay States thus shifted from the traditional indigenous urban areas of Kuala Kangsar, Klang, Sri Menanti, and Pekan. To exacerbate the situation the new conurbations consisted chiefly of immigrant communities and, by their very character, received more than their fair share of Government attention. In 1895, for example, the only English schools were those established in the new capitals. The general British attitude towards providing English education was aptly summarized by Swettenham who believed that it could only be well taught in a very few schools and that it was inadvisable to provide children of an agricultural population with an indifferent knowledge of a language that would not equip the majority of them for the duties of life and only make them discontented with manual work.[142] English education in the Protected States was therefore the privilege of those living in the principal towns, the majority being Chinese and Indian. Hospital facilities too were restricted to the larger towns and catered mainly for the Chinese and a handful of Indians; the Malays hardly used them. It is unfortunate that these were some of the by-products of British administration, because what resulted was two societies that progressed at different speeds, the urban and largely immigrant sector received all the plums and the rural and largely Malay sector remained neglected.

1. For a detailed account of the geographical and geological characteristics of the country, see Ooi Jin Bee, *Land, People and Economy in Malaya*, London, 1963, pp. 14–20.

2. In size Pahang is 13,873 square miles; Perak, 7,890 square miles; Selangor, 3,166 square miles; and Negri Sembilan, 2,550 square miles.

3. T. J. Newbold, *Political and Statistical Account of the British Settlement in the Straits of Malacca*, London, 1839; reprinted Kuala Lumpur, 1971, Vol. 1, p. 418.

4. Ooi Jin Bee, op. cit., p. 105.

5. A full analysis of traditional Malay economic techniques can be found in R. Firth, *Malay Fishermen: Their Peasant Economy*, London, 1946; and R. Firth, *Housekeeping among Malay Peasants*, London, 1966.

6. It was estimated that in 1835–6 the population of Perak was 35,000; Selangor 12,000; Rembau 9,000; Sungei Ujong 3,600; Johol 3,080; Jempol 2,000; Jelebu 2,000; Sri Menanti 8,000; and Pahang 40,000. See Newbold, op. cit., p. 418.

7. J. M. Gullick, *Indigenous Political Systems of Western Malaya*, London, 1958, p. 21.

8. Gullick, op. cit., p. 44.

9. Ibid., pp. 95–8.

10. Khoo Kay Kim, 'Nineteenth Century Malay Peninsula–1', in Zainal Abidin bin Abdul Wahid (ed.), *Glimpses of Malaysian History*, Kuala Lumpur, 1970, pp. 51–3.

11. This early period coincided with the growth of Indian influence in the region and is adequately analysed in H. G. Quaritch-Wales, 'Archaeological Researches in Ancient Indian Colonisation', *JMBRAS*, Vol. XVIII, No. 1, 1940, pp. 1–85; A. Lamb, 'Miscellaneous Papers on early Hindu and Buddhist settlement in northern Malaya and South Thailand', *FMJ*, Vol. VI, New Series, 1961; P. Wheatley, *The Golden Chersonese*, Kuala Lumpur, 1961, pp. 177–204; K. A. Nilakanta Sastri, *The Colas*, Madras, 1955, pp. 209–20; R. O. Winstedt, *The Malays. A Cultural History*, Singapore, 1947, pp. 20–31, 73–88, 145–52.

12. The best, although not exactly contemporary, account of the Malacca Sultanate is the *Sejarah Melayu*. C. C. Brown, 'The Malay Annals', *JMBRAS*, Vol. XXV, Parts 2 and 3, 1952.

13. For details see M. A. P. Meilink-Roelofsz, *Asian Trade and European Influence in the Indonesian Archipelago between 1500 and about 1630*, The Hague, 1962.

14. The Portuguese and Dutch periods of Malaysian history are well discussed in Meilink-Roelofsz, op. cit., pp. 136–42; Tomé Pires, *Suma Oriental*, translated by Armando Cortesão, London, 1944, Vol. II, pp. 278–81; I. A. Macgregor, 'Notes on the Portuguese in Malaya', *JMBRAS*, Vol. XXVIII, Part 2, 1955, pp. 5–41; D. K. Bassett, 'The Historical Background, 1500–1815', in *Malaysia: A Survey* (ed.) Wang Gungwu, London, 1964, pp. 113–27; D. K. Bassett, 'European Influence in the Malay Peninsula, 1511–1786', *JMBRAS*, Vol. XXXIII, Part 2, 1961, pp. 106–21; S. Arasaratnam, 'International Trade and Politics in Southeast Asia 1500–1800', *JSEAH*, Vol. 10, No. 3, 1969, pp. 391–581.

15. British activities in the Straits Settlements are analysed in P. J. Begbie, *The Malay Peninsula*, Madras, 1834; reprinted Kuala Lumpur, 1967; H. P. Clodd, *Malaya's First British Pioneer: The Life of Francis Light*, London, 1948; K. G. Tregonning, *The British in Malaya*, Tuscon, 1965; C. M. Turnbull, *The Straits Settlements 1826–67: Indian Presidency to Crown Colony*, London, 1972; C. M. Turnbull, 'The Nineteenth Century', op. cit., pp. 128–37.

16. N. Tarling, 'British Policy in the Malay Peninsula and Archipelago 1824–71', *JMBRAS*, Vol. XXX, Part 3, 1957, pp. 9–18, reprinted Kuala Lumpur, 1969; L. A. Mills, *British Malaya 1824–1867*, first published in *JMBRAS*, Vol. III, Part 2, 1925; reprinted Kuala Lumpur, 1966.

17. For details see N. Tarling, *Piracy and Politics in the Malay World*, Melbourne, 1963; C. N. Parkinson, *British Intervention in Malaya 1867–1877*, Singapore, 1960.

18. The treaties were Captain H. Burney's Treaty of 1826 with Thailand; in the case of Perak there were W. S. Cracroft's Treaty of 1818, John Anderson's Treaty of 1825, and Captain James Low's Treaty of 1826; Selangor was a party to W. S. Cracroft's Treaty of 1818, and John Anderson's Treaty of 1825; Rembau signed R. Ibbetson's Treaties of 1831 and 1832, and Naning concluded a treaty with Lieutenant-Colonel Taylor in 1801. See W. G. Maxwell and W. S. Gibson (eds.), *Treaties and Engagements affecting the Malay States and Borneo*, London, 1924, pp. 77–81, 20–5, 30–3, and 57–9.

19. Sir Harry St. George Ord was an officer in the Royal Engineers who joined the Colonial Service in 1855 as Commissioner of the Gold Coast. Two years later he became Lieutenant-Governor of Dominica and in 1861 was transferred to Bermuda as Governor. In 1864 he returned to West Africa as Special Commissioner, a post he occupied till his appointment to Singapore.

20. A. E. H. Anson was Lieutenant-Governor of Penang from 1867–82. For periods in 1871, 1877, and 1879 he administered the Government of the Straits Settlements in the absence of the Governor. After his retirement he wrote a book, *About Others and Myself 1845–1920*, London, 1920.

21. These factors were supplemented by a general change in attitudes towards the concept of imperialism in British intellectual circles. For details of this see C. A. Bodelsen, *Studies in Mid-Victorian Imperialism*, London, 1960; J. E. Tyler, *The Struggle for Imperial Unity, 1868–1895*, London, 1938; W. L. Langer, *The Diplomacy of Imperialism*, 2nd ed., New York, 1956, Chapter III; R. Koebner and H. D. Schmidt, *Imperialism*, Cambridge, 1964.

22. The four main divisions of Negri Sembilan are Sungei Ujong, Rembau, Jelebu and Johol.

23. A full analysis of this period can be found in E. Sadka, *The Protected*

Malay States 1874–1895; C. D. Cowan, *Nineteenth Century Malaya: the Origins of British Political Control*; Parkinson, *British Intervention in Malaya*; Khoo Kay Kim, *The Western Malay States 1850–1873*.

24. W. H. Read, a prominent Singapore businessman, Chairman of the Straits Settlements Association and the Singapore Chamber of Commerce, was on friendly terms with some Malay rulers, and in 1866 held the Klang Revenue Farms in partnership with Tan Kim Cheng. He was also closely connected with interests promoting telegraph lines through the Peninsula and the opening of the mines in Selangor. J. G. Davidson, the nephew of James Guthrie of Guthrie and Company, was the legal adviser and financial backer of Tunku Dziauddin of Selangor. He planned to float the Selangor Tin Mining Company to exploit mineral resources there. Later, in 1875, he was appointed British Resident in Selangor and was transferred in 1876 as Resident of Perak. In February 1877 he resigned from Government service and returned to his law practice in Singapore. Tan Kim Cheng was a Singapore merchant and a leader of the Chi Hin secret society, who advanced large sums of money to Sultan Abdullah of Perak. He was the son of TowkayTanTock Seng. W.T. Lewis began his connexion with the Straits Settlements in Penang and in 1826 he went to Malacca as Assistant Resident. The rest of his career, lasting some fifty-four years, was spent in Penang and he was described as the 'evil genius' behind the Naning War of 1831–2 (K. G. Tregonning, *History of Modern Malaya*, Singapore, 1964, p. 111). Before he retired in September 1860 he was Resident Councillor and Commissioner of Police, Penang, and this gave him considerable influence in Perak. In April 1861 he persuaded Sultan Jaafar of Perak to grant him sole rights to farm the territory of Krian and this venture, although unsuccessful, was the first attempt to develop large-scale commercial agriculture in Perak.

25. The Tanjong Pagar Dock Company was formed in 1864 with a capital of $200,000. For a detailed account of the activities of this company, see G. Bogaars, 'The Tanjong Pagar Dock Company, 1864–1905', *Memoirs of the Raffles Museum*, No. 3, December 1956. The Eastern Asia Telegraph Company was formed in London in 1867 with an initial capital of £150,000. The company hoped to set up a telegraph line from Rangoon to Singapore with a branch line across Thailand, and later to Hong Kong in the north and Java and Australia in the south. W. H. Read and W. Paterson were the principal people involved in the Straits Settlements and by 1866 had secured concessions in Kedah, Selangor, and Johor. The scheme, however, did not materialize because by 1870 the preference for submarine cables had gained considerable support. See Khoo Kay Kim, *The Western Malay States*, pp. 103–6.

26. Sustained tin mining by the Chinese in the Malay States began around 1824, the chief centres being Lukut and Sungei Ujong. It was estimated that in 1824 there were 200 Chinese at Lukut and 1,000 in Sungei Ujong in 1828. In addition about 400 were working in Perak. See Newbold, *Political and Statistical Account of the British Settlements*, Vol. II, p. 100. In the 1850s the Chinese population in Kanching, Ampang, and Selangor increased rapidly. The discovery of tin in Larut, Perak, meant that by 1862 there were 20,000–25,000 Chinese miners there. See R. N. Jackson, *Immigrant Labour and the Development of Malaya*, Kuala Lumpur, 1961, pp. 33–5. The best detailed account of tin mining in Malaya is Wong Lin Ken, *The Malayan Tin Industry to 1914*, Tuscon, 1965.

27. According to Cowan there was no significant investment in Perak but in

Selangor advances were made to get mines started and, after 1866, to finance different warring factions in the civil war. Most of the early capital was supplied by Malacca Chinese merchants and by the British firm of Neubronner & Co. In all, the investment in mines was between $500,000 and $1,000,000. When the civil war broke out in earnest in 1870, Singapore merchants played a vital part in events in Selangor, but it is impossible to gauge the size of the political loans that were granted. Some idea, however, can be obtained from the fact that the war debts of Tunku Dziauddin amounted to $300,000. See Cowan, *Nineteenth Century Malaya*, pp. 138–9. In July 1872, 12,000 Chinese miners, financed largely by British capital, worked along the Klang River. See Khoo Kay Kim, *The Western Malay States*, p. 86.

28. For details, see Sadka, *The Protected Malay States*, pp. 324–63.

29. V. Purcell, *The Chinese in Malaya*, London, 1948; new ed. Kuala Lumpur, 1967, p. 6.

30. Governor to CO, 12 September 1895, printed in *Straits Settlements Legislative Council Proceedings*, Paper No. 36, 1895, p. C127.

31. P. C. Campbell, *Chinese Coolie Emigration to Countries Within the British Empire*, London, 1971, pp. 3–4.

32. W. L. Blythe, 'Historical Sketch of Chinese Labour in Malaya', *JMBRAS*, Vol. XX, Part 1, June 1947, p. 70.

33. Report on the Commission of Enquiry into the state of Labour in the Straits Settlements and Protected Native States, 1891, *Straits Settlements Legislative Council Papers*, 1891; Jackson, *Immigrant Labour and the Development of Malaya*, pp. 70–1.

34. The best accounts of secret society activities in Malaya can be found in W. L. Blythe, *The Impact of Chinese Secret Societies in Malaya*, London, 1969; M. L. Wynne, *Triad and Tabut: A Survey of the Origin and Diffusion of Chinese and Mohamedan Secret Societies in the Malay Peninsula AD 1800–1935*, Singapore, 1941, distributed in 1957; L. F. Comber, *Chinese Secret Societies in Malaya: A Survey of the Triad Society from 1800 to 1900*, New York, 1959.

35. Jackson, *Immigrant Labour and the Development of Malaya*, pp. 71–4.

36. Blythe, *JMBRAS*, Vol. XX, Part 1, 1947, pp. 74–7.

37. This varied between $3 and $13 per head according to circumstances, supply, and demand. Notes on Chinese labour by H. C. Ridges, Protector of Chinese, Selangor, and Negri Sembilan, and J. S. Paschal, President, Miners Association, Selangor, *FMS Annual Report, 1903*, Kuala Lumpur, 1904, CO 576.

38. J. B. Massy-Leech to RG, 6 April 1904, in *FMS Annual Report, 1904*, Kuala Lumpur, 1905, CO 576. The Chinese mining population of Kinta rose from 5,242 in 1884 to 25,000 in 1887. Jackson, *Immigrant Labour and the Development of Malaya*, p. 81. The registration system is well discussed in Wong Lin Ken, *The Malayan Tin Industry*, pp. 182–4.

39. Hugh Low, born in 1824, came from a family with horticultural interests. At nineteen years of age he went on a botanical tour of Borneo where he came under Raja James Brooke's patronage. He was Secretary of the Government of Labuan in 1848 and for the next twenty-nine years held various posts in the administration. He was appointed Resident of Perak in February 1877 and remained there till his retirement in 1889. He wrote *Sarawak, its Inhabitants and Productions*, London, 1848, and translated 'Selesilah of the Rajas of Brunei', *JSBRAS*, No. 5, 1880, pp. 1–35.

40. The bulk of the Chinese capital came from Penang, *Perak Annual Report*, 1899, *Perak Government Gazette*, 1900; see also J. C. Jackson, *Planters and Speculators*, Kuala Lumpur, 1968, pp. 155–62; Jackson, *Immigrant Labour and the Development of Malaya*, pp. 91–2.

41. Jackson, *Immigrant Labour and the Development of Malaya*, p. 93; Jackson, *Planters and Speculators*, pp. 176–207.

42. I. L. Bird, *The Golden Chersonese, and the Way Thither*, London, 1883; reprinted Kuala Lumpur, 1967, p. 357.

43. H. Clifford, 'Miscellaneous Essays: Rival Systems and the Malayan Peoples', *North American Review*, Vol. 177, 1903, pp. 399–409.

44. Ibid.

45. The first proposal was the brainchild of Towkay Loke Yew, a principal employer of Chinese labour in Selangor and Pahang, and a member of the Selangor State Council. The Acting High Commissioner, J. A. Swettenham, approved the scheme in May 1898 but nothing came of it. The second proposal was from G. T. Hare, the Secretary for Chinese Affairs and would have cost the Government $10,000 or $20,000 over a period of six months. The Resident-General, Frank Swettenham, opposed the idea because he did not believe that money was the problem in the importation of labour. The third scheme was put forward by J. P. Rodger, the Resident of Selangor, and supported by the High Commissioner who did not object to moderate loans being granted on good security. RG to HC, 2 February 1899, in Governor to CO, Desp. No. 26, 17 February 1899, CO 273/1899.

46. Acting Governor, SS, to CO, Desp. No. 307, 14 December 1899, CO 273/1899.

47. H.B.M.'s Consul Canton to British Ambassador, Peking, 22 February 1900, in FO to CO, 2 May 1900, CO 273/1900.

48. The total in 1901 was 676,138 as compared with 418,509 in 1891. *Report on the Census of the FMS, 1901*, Kuala Lumpur, 1901.

49. RG to HC, 26 March 1903, enclosure in Governor to CO, Desp. No. 343, 23 June 1903, CO 273/1903.

50. Report by Dr. Luehring, 26 October 1903, in Acting Governor, SS, to CO, Desp. No. 698, 31 December 1903, CO 273/1903.

51. B. F. Van Dyke, 'Sitiawan', *The Malaysia Message*, Vol. 8, No. 8, May 1904, pp. 7344.

52. L. E. H. Luehring, 'Notes from Perak', *The Malaysia Message*, Vol. 8, No. 5, February 1904, p. 49.

53. Report by W. Cowan, Protector of Chinese Perak, 10 March 1904, in HC to CO, Desp. No. 182, 19 April 1904, CO 273/1904.

54. Purcell, *The Chinese in Malaya*, p. 151.

55. C. W. C. Parr, *Report of the Commission appointed to enquire into the conditions of indentured labour in the Federated Malay States*, Kuala Lumpur, 1910.

56. Ibid.

57. The area under sugar cane fell from 7,128 acres in 1909 to 3,759 acres in 1910. This was reduced to 2,133 acres in 1911 and to nothing in 1913. See Jackson, *Immigrant Labour and the Development of Malaya*, p. 156.

58. Jackson, *Immigrant Labour and the Development of Malaya*, p. 156.

59. The best accounts of Indian immigration and the activities of Indians in

Malaya are K. S. Sandhu, *Indians in Malaya*, London, 1969; J. N. Parmer, *Colonial Labor Policies and Administration*, New York, 1960; S. Arasaratnam, *Indians in Malaysia and Singapore*, Kuala Lumpur, 1970; U. Mahajani, *The Role of Indian Minorities in Burma and Malaya*, Bombay, 1960.

60. N. E. Marjoribanks and A. T. Marakayyar, *Report on Indian Labour Emigration to Ceylon and Malaya*, Madras, 1917.

61. The Hill Estates in Sungei Ujong were an example of this. T. H. Hill to Resident, Selangor, 19 March 1884, SGR, 1884.

62. S. Nanjundan, *Indians in the Malayan Economy*, New Delhi, 1950, p. 21.

63. Resident, Selangor, to Selangor Planters, 19 February 1891, SGR, 1891.

64. Report on a visit to Southern India by E. V. Carey, Chairman, Selangor Planters' Association, 27 June 1895, SGR, 1895.

65. E. V. Carey to Governor, 30 April 1894, SGR, 1894.

66. This was Ordinance No. 5 of 1884 and its object was to free Indian emigration from as many restrictions as possible in order to encourage labourers to seek employment in Malaya.

67. Parmer, *Colonial Labor Policy and Administration*, p. 20.

68. Jackson, *Immigrant Labour and the Development of Malaya*, p. 105.

69. For details see Sandhu, *Indians in Malaya*, pp. 88–103.

70. T. H. Hill with A. B. Rathbone pioneered European coffee-planting and owned extensive estates in Selangor and Sungei Ujong. Hill came to Malaya from Ceylon and knew well the nature, habits, and language of the Tamil labourer. He also enjoyed the confidence of the rest of the planting community. OAG, SS, to CO, Desp. No. 228, 22 June 1901, CO 273/1901. A. B. Rathbone wrote *Camping and Tramping in Malaya*, London, 1898.

71. Correspondence and Papers relating to the supply of indentured Indian Immigrants for FMS and SS and the improvement of the system of recruiting, *Straits Settlements Legislative Council Proceedings*, Paper No. 11, 1903.

72. A term of 600 days was substituted for the two-year contract, wages were fixed at 7 annas for males and 5 annas for females, and provisions were made to prohibit employment at places where conditions were unsatisfactory.

73. Born in 1850, W. T. Taylor joined the Colonial Service in 1876 when he went to Cyprus as Collector of Customs and Excise at Larnaka. In 1882 he became Chief Collector of Customs and later Receiver-General and Chief Collector of Customs and Excise. In 1895 he was transferred to Ceylon as Auditor-General and on four occasions acted as Colonial Secretary. He was appointed Colonial Secretary, Straits Settlements, in June 1901 and was promoted to Resident-General on 1 January 1905, a post he occupied till his retirement on 30 September 1910. See J. H. M. Robson, *Records and Recollections 1889–1934*, Kuala Lumpur, 1934, p. 106.

74. *Indian Immigration Department Annual Report*, 1906.

75. J. Turner owned estates in Penang and Province Wellesley, was President of the Malay Peninsula Agricultural Association and the Perak Planters' Association, and a Legislative Councillor.

76. The fund provided free passage and board to all bona fide Indian emigrants, maintained recruiting depots in India and quarantine stations in Malaya, and paid for all other legitimate expenses from the time that the labourers were recruited in India until their arrival at their place of employment in Malaya. The

Enactment was amended to improve it in 1908, 1909, 1911, and 1913. See Sandhu, *Indians in Malaya*, p. 63.

77. Jackson, *Immigrant Labour and the Development of Malaya*, pp. 116, 120.

78. F. A. Weld, born in 1823, migrated from England to New Zealand in 1844 to farm sheep. After a spell in the New Zealand General Assembly, he became Minister for Native Affairs in 1860, and Premier in 1864–5. He left New Zealand in 1867 and served as Governor of Western Australia (1869–74), and Governor of Tasmania (1875–9), before coming to Singapore. He retired in 1887 and died four years later. For more details, see A. Lovat, *The Life of Sir Frederick Weld, GCMG: A Pioneer of Empire*, London, 1914.

79. *Straits Settlements Legislative Council Proceedings*, 1887, p. C.199.

80. Governor to CO, Desp. No. 397, 24 September 1887, CO 273/1887.

81. The most noteworthy example of this practice was British India, where the Muslims were used as a political counterpoise to the more numerous Hindus.

82. For details of Malay vernacular education in the period before 1896, see F. A. Swettenham, *British Malaya*, pp. 257–9; W. R. Roff, *The Origins of Malay Nationalism*, Yale, 1967, pp. 126–7; Sadka, *The Protected Malay States*, pp. 293–6.

83. Sadka, *The Protected Malay States*, pp. 324–5.

84. E. M. Merewether, *Report of the Census of the Straits Settlements taken on the 5th April 1891*, Singapore, 1892. Merewether joined the Straits Settlements Civil Service as a cadet in 1880. He was appointed Assistant Colonial Secretary in 1897 and subsequently acted as Treasurer and Resident Councillor, Malacca. In December 1901 the Colonial Office, on Swettenham's recommendation, approved his promotion to Resident of Selangor but in June 1902 he was transferred to Malta as Lieutenant-Governor.

85. J. E. Nathan, *The Census of British Malaya, 1921*, London, 1922.

86. According to J. S. Furnivall a plural society is one in which economic forces are exempt from control by social will, each racial group living side by side but separately, with a division of labour along communal lines. Such a society is made up of separate racial sections, each of them being aggregates of individuals rather than a corporate whole, and of individuals who lead incomplete social lives. See J. S. Furnivall, *Colonial Policy and Practice: A Comparative Study of Burma and Netherlands India*, London, 1948, pp. 303–12.

87. The operative clause of the Pangkor Engagement of 20 January 1874, which gave birth to the Residential system, was the sixth which specified 'That the Sultan receive and provide a suitable residence for a British officer to be called Resident, who shall be accredited to his Court, and whose advice must be asked and acted upon on all questions other than those touching Malay Religion and custom'. See Maxwell and Gibson, *Treaties and Engagements*, pp. 28–9. The word 'custom' itself was very vague and could be interpreted as almost anything.

88. Tunku Dziauddin originated from Kedah and was the son-in-law of Sultan Abdul Samad of Selangor. From about 1870–4 he ruled over Klang and Kuala Selangor, using traditional methods of administration where possible. For Davidson see note 24.

89. The most noteworthy of these was the establishment of a Government Treasury and the organization of a police force. See Swettenham, *British Malaya*, pp. 217–20.

90. For details see Sadka, *The Protected Malay States*, pp. 79–82.

91. Abdullah Muratham Shah was the major Perak chief who invited the

British to send a Resident to Perak on condition that they recognized him as Sultan. He was considered to be frivolous and unable to concentrate on anything 'beyond his immediate desires and fancies, his opium smoking and other excesses, his changes of mind, evasions, and delays'. See ibid., pp. 47 and 80. In 1876 he was found guilty of being involved in the conspiracy to kill Birch and was exiled to the Seychelles, ibid., pp. 92–4.

92. J. W. W. Birch joined the Colonial Service in 1846 in the Department of the Commissioner of Roads, Ceylon. In 1870 he was appointed Colonial Secretary of the Straits Settlements and in 1874 was posted as Resident in Perak.

93. A full account of Birch's tenure in Perak may be found in M. A. Mallal, 'J. W. W. Birch: Causes of his Assassination', unpublished M.A. Thesis, University of Malaya, Singapore, 1952; and R. O. Winstedt and R. J. Wilkinson, 'History of Perak', *JMBRAS*, Vol. XII, Part 1, 1934.

94. W. Jervois, born in 1821, attended the Royal Military Academy, Woolwich, and was commissioned in the Royal Engineers in 1839. Between 1856 and 1875 he was Assistant and Deputy Inspector-General of Fortifications and reported on defence installations in Canada, the West Indies, India, and Burma. After serving as Governor in Singapore he became Governor of South Australia in 1877 and of New Zealand from 1882 till 1889.

95. Sadka, *The Protected Malay States*, pp. 98–101.

96. Quoted in Swettenham, *British Malaya*, pp. 216–17.

97. Born in 1846, W. E. Maxwell was the son of Sir Peter Benson Maxwell, Chief Justice of the Straits Settlements, 1867–71. He qualified as a lawyer in 1867 and from 1869 to 1878 served as a magistrate in various parts of the Straits Settlements. From August 1876 to 1882 he was Assistant Resident, Perak, and later became Commissioner of Lands, Straits Settlements. After acting as Resident Councillor, Penang, between 1887 and 1889, he was appointed Resident in Selangor. In March 1892 he went to Singapore as Colonial Secretary and acted as Governor from September 1893 to January 1894. In 1895 he went to the Gold Coast as Governor and died two years later. He wrote extensively, especially on land problems. His two books were *Straits Settlements, Present and Future Land Systems*, Rangoon, 1883, and *Memorandum on the Introduction of a Land Code in the Native States in the Malay Peninsula*, Singapore, 1894.

98. Acting Governor to all Residents, 19 December 1893, SGR 1895.

99. The other districts of Selangor were Kuala Lumpur, Kuala Langat, Ulu Langat, and Ulu Selangor.

100. Batang Padang, Kuala Kangsar, Larut, Lower Perak, and Upper Perak were the remaining districts.

101. Resident, Selangor, to Col. Sec., 7 December 1877, SGR, 1877.

102. Col. Sec. to Resident, Selangor, 3 June 1876, SGR, 1876.

103. E. Innes, *The Chersonese with the Gilding Off*, London, 1885; reprinted Kuala Lumpur, 1974, Vol. 1, pp. 49–72.

104. After several years' service in the Royal and Indian Navies, B. Douglas was appointed harbour-master of South Australia in 1854, during which time he surveyed parts of the South Australian coast. He was then selected to be Resident of the Northern Territory, and after four years in that capacity arrived in Singapore in 1874 to assume duties as Police Magistrate. In November 1875 he was appointed Assistant Resident, Selangor, and was promoted to Resident in 1876. Douglas resigned in 1882 and died in Canada in 1906.

105. In theory these officials were supposed to attend State Council meetings, act in judicial capacities when so authorized, help the police in the repression and prevention of crime, settle or arbitrate in cases too petty to be brought before the legally constituted courts, carry out such Government directives as were issued from time to time, keep bridle tracks and other means of communications open, and report in detail on any mining and agricultural lands disputes. Resident, Selangor, to Governor, 9 June 1882, SGR, 1882.

106. Resident, Selangor, to Governor, 9 June 1882, SGR, 1882.

107. Governor to Col. Sec., 14 April 1882, SGR, 1882.

108. Yap Ah Loy, a *Kheh*, was born in 1837 and had come to Malacca from the Kwangtung province of China at the age of seventeen. For a time he worked as shop assistant, mine cook, and pig dealer around the mines of Lukut and Sungei Ujong but then enrolled as a fighting man in the employ of the Capitan China of Sungei Ujong. At the age of twenty-six he became Capitan China of Sungei Ujong before moving on to Kuala Lumpur. In 1868, with the aid of Chinese and Malay leaders in the area, he succeeded to the office of Capitan China of Kuala Lumpur. Between 1870 and 1872 he fought for Kuala Lumpur on the side of Tunku Dziauddin and when the State's administration was taken over by the British he was recognized as Capitan and sat on the State Council. In 1880, when the Resident moved his headquarters from Klang to Kuala Lumpur, Ah Loy's power was seriously curtailed. He died in April 1885. For details see S. M. Middlebrook, 'Yap Ah Loy', *JMBRAS*, Vol. XXIV, Part 2, 1951, pp. 1–127; J. M. Gullick, 'Kuala Lumpur, 1880–1895', *JMBRAS*, Vol. XXVIII, Part 4, 1955, pp. 5–172.

109. HC to CO, Desp. No. 328, 4 September 1902, CO 273/1902; and Sadka, *The Protected Malay States*, pp. 390–1.

110. Report of the Acting Assistant Resident, Selangor, 8 April 1875, SGR, 1875.

111. Governor to Col. Sec., 14 April 1882, SGR, 1882.

112. Letter of Authority and Regulations for the Guidance of Native Penghulus, *Straits Settlements Legislative Council Proceedings*, No. 23, 1883.

113. Acting Resident, Selangor, to Collector and Magistrate, Ulu Selangor (Macarthy), 1 December 1883, SGR, 1883.

114. These included the Judicial, Land, Mining, Survey, Public Works, Education, and Audit Departments.

115. Memorandum on the District Officer, by W. E. Maxwell, 11 April 1890, SGR, 1890.

116. The District Officer, by Maxwell, 11 April 1890, SGR, 1890.

117. For more details see Sadka, *The Protected Malay States*, pp. 176–95. The membership of the Selangor State Council comprised Tunku Dziauddin, the Viceroy; Captain Bloomfield Douglas, the Resident; J. Innes, Collector and Magistrate, Langat; Syed Zin, Superintendent of Public Works; Yap Ah Loy, the Capitan China; Raja Kahar, the Sultan's son; and the Tunku Panglima Raja. Governor to CO, Desp. No. 88, 22 March 1877, CO 273/1877.

118. Bird, *The Golden Chersonese*, p. 217.

119. Among the chiefs who felt slighted were Tunku Dziauddin, Syed Zin, the Tunku Panglima Raja, Raja Musa, and Raja Mahmood. Innes to Kimberley, 2 May 1882, SGR, 1882.

120. 1 *bhara* is equivalent to 400 lb. or 300 *kati*.

121. *Selangor State Council Minutes*, 25 August 1877, Klang.

122. *Selangor State Council Minutes*, 21 April 1880, Kuala Lumpur.

123. Col. Sec. to Resident, Selangor, 17 May 1898, enclosure No. 1 in Instructions to the British Resident and other papers relating to the Protected Malay States, Cmd. 2410, *Parliamentary Papers*, Vol. LI, 1879.

124. J. P. Rodger was born in 1851, educated at Cambridge, and qualified as a lawyer in 1877. In 1882, while travelling in Malaya, he accepted an appointment as Chief Magistrate and Commissioner of Lands, Selangor. He spoke Malay and enjoyed cordial relations with both Malays and Chinese. In 1888 he was appointed Resident of Pahang and later, in 1896, became Resident of Selangor. His last appointment in Malaya was as Resident of Perak, 1902. On his retirement from Malaya in 1903, he went as Governor to the Gold Coast.

125. F. A. Swettenham, *Footprints in Malaya*, London, 1942, p. 9.

126. Abdul Samad became Sultan in 1857 but the confused political situation in Selangor led him, in 1866, to appoint his son-in-law from Kedah, Tunku Dziauddin, Viceroy of the State. The British regarded him as an odd eccentric with no interest in active politics and content to lead a simple life. He was very interested in the daily life of Langat and spent most of his time wandering around the village simply dressed, watching cock fights, and smoking opium. For more details see Sadka, *The Protected Malay States*, pp. 167–70; J. M. Gullick, 'A Careless Heathen Philosopher', *JMBRAS*, Vol. XXVI, Part 1, 1953; Innes, *The Chersonese with the Gilding Off*, pp. 38–9; C. D. Cowan, 'Sir Frank Swettenham's Perak Journals', *JMBRAS*, Vol. XXIX, Part 4, 1951, p. 114.

127. On three of these occasions, 19 February 1884, 22 October 1885, and 27 January 1886, the Council met in Kuala Lumpur and the Sultan did not want to travel there. The fourth time was on 27 September 1884 when the Sultan's son and heir, Raja Musa, died.

128. *Selangor State Council Minutes*, 1883–7.

129. An interesting traveller's account of the ceremony can be found in Bird, *The Golden Chersonese and the Way Thither*, p. 230: 'The Sultan sat on a high-backed carved chair or throne. All the other chairs were plain. The Resident sat on his right, I on his left and on my left the Raja Moussa, with other sons of the Sultan, and some native princes. Mr. Syers acted as interpreter. Outside there were double lines of military police, and the bright adjacent slopes were covered with the Sultan's followers and other Malays. The balcony of the audience hall, which has a handsome balustrade, was full of Malay followers in bright reds and cool white. . . . The Resident read the proceedings of the Council of the day before, and the Sultan confirmed them. The nominal approval of measures initiated by the Resident and agreed to in Council, and the signing of death warrants are among the few prerogatives which High Highness retains.'

130. *Selangor State Council Minutes*, 13 January 1888, Kuala Lumpur.

131. Maxwell justified his actions to the Governor, Sir Cecil Clementi Smith, by asserting that publication of opinions voiced by some members of the Council might make it difficult, under special circumstances, to obtain a genuine expression of views. The Resident believed that on occasions a Malay member might be willing to support a certain policy but would prefer not to let the general population know what his advice had been. Maxwell also feared that some members might be encouraged, by the publicity printing brought, to earn popularity by opposition. Resident to Col. Sec., 10 March 1890, SGR, 1890.

132. W. H. Treacher was born in 1849 and joined the Labuan service in 1871. Ten years later he became the first Governor of British North Borneo. In 1888 he was appointed Secretary to the Perak Government and became Resident of Selangor four years later. With Federation, in 1896, he succeeded Swettenham as Resident of Perak and was promoted to Resident-General in 1902. He retired in 1904.

133. *Selangor State Council Minutes*, 11 April 1893, Kuala Lumpur.

134. C. C. Smith was Colonial Secretary of the Straits Settlements from 1878 to 1885, before being appointed Governor.

135. *Selangor State Council Minutes*, 12 December 1893, Kuala Lumpur.

136. *Selangor State Council Minutes*, 12 June 1894, Kuala Lumpur.

137. *Perak State Council Minutes*, 21 June 1892, Taiping.

138. *Perak State Council Minutes*, 19 December 1892, Taiping.

139. The Governor's interference was not confined to specific subjects and embraced a wide range of Councils' deliberations. The Colonial Office, by contrast, never interfered directly with the affairs of the Councils.

140. The duty from tin in Perak increased from $140,292 in 1877 to $1,669,707 in 1895. In Selangor the returns were $1,520,927 in 1895 compared with $111,920 in 1878, while in Negri Sembilan they were $164,712 in 1895 and $27,901 in 1884. Pahang, the last State to come under British protection, did not possess much tin and the figures were $1,910 in 1889 which increased to $24,467 in 1895. The total revenue for Perak in 1877 was $312,872 and $4,033,611 in 1895. The figures for Selangor were $189,897 in 1878 and $3,805,211 in 1895, for Negri Sembilan $121,175 in 1884 and $535,442 in 1895, and for Pahang $30,390 in 1889 and $106,743 in 1895. Special General Return, *FMS Annual Report, 1896*, Taiping, 1896, CO 576.

141. Details of urbanization may be found in N. Ginsburg and P. E. Roberts, *Malaya*, Singapore, 1958, pp. 52–61; Ooi Jin Bee, *Land, People and Economy in Malaya*, pp. 169–73; Hamzah Sendut, 'Pattern of Urbanisation in Malaya', *MJTG*, Vol. XVI, 1962, pp. 114–30; P. P. Courtenay, *A Geography of Trade and Development in Malaya*, London, 1972, pp. 246–53; Anon., 'Towns', in *Twentieth Century Impressions of British Malaya* (eds.) A. Wright and H. A. Cartwright, London, 1908, pp. 303–13; E. Cooper, 'Urbanisation in Malaya', *Population Studies*, Vol. V, Part 2, pp. 117–31.

142. Perak Annual Report, 1890, Cmd. 6576, *Parliamentary Papers*, Vol. LVI, 1892; Chai Hon Chan, *The Development of British Malaya, 1896–1909*, p. 227.

II

FEDERATION AND THE RESIDENT-GENERAL

BY 1895 it became clear to British officials in the Straits Settlements and London that the Residential System had become increasingly unworkable and had not fulfilled the expectations of the Colonial power. The proponents of change blamed failure on the lack of uniformity within the Protected States.[1] Dissatisfaction was also expressed over the role of the Governor's chief assistant, the Colonial Secretary, who was the principal channel of communication between the Residents on the one hand and the Governor and Colonial Office on the other, and advised the Governor on all matters concerning the Malay States.[2] In the beginning this arrangement had not seemed manifestly disadvantageous, but as the years went by the knowledge and experience of the Residents increased considerably and out-stripped that of the Colonial Secretary to such an extent that a separate but subordinate officer known as the Assistant Colonial Secretary for Native States[3] had to be appointed to deal with the Protected States. The rapid progress in the work of settlement and organization forced Residents to act on their own initiative and did not leave them with the time to carry on extended correspondence with Singapore. They were increasingly driven to act independently and created a situation where more and more discrepancies appeared between one State and another, especially in administrative regula-tions, land laws, mining rules, fishing regulations, court practices, and attitudes towards Malay traditions and customs. This was obviously unsatisfactory and there were several complaints; no Resident was disposed to give way and controversies often occurred which had to be referred to the Governor for final decision. There were also times when a Resident died or was removed from office and the new incumbent proceeded promptly to upset much of what his predecessor had done. The matter was further complicated because it was always possible that an officer with no knowledge of Malaya could be appointed Colonial Secretary; his proximity to the

Governor put him at a great advantage and on issues where he disagreed with any particular Resident recourse to the Secretary of State was inevitable.[4] Some form of standardization was considered essential and the necessity to appoint an officer with such responsibilities, resident in the Malay States, was widely recognized by the British as being imperative.

The first official suggestion for some kind of a federation originated from C. P. Lucas[5] of the Colonial Office in March 1892[6] and was based on discussions he had had with Swettenham.[7] The document proposed a union or federation of states with a common administration and common finances and it was hoped that these arrangements would result in greater efficiency and economy. Although the Governor, who would also take on the title of High Commissioner of the Malay States, was expected to retain overall control the scheme envisaged the appointment of a Resident-General who was to be the Chief British Officer in the Peninsula and who would visit, inspect, and supervise the States. Other proposals included the establishment of a common treasury, the creation of federal departments,[8] the setting up of a High Court, and the institution of a unified Civil Service.[9]

The idea was expounded again by Swettenham in August and September 1893 when he suggested a federation under a Resident-General and underlined the need for uniformity, the wisdom of pooling resources, the advantages of having a unified Civil Service, and common defence arrangements.[10] Further negotiations, discussions, and consultations among British administrators ensued and the consensus was that the best solution would be a federation with one system of administration and a common purse, the idea being that the stronger and more wealthy states would help the weaker and less prosperous. In 1894 and early 1895 the Governor, C. B. H. Mitchell,[11] visited the Protected States, conferred with the Residents and other influential personalities in the Straits Settlements and on the Peninsula, and concluded that the system in existence was cumbersome and highly unsatisfactory.[12] What was needed, therefore, was the preparation of the political instrument that would indicate the consent of the Malay Rulers to the idea of some sort of union and at the same time set out the scope and obligations of the bond, and an administrative scheme that would ensure its efficient working. Mitchell recommended that a British officer be sent to the various states to explain the plan and obtain the agreement of the Rulers.[13] Swettenham was selected for the task and was advised that a neces-

sary preliminary was to arrange a careful translation of the draft
Federation Agreement into Malay so as to avoid any ambiguities in
the English text. Great tact was called for in explaining to the Sultans
that the object of Federation was to advance the common good of
the States without in any way diminishing their powers and privileges.[14] Indeed, in approving the Draft Treaty the Secretary of
State for the Colonies, Joseph Chamberlain, had insisted that

... no pains should be spared to safeguard the position and the dignity of the
Native Rulers, to invite them to co-operate as fully as heretofore with the British
Advisers in promoting the advancement of their respective territories and subjects, and to give them the assurance that such changes as shall be made are solely
intended to promote strength by combination, uniformity of policy and harmony
of purpose.[15]

The Sultans were also to be assured that Federation would strengthen
the powers of the States in the administration of justice, the suppression of crime, defence against aggression, means of communication,
and give them the increased strength that combination for a common
purpose implied.[16]

Swettenham's first stop was at Kuala Kangsar where he met
Sultan Idris Mershid-el Aazam Shah of Perak, the most influential
and economically powerful of the Protected States Sultans. Idris,
born in 1849, was the grandson of Sultan Abdul Malik Mansur Shah
(1806–25), and son-in-law of Sultan Yusuf, Regent (1877–86) and
Sultan (1886–7).[17] In his younger days, 1874–5, he was a constant
companion of Sultan Abdullah but, after the assassination of
J. W. W. Birch, he detached himself from Abdullah's group and,
with Yusuf, was prepared to co-operate with the British. He was
appointed Sultan in 1887 with the help of the British, although,
according to the Perak system of rotation, he was not in the direct
line of succession. Idris had a smattering of English and was a 'loyal
and enthusiastic imperialist'.[18] In the circumstances it was hardly
surprising that the Sultan at once signed and sealed the document
carried by Swettenham.[19]

In Pahang, the British emissary saw Ahmad Maatham Shah
Ali who took the title of Sultan in 1882 and was so proclaimed
by his chiefs in 1884.[20] His was not only the most recent of the Malay
States to have accepted a British Resident but was also the most
reluctant. Although induced in 1887–8 to accept a British officer, the
Sultan retained a capacity for leadership and a military genius which
came to the fore in the disturbances of 1892.[21] A strong, independent
personality, he was a Sultan of the old school who still had to be

reckoned with. On the occasion of Swettenham's visit he proved to be stubborn and took the better part of four hours before he signed the Federation Agreement.[22]

Selangor was Swettenham's next stop and Sultan Abdul Samad[23] posed few problems. Swettenham knew the Sultan well, had got on with him when he was Resident of Selangor, and obtained his signature within an hour.[24] The State of Negri Sembilan posed somewhat peculiar problems because the territory had, initially, consisted of six small states each under the control of a chieftain. A Confederation of Sri Menanti, Rembau, Tampin, and Johol was effected by the British in 1889 and to this were added Sungei Ujong and Jelebu in 1895. When Swettenham went there in 1895 the overall suzerainty of the Yang-di-Pertuan Besar had not been regularized[25] and he was forced to obtain the agreement of a number of territorial chiefs. The Dato Bandar of Sungei Ujong agreed, on behalf of himself and the Dato Klana, after half an hour. The Dato of Jelebu took a further half hour and the Yam Tuan of Sri Menanti with the Datos of Johol, Rembau, and Tampin took a total of three hours.[26]

The choice of Swettenham to accomplish this delicate mission was not without significance. In addition to being the most experienced of the British administrators he knew every one of the Rulers personally and what was most important, had the strong and dominant personality which would have overcome the reluctance of any Malay chief. Exactly what he told the Rulers is not a matter of record, but the speed of the whole operation suggests that little effort was made to explain the several ramifications that would have become consequent upon Federation. It is significant that Swettenham went first to the Sultan of Perak. Besides being the State where the Residential System had originated it was also the most prosperous. From the political, and indeed the psychological, point of view, therefore, the signature of Idris was an encouragment for the others to follow suit.[27] Some indication of what might have been discussed at that meeting was later outlined by E. W. Birch[28] who claimed that Swettenham gave a solemn pledge to the Ruler that the Treaty would not introduce any radical changes.[29]

Swettenham's anxiety to get the Draft document quickly signed prevented the Sultans from either consulting with their premier chiefs, or discussing the proposals in their State Councils; and the British emissary was quite aware that in this respect the Rulers had failed in their duty to the people. What is more interesting is that the Federation scheme was a profound secret until it became an accomplished fact. There was no indication that the Sultans desired a change, no public discussion of the proposals, and the subject was never even mentioned in any of the local newspapers. Once the Treaty was signed the British were in no particular hurry to implement the plan. Although the agreed details of the scheme were published in the Straits Settlements Gazette on 23 August 1895, implementation did not take place until 1 July 1896—a whole year after the Agreement was signed. One of the reasons for the delay was the suggestion that the Treaty was premature and the Government found itself unable to carry it into effect.[30]

The Treaty of Federation contained five articles. The first two indicated that the various Rulers agreed to 'place themselves and their States under the protection of the British Government' and 'to constitute their countries a Federation, to be known as the Protected Malay States' which were to be administered 'under the advice of the British Government'. Article three stated that the arrangement did 'not imply that any one Ruler or Chief shall exercise any power or authority' over any other State. The most significant innovation, however, was the creation of a Resident-General provided by clause four:

The above-named Rulers agree to accept a British Officer, to be styled the Resident-General, as the agent and representative of the British Government under the Governor of the Straits Settlements. They undertake to provide him with suitable accommodation, with such salary as is determined by Her Majesty's Government, and to follow his advice in all matters of administration other than those touching the Muhammadan religion. The appointment of the Resident-General will not affect the obligations of the Malay Rulers towards the British Residents now existing or hereafter appointed to offices in the above-mentioned Protected States.[31]

The first part of article five made provision for one State to aid another in respect of men, money, or 'other respects as the British Government through its duly appointed officers may advise' and, if required, provide troops for the defence of the Straits Settlements. The final part of the last article confirmed that: 'Nothing in this Agreement is intended to curtail any of the powers of authority now held by any of the above-named Rulers in their respective States, nor does it alter the relations now existing between any of the States named and the British Empire.'[32] No mention was made of the title of 'High Commissioner' and the name 'Federated Malay States' was conspicuously absent. The Treaty did not admit the grant of executive control, alter the powers of Residents in relation to the Sultans, or give the Resident-General executive control of the separate states. The constitutional position of the Malay States was not altered and the British representative was accepted only in an advisory capacity.

The use of the term 'federation' in the context of the new arrangement raises important conceptual arguments because in the case of the Malay States the British made no attempt to create a federation in the legislative sense of the word. Basically, federal government is one where the functions of government are 'divided in such a way that the relationship between the legislature which has authority over the whole territory and those legislatures which have authority over parts of the territory is one of co-ordinate partners in the government process'.[33] A true federation, in other words, involves the surrender of certain often specified state rights to a central authority, and a division of powers among bodies with limited and co-ordinate authority.[34] The Constitution of the Commonwealth of Australia, enacted in 1900, was a clear example of a federal constitution. It established an administration for the whole country which, within a sphere, exercised powers independently of the state governments; while the state governments, within a sphere, could act independently of the Commonwealth Government. Neither the States nor the Central Government, acting alone, could alter the other's power as laid down in the Constitution. The Canadian Constitution of 1867 divided powers between provincial and Dominion legislatures so that the provinces had exclusive legislative control over a list of specified subjects and the Dominion had exclusive legislative control over the rest which were also specified, but not exhaustively.[35] In the case of the Malay States, however, the Federation Treaty (1895) did not establish a proper central government and, in fact, not only did it not apportion powers but expressly preserved all existing State rights. Either the use of the term 'federation', as applied to the union of Perak, Selangor, Negri Sembilan, and Pahang, was due to the ignorance of those employing it, or it was a deliberate attempt to create a legalistic misnomer.[36]

In the wider perspective of British imperial policy there had also occurred a trend which favoured the constitution of federations. Throughout the 1870s and 1880s, imperialists in Britain had striven to devise a better system of regulating relations between the mother country and its colonies. Various proposals were promulgated but the principal ones were the admission of colonial representatives to the British Parliament, a federal constitution on the lines of the

Canadian or American models, and a Council of Advice consisting of representatives from the colonies. Of these the federal solution was most widely advocated, but it was only after Joseph Chamberlain became Colonial Secretary on 1 July 1895 'that the idea of a closer union of the British Empire was transferred from the region of nebulous aspiration to the sphere of practical politics'.[37] Chamberlain was the one person capable of providing the leadership to effect the consolidation of the British Empire and had pledged his faith in imperial federation as early as 1886.[38] The decision, therefore, to create some form of a Malayan federation might well have been a part of a larger pattern.

In practical terms the Federation Treaty carefully evaded recognition that the Residents, ever since the inauguration of the Residential System, were the actual rulers in their respective territories, and persisted in placing the newly-created Resident-General in the same theoretical framework of an officer offering authoritative advice without really governing. These scrupulous attempts to maintain the fiction of indirect rule might have been designed as a sop to the Malay sovereigns. No attempt was made to define the role and functions of the Resident-General, no specific guidelines for future administration were laid down, and all in all the document was remarkable for its loose phrasing and vagueness.

Detailed plans for the government of the Federated Malay States were, however, worked out separately and, according to Swettenham, the Resident-General as the representative of the Governor in the Peninsula based in Kuala Lumpur, was expected to travel extensively within the area and keep in close touch with Rulers and Residents and with every new administrative development. Without in any way undermining the status of the Malay Sultans he was expected to secure uniformity of practice in the four States. It was also contemplated that he would initiate beneficial schemes for the Federation and in this he would be aided by a number of new officers whose duties would be common to all the states.[39] The major changes, as anticipated, involved the powers of Residents. Under the new arrangements, they became the channels of communication between the Resident-General and State officials and unofficials; their link with the Governor was no longer the Colonial Secretary but the Resident-General. In the event of differences of opinion Residents could appeal to the Governor, through the Resident-General, but, pending the Governor's decision, the Resident-General's instructions were to be carried out. They were expected to prepare Annual State

Estimates and forward them to the Resident-General by 1 October for submission to the Governor. Their prerogative to make new appointments on the Fixed Establishment or on the Provisional and Temporary Establishment was taken away from them, and they were required to submit Annual Reports, according to a set format, to the Resident-General, by 15 April.[40]

State Councils were expected to continue and to conduct their business as hitherto, but it was clearly stated that they were merely legislative and advisory and would have no control over public expenditure. They were empowered to decide on the selection, remuneration, removal, and retirement of Malay officials subject to the approval of the Resident-General and the Governor. Even the drafts of all legislative measures to be presented to Councils had to be submitted by Residents to the Resident-General for transmission to the Governor, and no enactment could be published or implemented without the prior sanction of the Governor.[41]

British officers in the Malay States were constituted into a unified civil service eligible for promotion from one State to another without loss of seniority. Powers of magistrates, court practices, scales of fees, and other judicial procedures were to be standardized and a judge was to be appointed to go on circuit to the headquarters of each State, hear appeals, and, where possible, try capital cases. Another priority was to obtain an Attorney-General to draft all legal enactments, contracts, and other important documents, and to advise the Governor, Resident-General, and the Residents, on all legal matters. To preserve law and order, the organization and general direction of a Sikh force was entrusted to an officer to be known as the Commandant of the Malay States Sikhs.[42]

Among the projected Federal appointments were those of Chief Engineer to take charge of the Public Works Department, Chief Railway Engineer to advise on railway systems, by-laws, leave rules, and all matters affecting the construction and working of the Malay States Railways, Chief Auditor, Chief Surgeon, Chief Surveyor, Chief Commissioner of Lands and Mines, Commissioner of Police and Prisons, Inspector of Schools, and Inspector of Posts and Telegraphs. These officials would correspond direct with the Resident-General and receive instructions from him, but did not have the authority to issue instructions contrary to the rulings of Residents to State departments. Disagreements between Residents and Federal Officers were to be referred to the Resident-General, pending whose decision, the Residents' views were to prevail. These details indicated that the role of Federal Officers, at least initially, was to be purely advisory.[43]

The first Resident-General of the Federated Malay States was Swettenham and the appointment, in terms of suitability and experience, was widely expected.[44] As the premier official in the Malay States, he saw himself as the vital element in the territory's development and progress. His impeccable background gave him a first-rate understanding of the principal personalities, as good an idea of any single state as its Resident, and a far wider perspective of the Federation than anyone else. As the crucial link holding the Federal machinery of government together he personified unity of purpose and identity of treatment, he was expected to have the foresight and breadth of vision to initiate works and policies calculated to serve the best political and economic interests of the States.[45] Unquestionably the Resident-General was designed to be the guiding light and the source of all inspiration in finding answers to every possible problem. In theory, his authority could only be countermanded by the Colonial Office or the High Commissioner. Swettenham was fortunate in the sense that within the bureaucracy of the Colonial Office he enjoyed the staunch support of Lucas who drafted most of the despatches dealing with the Malay States from 1878 onwards. This was a great asset and a useful weapon in the arguments that Swettenham had with the Governor, C. B. H. Mitchell. Swettenham's ideas and concepts of the role of a High Commissioner evolved as a result of his earlier experiences as Resident. These had led him to believe that a Governor who spoke no Malay, was a stranger to the area, did not reside in the Malay States, and whose duties in the Straits Settlements were more than sufficient to occupy his time and energies, could not possibly efficiently oversee the activities of Residents. Such considerations had persuaded Residents to implement individual ideas and pursue independent policies. Whatever continuity of ideas emerged did so only when control of affairs was in the hands of officials who subscribed to the ideas of some particular Resident they had served under, or when a Resident of one of the States was able to coerce the Governor to insist on the adoption of a similar principle in another State.[46] So when he became Resident-General, Swettenham was determined to be the fount of power so far as the conduct of affairs within the Federation was concerned. His obvious ability and immense self-confidence combined with his extrovert character and firm opinions were qualities which contributed to his success as an administrator.

In the day-to-day administration of the States Swettenham had to rely on the Residents and assured them that, although they were obliged to act on his instructions, it lay within their rights, in the event of any disagreement, to appeal to the High Commissioner in Singapore. The Resident-General acknowledged the importance of Residents because they were local men known by sight throughout their respective States. They were accepted by Sultans and chiefs as 'their men' who would support them against anyone who threatened the interests of the States.[47] In other words, although Swettenham believed that he had undisputed control over his Residents he also recognized that they had important functions to perform in voicing State opinions and acting as custodians of State rights and privileges. On their part, the Residents were aware of their diminished authority consequent on Federation, but were prepared to work loyally and strenuously with Swettenham. To gauge the temper and feelings within the component States, Conferences of Residents were convened by the Resident-General, where important issues were fully discussed, and which provided a forum for the free exchange of ideas. When necessary, officials with specialized knowledge of particular subjects were asked to attend. These meetings thus were an embodiment of a kind of a Consultative Council to the Resident-General.[48]

As Resident-General, Swettenham had as his Residents, Treacher in Perak, Rodger in Selangor, the Hon. Martin Lister[49] and later E. W. Birch in Negri Sembilan, and Hugh Clifford[50] and Arthur Butler[51] in Pahang. He maintained cordial relations with them and there were no major disagreements during his tenure in this office. When Treacher was first appointed Resident in Perak under the Federation Scheme, he did complain about the status of his new post but his complaints were directed not at the Resident-General but the Colonial Office. He protested that, despite his promotion to Resident of Perak, his status had in fact been diminished. By being subjected to the control of the Resident-General he was deprived of 'all original and personal control and initiative in respect of the most important Departments' and feared that his new job was inferior even to that of Collector and Magistrate in the Indian Civil Service. The Colonial Office, however, warned Treacher that unless he acquiesced in the new arrangements he could not expect to be considered for any kind of promotion outside the Malay States.[52]

So far as the alienation of land was concerned, Swettenham empowered Residents to alienate, on behalf of the Sultans, and without reference to the Resident-General, six hundred and forty acres to any individual provided that the grant did not exceed an aggregate of this amount held in partnership or sole ownership by the same person.[53] In the case of mining land the Residents could make grants of up to three hundred acres.[54]

In 1896 the Colonial Office appointed a number of Federal Officers whose duties were meant to transcend narrow state boundaries. The original plan had been to appoint eleven such officers each in charge of a department but in the first year of Federation only seven were selected: they were the Judicial Commissioner, L. C. Jackson;[55] the Legal Adviser, T. H. Kershaw; the Commandant of the Malay States Guides and Inspector of Prisons, Colonel R. F. S. Walker;[56] the Commissioner of Police, H. C. Syers;[57] the Commissioner of Lands and Mines, H. C. Belfield;[58] and the Secretary for Chinese Affairs, G. T. Hare.[59] An Inspector of Schools, J. Driver, was appointed in 1897 and in 1899 the post of Auditor and Accountant was filled. When Swettenham was Resident-General these officers were not allowed to exercise executive powers. Theirs was a purely advisory role and the departments they advised remained separate entities, thus avoiding further erosion in the powers of Residents.

In discussions preceding Federation, British officials had envisaged the setting up of a Federal Council, on the lines of the *Bose-vaka-Turaga* of Fiji,[60] or of the *Pitso* of Basutoland, as a consultative and advisory body composed of those who were at that time members of the State Councils. Much emphasis was laid on the pomp and ceremony that would accompany meetings of the Council and it was hoped that these occasions would demonstrate to the Malay Sultans that the Federation Treaty had not diminished their dignity and prestige.[61] When Federation was effected on 1 July 1896, however, no such Council was established and the obvious problem of trying to fit the Sultans into the new arrangements still remained. There had been tacit agreement among the architects of the Federation that the status of the Rulers should not in any way be altered; but it was also recognized that for the objects of the scheme to be successfully realized the control of all major decisions and policies had to be exercised by the British administrators on the spot. Thus although the Treaty placed the Resident-General in the position of someone offering authoritative advice, and not really governing, this provision was never taken seriously. Swettenham insisted that by agreeing to the appointment of a Resident-General the Sultans had accepted that the British officer would exercise executive control. He repeated this view in October 1925 when he referred to 'a scheme of federation and administration which for the first time recognized the control instead of the advice of British officers'.[62] The British believed that the Sultans consented to the appointment of a Resident-General with the expectation that it would provide them with a representative with greater authority than that of any single Resident, support their interests, and plead their cause.[63]

The first few months of working the new system, however, saw a revived discussion on the need for Rulers' Conferences. Annual meetings were suggested, with the High Commissioner, if possible, presiding, and the Resident-General, the Malay Sultans, the Residents and members of State Councils attending to discuss matters affecting the mutual interests of the Malay States. It was believed that these gatherings, if carefully managed, would be most interesting and valuable. But the aspirations were never fully realized and although the first Conference did take place in July 1897 its significance was limited in that it was the first occasion when Rulers from the four Protected States had met in an atmosphere of peace and friendship. The assembly itself concentrated on maintaining this air of cordiality and informality, the accent was on social and sporting functions which were meticulously arranged and great pains were taken to ensure that everyone generally enjoyed themselves to the utmost. The only item of any consequence discussed was on the closing day of the Conference and concerned the appointment of *penghulu*. It was also decided that the meetings would not be convened annually but would be held as and when the Resident-General, with the approval of the High Commissioner, so decided.[64]

Thus Swettenham, during his tenure as Resident-General (1 January 1896–12 December 1901), succeeded through a combination of strength of character, tact, diplomacy, and foresight in launching the newly created entity which came to be known as the Federated Malay States. From the British point of view, he not only created an efficient and smooth-running administration but also presided over the emergence and growth of a common economic policy for the region. This was aimed at attracting capital, encouraging labour immigration, and assisting in the development of mineral and agricultural resources by the construction of roads, railways, and drainage and irrigation works.[65] As mentioned in Chapter I, during the period 1874–96 little had been done to examine the country's mineral resources and the total area under cultivation was insignificant. The only economic policy that existed was a *laissez-faire* one which encouraged prospective investors by expending revenue on railways and public works, provided loans at low rates of interest, alienated land on easy terms, and levied low taxes on new enterprises.[66]

Swettenham realized that it would be vain to presume that European investors would venture into tropical surroundings with manifest labour and transport problems unless profit prospects could be made attractive. According to him it was unrealistic to expect traders, miners, and planters to invest in the Federation for philanthropic reasons or for the purpose of raising the revenues of the territory for the public good.[67] An economic policy designed to lure the much-needed capital was, therefore, vital. In formulating the guidelines, the Resident-General saw the need for more coolies, extra cash, and better communications. He was, personally, most concerned with the extension of the railway network. Until Federation, railways had been constructed in order to establish direct communications between the mining centres of Perak, Selangor, and Negri Sembilan, and the seaports. The lines acted as feeders to the main waterway down the Straits of Malacca and linked Taiping to Port Weld, Kuala Lumpur to Klang, Seremban to Port Dickson, and Ipoh to Telok Anson. Swettenham's proposals for railway extension, for the first time, looked at the Federated Malay States as a whole. In Perak he wanted the Larut and Kinta systems linked at Chemor so as to ensure economy in working, good administration, and convenience to travellers. A track from Taiping to Kuala Prai was also envisaged as a means to opening up the Krian district and connecting the Larut tinfields with Penang harbour. On a broader front it was just as important to couple the Perak and Selangor systems with a line that would traverse a rich but almost untouched district where gold and tin workings had opened up and where there was a large amount of good agricultural land. In Pahang, a line was planned from Kuala Lipis to a point on the road between Kuala Kubu and Kuala Lipis. This would serve the mines at Raub, Tras, and Penjam, and encourage the speedy development of the richest known mining area in the State. The final element in Swettenham's blueprint was a line from the southern end of the Selangor Railway at or near Cheras, to join up with the Sungei Ujong Railway at Seremban.[68]

An essential element of Swettenham's policy was that the works should begin as soon as possible and not follow the pattern of pre-Federation railway construction when approximately fifteen years elapsed in producing one hundred and fifty miles of track. The advantages of an efficient railway system had by 1897 become obvious. The receipts from the Perak and Selangor network represented 8 per cent on the invested capital and the extra two hundred miles of railway would open up valuable mining and agricultural areas, provide a rapid and cheap transport system, and link the western Malay states with the ocean-going steamers at Penang. The project was expected to cost £1,000,000 and to pay for this Swettenham proposed to raise a loan of £500,000 in England at favourable rates of interest.[69]

The Governor, C. B. H. Mitchell, was more cautious and preferred to regard railway extensions in the context of the available resources of the country and the natural traffic advantages already afforded by roads, rivers, or other means of communication. He did not think the potential revenues of the Federated Malay States justified a policy where railway extensions would be financed through a loan. The Governor maintained that a pattern of waterways and good roads, together with cheap available labour and materials for utilizing both, would sorely handicap a railway as soon as it left the points beyond which it would be used for heavy traffic, the assumption being that the heavy traffic would find its way by the cheapest method to and from the port of shipment.[70] The Colonial Office initially agreed with Mitchell and, since the traffic was not sufficiently assured for an ambitious scheme, preferred to proceed gradually, using the resources of the states rather than resort to borrowing.[71] The Resident-General, however, persisted in arguing his case strongly[72] and was supported this time by Lucas and Sir Montague Ommaney within the Colonial Office. The latter advocated a policy of early action because the time factor was vital and he wanted Swettenham to submit a definite programme of construction. He hoped that, allowing for time delays for the completion of surveys and preliminaries, the railway network would be completed in four years.[73] As a result of these recommendations the Secretary of State for the Colonies, Chamberlain, showed willingness to reopen the entire question, and, as a consequence of further discussions, decided to sanction Swettenham's plans. Chamberlain believed that railways in the Federation would be financially remunerative and the added administrative and political advantages were obvious in the sense that the railway network would tend to consolidate the union of the four States. The Secretary of State had great confidence in the Resident-General's experience and good judgement and hoped that Swettenham would superintend the implementation of the railway policy.[74] In the light of subsequent developments, however, the pace of economic progress and the increased revenue from this matched the speed of construction, and the necessity to raise a loan in England did not arise.[75] The optimism and the convictions of Swettenham were thus eminently vindicated and the railways, as an integral element of the economic policy, remained a source of great pride to him.

A liberal land alienation programme was also high on Swettenham's list of economic priorities. All land already alienated or due to be alienated in the first five years of Federation was made secure from reassessments in perpetuity. The idea was to develop permanent cultivation and stake agricultural plantations; and it was considered necessary and practical to offer such concessions, especially because most of the planters interested in the Malay States came principally from countries where there was no enhancement of assessments. As such they resented the imposition of any liability to increased assessment on land they might occupy.[76] No limit was placed on the area of land that could be alienated, although grants in excess of six hundred and forty acres were subject to stringent conditions; the object was to encourage the bona fide planter and discourage the land speculator.[77] A Federal Land Enactment embodying these principles was passed in 1897 and formed the basis of British land policy till March 1903 when an enactment to consolidate and amend the law relating to land was passed.[78]

The problems arising from a shortage of suitable labour and the measures taken to overcome them have already been discussed in Chapter I. It is, therefore, only necessary to state here that British immigration policies were stoutly defended on economic grounds. Most British administrators regarded the Malay as naturally indolent and unwilling to become involved in any work which required extreme and continuous toil. Hence, Swettenham, Clifford, and the other decision-makers argued that the resources of the country could only be adequately developed if all restrictions on immigration could be removed.[79]

In February 1901, Swettenham was promoted to Governor of the Straits Settlements and High Commissioner for the Federated Malay States and he was succeeded as Resident-General by Treacher (13 December 1901 – 31 December 1904). Unlike Swettenham, the new Resident-General was not a Malay scholar and his knowledge of the language was only good enough to enable him to function without the aid of an interpreter. In terms of experience his years of service in the Malay States in various capacities gave him a good knowledge of the country and a valuable insight into Malay character. To his disadvantage he was shy and retiring and never really mixed freely with the Malays or took any special interest in studying their way of life. He had the kind of ability which tended to produce a safe rather than a brilliant administrator, and although he was conscientious and hard-working, strength of character and quickness of decision were not his forte, and he preferred to take the pleasant or popular course. It was alleged that he was inclined to waver under the stress of contradictory advice which was often sought rather than offered.[80] His integrity was suspect and it was believed that he was predisposed to 'take more than was good for him' but no concrete evidence on this subject was profferred.[81]

Treacher's main rival for the post was the Resident Councillor of Penang, who was also Acting Colonial Secretary, C. W. S. Kynnersley. Kynnersley had joined the service in 1872, was much experienced, spoke good Malay, got on well with people, and seemed well qualified for the position. Against these positive qualities was an apparent want of decision and a scant personal knowledge of the Malay States.[82] The possibility of appointing a complete outsider was considered but was rejected on the grounds that someone without any experience of Malaya would certainly be unpopular with Malay Sultans.[83] The ultimate decision, however, rested with the Colonial Office, who after much discussion chose Treacher because of his generally sound ideas; but the lingering doubts that surrounded his personality were manifested in the requirement that he would be obliged to retire from the service on attaining the age of fifty-five, a requisite which allowed him a maximum of four years as Resident-General.[84]

From the beginning of Treacher's tenure of office it was clear that the change in personalities would be accompanied not only by a change in policies but also in methods of administration and outlook. The absence of any particularly influential friends at the Colonial Office and the fact that he did not enjoy the unqualified confidence that Swettenham had inspired, ensured that policies originating from him were bound to be closely scrutinized. He was placed at a further disadvantage because the new High Commissioner was Swettenham and the Colonial Office placed more emphasis on, and gave more credence to, the opinions and recommendations of the acknowledged expert on Malayan affairs. Thus, a situation was created where an admittedly weak Resident-General, working under the looming shadow of an extremely successful predecessor, tried in vain to maintain the momentum and harmony that had been established. In those circumstances Treacher, perhaps predictably, tended to play safe and make as few decisions as he possibly could. The High Commissioner was increasingly called upon to pass judgement on matters concerning the Federated Malay States. In August 1902, for example, an abstract of the Proceedings of a Conference of Residents held in Kuala Lumpur was prepared which recorded the issues that had been discussed. The astonishing feature of this document was that almost every single question to arise was referred to Swettenham together with the resolution of the Residents. The predicament was intensified because the High Commissioner was unable, in many instances, to agree with the resolutions adopted by the Conference.[85] The Colonial Office glossed over this peculiar situation by attributing it to Treacher's character and personality and to the fact that that particular Residents' Conference was concerned chiefly with matters of organization incidental to the systematization of the four states. It was hoped that as the Federation became better organized the need to discuss such questions and to refer them to the High Commissioner would gradually become minimal.[86]

Treacher inherited an administrative system which had been largely shaped by Swettenham's identity. The non-existence of formally established guidelines and rules, the vagueness of the Federation Treaty, and Swettenham's personal vision, allowed him a great deal of scope for experimentation and flexibility. Treacher, on the other hand, was unable to provide the same kind of inspirational leadership and was more comfortable working within formalized structures. In January 1902, therefore, he convened a meeting of Residents and successfully persuaded them to agree to create federal departments with officers responsible for and in administrative charge of their respective departments.[87] The Resident-General also issued a series of executive orders which spelt out in detail the powers and duties of federal officers.

The presence of Swettenham as High Commissioner affected administrative procedures in the Malay States, since it would have been highly unusual for the ex-Resident-General, who had spent so many years of his career in the Federation, to have dissociated himself, to any large extent, from developments there. Swettenham's enthusiasm for, and commitment to, the Peninsula was much too emotional, and the presence of a large number of friends on the mainland ensured a continuing interest. Treacher was directed to submit Annual Estimates of Revenue and Expenditure, and to go through them, in detail, with the High Commissioner. Every set of State Council Minutes and Proceedings, and all Residents' and Federal Heads of Department reports were also required by Singapore. Proceedings of the Assembly of Rulers, Resident-General, Residents and members of State Councils had to be conducted in the presence of the High Commissioner, and the Proceedings of Residents' Conference had to be reported to Swettenham in detail. He also travelled extensively through the Malay States, met whosoever he liked, and discussed Federation affairs with the Resident-General, Malay Sultans, and Residents whenever the need arose.[88]

This changed relationship between the Resident-General and the High Commissioner remained a feature of government until the inauguration of the Federal Council in 1909. In April 1904 Swettenham was succeeded as Governor and High Commissioner by Sir John Anderson (16 April 1904 to 1 September 1911). This was a departure in itself because Anderson, born in 1858, had spent his entire career, before coming to Singapore, within the portals of the Colonial Office. He had joined in 1880 as a second-class clerk and was appointed private secretary to Sir Robert Meade, Permanent Under-Secretary of State for the Colonies, in 1892. In 1897 he was promoted to first-class clerk and in 1901 had accompanied the Prince of Wales on a tour round the British Empire. Anderson's lack of colonial experience did not matter much so far as the Straits Settlements were concerned, but seen in the context of the Federated Malay States the handicap was more apparent. To make matters worse, Treacher left his post in September 1904, and it became necessary to appoint a new officer to that position. Largely due to the recommendations of Anderson, W. T. Taylor[89] was selected for the job. The High Commissioner had great confidence in him (as a man of spare build he came to be known as *ikan kering*, dried fish, by the Malays) and was convinced that he would exert with complete satisfaction the large amount of responsibility entrusted to him.[90] The Colonial Office was not as enthusiastic because Taylor was almost fifty-six years old, was by no means a clever man, and his Ceylon experience, which Anderson considered to be a special qualification for the better organization of the Federation service, could hardly be called an asset, since it was the worst structured in the East.[91] The appointment, however, was sanctioned despite the fact that Taylor spoke no Malay. This last factor was significant because it was desirable that a Resident-General should be capable of communicating with Malay Sultans in their own language. An inability to do so was bound to cause loss of confidence and make it impossible for Taylor to fathom the true feelings and wishes of the Rulers.[92] At this point it may be worth bearing in mind that the Malay is by nature a very polite and courteous individual and any criticism that he might have is invariably couched in figurative language, and for someone unfamiliar with Malay language and culture to grasp the essence of any communication was indeed a mammoth task.

Taylor's period as Resident-General (1 January 1905 – 30 September 1910) was distinguished only by its pedestrianism. It did not take Anderson long to find his feet and his quick brain and dominating personality, combined with his undoubted administrative capabilities,[93] drew him increasingly into the affairs of the Federated Malay States. His Colonial Office background and the years spent in Whitehall provided him with an excellent entrée to the seat of much power, and ensured for him a significant deal of sympathy and support. Taylor's role, on the other hand, deteriorated to such an extent that he became the mouthpiece of the High Commissioner, and the third Resident-General's term of office set the scene for the abolition of the post and its replacement by the Chief Secretary to the Government. Towards the end of his tenure Taylor was driven to the point of openly expressing his dissatisfaction and it was widely acknowledged that on several issues he did not see eye to eye with Anderson.[94]

The eras of Treacher and Taylor witnessed major changes so far as the Residents' authority was concerned. The first blow was struck by Treacher in January 1902 when he created Federal Departments with responsible federal officers in control. The consequence of this was that powers of Residents were to a great extent taken away from them and transferred to the heads of Federal Departments, who acquired control of the departments and administered them subject to the authority of the Resident-General rather than the Residents. This led to the growth of a system which, as a by-product, contained one of the principal characteristics of a truly federal structure, namely, the division of powers between State governments and the central administration, the Resident-General representing the latter, but it was clearly not the system agreed to by Malay Sultans and supported by the Residents when the Treaty of Federation was signed. This modified arrangement developed in spite, and not because, of the Treaty which had not anticipated such a progression and had, therefore, made no effort to define the division of powers between the Central and State Governments. The result was that the

Resident-General, by virtue of his control over the Residents, became the virtual head of all State Governments while there was nothing that protected the States against the continuous encroachment of the Central Government.[95] The Residents discovered that even in matters solely affecting the States their directives were liable to be completely reversed by the Federal Secretariat.[96]

The reforms formally centralized the administration and put it firmly in the control of the Resident-General and his Secretaries. His authority, through the Federal Officers, became more immediate and, therefore, more effective. The Residents were somewhat confused because, while being held responsible for the administration of their States, they were forced to share this responsibility with a number of federal and quasi-federal departments:[97] they were the spokesmen for Sultans but responsible to the Resident-General and the High Commissioner. With the steady growth in the powers and functions of Central Government, Residents became the core of those parochial State interests which sought to oppose centralized and uniform administration. Centralized budgetary control encroached further on their hold over public finances. They had to submit their Draft Annual Estimates to the Resident-General for approval, were not allowed to make any new appointments, could not increase salaries outside approved schemes, or include any change of a permanent nature without the consent of Kuala Lumpur.[98]

Early in 1904, the judicial functions of Residents disappeared with the abolition of Residency Courts and the removal of appeals from the Sultan-in-Council to the Judicial Commissioner's Court. Changes also occurred in the legislative process, and Residents, who had previously dominated the proceedings, were forced to surrender control of specific subjects through State enactments. In the absence of a central legislature, all draft measures required the approval both of the Resident-General and the High Commissioner before they could be considered by State Councils and, when passed there, they needed the final sanction of the High Commissioner before they could be gazetted and enforced.[99] In practice, all legislative business was centralized in Kuala Lumpur and State Councils, essentially, acted as rubber stamps. The initiation and content of all legislation was manipulated by the Resident-General's Office and although the Rulers, Residents, and Federal Officers could propose legislation, the Resident-General's approval was vital before the legislative wheels turned.

The Residents, however, remained the chief executive officers responsible for the administration of their states. They supervised the working of the many state departments as well as those quasi-federal departments which came under their portfolio. The Residents were held accountable for the success of public works and no project could be embarked upon without their advice, even in circumstances where they had not recommended it in the first place.

In attempting to walk the tightrope between increasing general prosperity of their states and maintaining an influence and control over their administrations, and protecting them against central government encroachment, the Residents came into conflict with the Resident-General and the High Commissioner. Rodger, Birch, Douglas, and C. Wray[100] were all inveterate champions of State rights. In 1897, when he was Acting Resident in Perak, Rodger expressed his misgivings on the creation of a Federal Department of Chinese Affairs and favoured the grant of increased powers to local State officials to deal with problems facing the Chinese population.[101] He criticized the formation of a single police force and complained about the long delays which resulted from having to refer matters to the Resident-General and the High Commissioner.[102] When the Railway Enactment, 1903, was forced on Perak, Rodger, the Resident, charged that sections of that legislation infringed upon State rights, and referred Treacher to the Pangkor Engagement as modified by the Treaty of Federation. The Resident-General reacted by saying that 'Mr. Rodger (the Resident of Perak) constantly refers me to the "constitution" of Perak based on the Pangkor Engagement and modified by the Federal Engagement. But as in the case of Great Britain the "constitution" is not tied down within the terms of written engagements, but fortunately is capable of growth and expansion with the approval of the Ruler for the time being as conditions change and the prosperity of the State increases',[103] and he went on to quote Swettenham to the effect that references to the Pangkor Engagement were not quite appropriate. Treacher's reference to the constitution of Britain was unfortunate and showed a failure to comprehend that a federal-type constitution had to be rigid, written, and incapable of the *ad hoc* development that had characterized the growth of the British Constitution.[104]

Clifford was another Resident who, during his stay in Pahang, criticized his superiors and expressed dissatisfaction with the manner Federation had affected his powers. There is no record of any specific incident that Clifford was involved in, but an insight into this side of his character was provided by Anderson when he discovered the possibility that the former Resident of Pahang might succeed Taylor as Resident-General.[105] The High Commissioner pleaded with the Colonial Office not to appoint Clifford because, as Resident, he had been vain and 'given to playing his own hand, only he is more cunning about it'.[106]

The most forthright and prolonged resistance to the expansion of the central government, however, emanated from Birch. In 1904, when he was appointed Resident of Perak, he began a vociferous campaign against the tendencies towards centralization. Early in 1905 he acquired, for the public service, a house and a plot of land in Ipoh, in exchange for certain tin-bearing lands in Kinta. The affair began on 4 January 1905 when a British businessman, G. M. Donald, offered to transfer to the Perak Government three acres of land, valued at $5,000, as a site for a Forest Station, in exchange for mining land. In addition, because he required ready cash to carry out a contract in Pahang, Donald was anxious to sell his house which stood on six acres of land, the whole property being valued at between $20,000 and $25,000. Birch did not think it necessary to consult either the Resident-General or the High Commissioner, and directed the Kinta District Officer, E. J. Brewster, to study the proposition. Brewster found that:

1. Messrs. Aylesbury and Garland, a firm of British businessmen in Ipoh, had, a few months previously, asked for $3,000 for half an acre of land directly opposite the block of land offered by Donald to the Forest Department. Donald's land was conveniently located and the valuation of $5,000 was a realistic and fair one.

2. The house situated on the six acres of land was worth approximately $20,000 and since Ipoh was desperately in need of Government quarters it was recommended both lots of property be taken over by the State in exchange for fifty acres of mining land.

Birch personally inspected the properties and was sufficiently impressed to offer Donald forty acres of mining land, which the latter accepted, and in return obtained the title deeds for both the blocks.[107]

Taylor, the Resident-General, was incensed and informed Birch that the procedure employed by the Resident was extremely irregular. According to him, Birch should have provided for the acquisitions in his Annual Estimates for Expenditure or, if the case had been an urgent one, he should have applied for, and obtained, special sanction. The Resident not only failed to do this but also omitted to communicate with the High Commissioner or the Resident-General informing them of the detailed circumstances, with a view towards obtaining covering authority. As it was, nothing was known of the transaction in the Resident-General's Office until attention was drawn to it by an entry in the Resident's Estimates for 1906, of $1,000 for special repairs to the Judge's quarters in Ipoh. In the Public Works Department column of these Estimates, it was stated that the building was purchased from Donald and needed extensive repairs.[108] Birch, in his defence, rightly argued that this method of land acquisition was frequently employed between May 1892 and April 1900.[109] He charged that the position and authority of Residents was being seriously altered and represented an infringement of the Federation Agreement. In an obvious allusion to Taylor's Ceylon background, he stated that a Resident in the Malay States occupied a totally different position, and played a different sort of role from a Government Agent of a Ceylon province, and any restriction of the former's powers would only delay administration and cause irritation.[110] But both Taylor and Anderson concluded that Birch had overstepped his authority and, while the High Commissioner was quick to acknowledge that the Resident was one of the most energetic, zealous, and able men in the service, commented that his impatience and impetuosity were a constant cause of worry to his superiors. Anderson was so displeased with Birch that, before going on home leave in 1906, he conferred with Taylor about who would act as Resident-General, and decided that whoever it was it would not be Birch.[111]

In June 1907, Birch was confirmed as Resident of Perak, and in July of the same year his independent stance again surfaced. He submitted proposals to stage a grand Mining Exhibition in Ipoh some time in 1909. It was hoped that the project would result in the introduction of new processes in the tin mining industry and induce proprietors to adopt labour-saving devices and machinery.[112] The Resident committed the Government to a large amount of expenditure without consulting either the Resident-General or the High Commissioner. Anderson was furious and reported to the Colonial Office that if Birch continued to make high level decisions without prior consultation, neither the Resident-General nor the High Commissioner could be held responsible for the future administration of Perak. Birch's zest and enthusiasm for his work could not excuse or justify the public advocacy of an arrangement which visualized the Federal Government paying for the travel and hotel bills of every person likely to benefit, to visit every mine in the world where machinery was utilized. Anderson was satisfied that the fifty-year-old

Birch, who had spent over thirty years in the service, had got his health and capacity for self-restraint seriously impaired by the tropical climate. It had also increased his undiscriminating taste for popular fads and made him a demoralizing influence on the rest of the Government service. The High Commissioner proposed that he should be forced to retire on his existing pension or transferred as Governor to one of the Australian states, like Tasmania, where the climate might 'restore his health and mental balance' and where his enthusiasm could find a safe and natural vent.[113] These were strange and surprising recommendations about an officer who, only six months previously, had been given a clean bill by being confirmed as Resident. The Colonial Office accepted the proposition that Birch was not an easy personality to deal with, but Anderson's harsh proposals were hardly suited to the case.[114] Accordingly, a reprimand was advised,[115] but, for reasons that were left unstated, Anderson later recommended that all action on Birch be suspended.[116]

Birch could not evade the limelight for long and in April 1908 he was again at the centre of a controversy. This was because he allowed two doctors in Government service, Fox and Cooper, to retain, simultaneously, their brothel practice. Anderson confessed that the position and authority of Residents within their States was significant, although vague, and that the extent of the right of the Resident-General and the High Commissioner to interfere was equally ill-defined and liable to be challenged. In those circumstances, unless Residents adhered closely to the known policies of the Resident-General and the High Commissioner, it would become impossible for them to discharge to satisfaction their responsibilities to the Government. Birch, the High Commissioner insisted, was fully aware that it was the declared policy of the Government to divorce the Government's Medical Service from brothel practice; yet when an opportunity arose to give practical effect to that policy, the Resident used the discretion vested in him deliberately to obstruct that policy. To aggravate the situation, Birch allowed to pass unnoticed a series of impertinent letters from Cooper to the head of his Department, Dr. Wright. The episode was considered by Anderson as yet another example of the Resident's passion for popularity which blinded him to the necessity of maintaining the dignity of his office and the discipline of the Government service. The call for the compulsory retirement of Birch was repeated by the High Commissioner.[117] The Colonial Office examined the charges against the Resident in detail and although none of them, taken singly, justified more than a reprimand, taken together they were more serious. Even so, compulsory retirement was considered to be unduly harsh and it was only the desire to save Anderson further embarrassment that the Colonial Office decided, reluctantly, to endorse the High Commissioner's recommendation.[118] Before the decision could be carried out Birch, who was then on leave in England, was summoned to the Colonial Office and interviewed by an Under-Secretary, R. A. Antrobus. The Resident was informed of the proposed course of action and pleaded to be allowed to serve a further two years by which time the education of his children would be completed.[119] The case was then referred to the Secretary of State and a further interview was arranged for Birch. As a result of the meeting the Resident was allowed to return to his post but was told in no uncertain terms that if the High Commissioner was given any further cause for complaint, he could expect no more compassion.[120] This rebuke had its expected results and on his return to Perak, Birch made every effort not to cause annoyance to his superiors.[121]

So far as State Councils were concerned, there were calls for the enlargement of their functions. European business and commercial interests pressed for the inclusion of their representatives on the Councils and, in the case of Perak and Selangor, this was acceded to. The prerogative for nomination was, however, in the hands of the Residents and this often led to the nomination of quiet men who could be depended on to fill the office with dignity, without being too pertinaciously energetic in asking embarrassing questions or making radical proposals. European unofficial opinion wanted a planting representative on each of the three Western Malay States Councils and suggested that the agricultural community of each State should submit two or three names for the Resident to select from. In Selangor they wanted an additional commercial or professional person on the Council, from names submitted to the Resident by the local chamber of commerce. In Perak, where a large number of Europeans were involved in tin mining, there were requests to have a European miner, as well as a European planter, on the Council.[122]

The scope of State Councils also attracted attention and a public discussion of the draft estimates was advocated. The right of members to ask reasonable questions would ensure that proper vigilance would be exercised on matters affecting the general public interest.[123] The Government, however, did not share the same sentiments for increasing the role of State Councils, and no tangible measures were introduced to alter their character in any way.

During Treacher's tenure as Resident-General, the Second Conference of Chiefs of the Federated Malay States was held in Kuala Lumpur in July 1903. The agenda for this meeting was more substantial than on the first occasion, and included the use of Malay as the official language, further employment of Malays in the Government Service, the provision of houses and *balei* for *penghulu*, the use of intoxicants by Malays, the planting of coconuts by Malays, the extension of padi cultivation, the encouragement of Chinese and Indian agricultural colonies, the investment of Federated Malay States funds in Johor railway construction, and the constitution of Islamic religious courts and appeals from them. The British, however, made it plain that it was not within the power of the Conference to make decisive judgements on these issues and that its role was confined to indicating general policy. The most unexpected and explosive incident of the Assembly was a speech in Malay, by Sultan Idris of Perak, on the final day of the meeting. This revealed the extent of the anxieties felt by Malay Rulers over the manner in which Federation had progressed.[124]

On the economic front, the successors of Swettenham continued to build on the sound base that had been established. By May 1903 the West-coast railway extensions were virtually completed and in July 1908 the Government purchased the Sungei Ujong Railway from the private company that had built and operated the line since July 1891. The total cost of railway construction amounted to over $54,000,000, the entire amount being met out of the surplus revenues of the Federation.[125] Land policy was also modified when in March 1903 an effort was made to consolidate and amend the law relating to land. The catalyst for the change was the introduction, and almost instant success, of a new agricultural crop, rubber. The long-standing reluctance of capitalists to invest in agricultural enterprises disappeared overnight and a flood of applications for extensive areas of land streamed in. The administration considered the possibility of alienating public land by auction, as was the practice in Ceylon and in the Straits Settlements, but the absence of a complete Revenue Survey of the Federation posed significant problems. So the established system was allowed to prevail with some modifications. Higher rents were imposed after the first five years of tenure while development progressed, and premiums were raised from two to four dollars per acre.[126] These represented only minimal actual increases and bore little relation to the massive profits subsequently made by the rubber companies.

The principal characteristic of British administration in the Federation was that all the important administrative, political, and economic policies emanated from those British officials resident in Malaya and the Straits Settlements. The role of the Colonial Office was very much that of an elder statesman who ensured that no glaring contradictions and legal loopholes existed. But there was a brief period between the initialling of the Treaty of Federation in July 1895 and its implementation on 1 July 1896, when it played a more active part in the proceedings. One of the first subjects to attract the attention of Whitehall bureaucrats was the future recruitment of cadets into the Federation Government Service. Until then the mode of selection had been one where the Governor in Singapore appointed, or nominated, officials for the consideration of the Secretary of State.[127] As a system it had worked satisfactorily but had two glaring faults; some men who had been unsuccessful in other areas or professions could be appointed to responsible positions, and the educational qualifications of some of the appointees were not sufficiently high. On the other hand, the arrangement had a couple of distinct advantages *vis-à-vis* the Malay population; some of the men selected came from good social backgrounds,[128] most of them were well-mannered, and often the children of officials who held high positions in Malaya in years past. The British administrators in the Malay States were convinced that it was a matter of some importance to the Malay mind that a man should be a gentleman. This was because the Malays in their own society laid considerable stress on qualities of gentility and courtesy, and were quick to distinguish a well-bred individual from his opposite. Value was also placed on an official whose father before him had carved out a distinguished career for himself, or who had achieved a position known to and recognized by the Malays. Malay chiefs, it was thought, welcomed as junior officials men bearing names such as Weld, Hose, Maxwell, or Irving, and for a young man coming out for the first time to the East it was a magnificent incentive to work in a land where his father's name was known and honoured.[129]

Colonial Office plans envisaged future recruitment through an open competitive examination to be held in London and open to all British subjects, irrespective of colour. British officials in Malaya feared that such a system would appoint to responsible positions men liable to offend the sensitive nature of the Malays and tread indiscriminately on their customs, traditions, and manners. The great learning and higher educational levels that open competition would bring was, they declared, not as essential as was supposed. A good average education, gentlemanly birth and ideas, ordinary common sense, a vigorous constitution, and a high level of physical fitness, were attributes more likely to succeed in the varied outdoor life which service in the Malay States entailed. As an alternative to the Colonial Office blueprint, they favoured selection by a system of 'close competition' which involved the nomination, by the Governor, of men within a certain age limit who would then compete against one another in an examination. This would ensure selection for those who not only possessed the virtues of good birth, gentle manners, and a rugged physique but also the added important qualifications of a proper education and potential administrative ability. In addition, it would represent a positive improvement on the existing system which had reached a stage where it was vital to weed out those who were unable to keep pace with the development within the Malay States.[130]

Another consideration emphasized by British officials in Malaya was that only a cadet of British parentage was equipped to grapple with the many facets of administration in the Federation. The rationale behind this claim was that no clear guidelines of governmental action existed, and cadets were employed to assist a British agent appointed to advise and, by his influence, guide the 'high spirited rulers of a race' which had accepted British counsel simply because it was British. To employ Indians, Sinhalese, or other non-Europeans to positions of responsibility was, therefore, inadvisable. The myth was repeated that in the East only the Europeans, and not all of them, could, when placed in arduous predicaments, exercise unflinchingly and with discretion a controlling authority over those with whom they came into contact.[131]

Both the Colonial Office and officials in Malaya were, therefore, agreed that something had to be done to improve what was clearly an unsatisfactory and outmoded form of recruitment. Offers of employment extended on an informal basis had led to the development of an old-boy network with all its seamy connotations. Once appointed to a State service the cadet was officially a member of the State establishment and a servant of the Sultan. In practice he was at the mercy of the Resident and no proper machinery existed to safeguard the tenure of officers.[132] So long as conditions were backward, living and social comforts primitive, and economic development sluggish, not many voices of dissent were heard about the procedure. With the decision to create the Federation, however, what had been small and diverse states were combined to form a significant territory. Conditions of service improved and economic progress held out distinct possibilities. A more formal arrangement to include security of tenure, pension regulations, and other well-defined procedures was essential,[133] and recruitment policy was a good starting point. The protestations of the men on the spot made little impression on Colonial Office thinking and the determination to introduce appointments by open competition was staunchly adhered to. In its original form the new system operated until 1904, but in that year a strange amendment took place. It was decided then that only persons of pure European descent would be eligible to sit for the examination.[134] No official explanation was given for this but, years later, it was suggested that it arose from representations made by Malay Rulers. In the absence of proof it is difficult to accept this explanation as it is most unlikely that the Sultans would have wanted to introduce a regulation which excluded their own sons and relatives, or that any thinking Malay could have failed to recognize the stigma. In any case the decision extended to the Straits Settlements Civil Service as well and the Sultans would hardly have interfered in the affairs of the Colony.[135]

This uncharacteristic concern of the Colonial Office with Malayan affairs arose again in a case involving the Resident-General designate, Swettenham. When informed that he had been selected as the first Resident-General, he was told that his salary would be $12,000 per annum, and a travelling allowance of $10 for every day that he spent outside his headquarters of Kuala Lumpur. Swettenham was outspoken in his disappointment because the salary was identical to that which he received as Resident of Perak. He appealed to the Colonial Office for reconsideration, pointing out that he had spent twenty-five of the best years of his life in trying tropical conditions and did not have many years of active service left.[136] The Governor, Mitchell, recommended payment of an entertainment allowance of $3,000 a year to Swettenham as he did not relish the prospect of beginning a difficult job with the 'foreman of works ready to strike'.[137] The Colonial Office was not in any conciliatory mood and maintained that the Resident-General had little cause for complaint.[138] He was accused of being unduly grasping and it was even mentioned that one of the reasons why he had taken so much trouble over the federation project was that he expected to be personally rewarded.[139] The Colonial Office strongly believed that the principle of federating the Malay States was urgently advocated by officials in Malaya and the

Straits Settlements only because everyone concerned hoped to come out of it materially better off. In this light, therefore, any concessions to Swettenham would certainly have sparked off a string of requests from those below him. Whitehall was anxious to destroy unequivocally any ideas that federation had been created for the personal benefit of individual officers.[140]

In assessing this early role of the Colonial Office its uncompromising stance was understandable and logical, because it felt that until 1 July 1896 the onus of responsibility lay in Whitehall. Mitchell was busy enough looking after the Straits Settlements, and saddling him with added responsibilities during the interim period did not make any sense. So far as the issues themselves were concerned, the objections from British officials in Malaya to the system of open competition were regrettable, and reflected an inferiority complex among some of them. Swettenham's niggardly concern for dollars and cents embarrassed his friends, delighted his enemies in the Colonial Office, threw him open to charges of personal aggrandizement, and somewhat tarnished his image in London.[141]

Looked at in its entirety the phase of the Resident-General successfully achieved the declared administrative objects of Federation. The Colonial Secretary was relieved of all concern with Malay States affairs, the Governor, who became High Commissioner for the Federated Malay States, was provided with an adviser in the form of the Resident-General, who was in close contact with the Sultans and the Residents of the four states, knew all the officials, the influential people, and the work proposed or in progress, and could speak in sympathy with the interests and aspirations of the territory; the Resident-General was also closely involved with officials, planters, miners, and traders concerned with the economic development of the Federation. Continuity and uniformity of administration was also introduced in instances where identical circumstances existed.

While the objectives were approved by and had the support of all British officials in London, the Straits Settlements and the Malay States, the methods employed in accomplishing the ends were as varied as they were numerous. The main reason for this was, of course, the absence of a proper written constitution and the amorphous conditions that resulted. Much depended on the men on the spot and the constant interaction taking place between them. The dominant personalities of the era were, undoubtedly, Swettenham and Anderson, and it was their guiding force and strength that propelled the Federated Malay States. Of the two, Swettenham's tenure of office was the less stormy and turbulent. He possessed the obvious advantages of having spent his entire career in the region and being more than proficient in the Malay language. This infinite knowledge of the area and its personalities permitted him to depend more on an informal system than on a rigid and inflexible one. By operating a combination of tact, diplomacy, and firmness, he succeeded in imposing on the system an aura of peace, order, and efficiency. Anderson, through his lack of Malayan experience and his physical presence in Singapore, did not enjoy the same degree of camaraderie with either the other British officers or the prominent local personages. In order to give practical effect to his ambition to play a significant role in the affairs of the Federation, it was necessary for him to devise and implement more rigid administrative techniques which were supported as well as opposed by British officials and Malay Rulers alike. The imperfections and weaknesses of his principal Resident-General, Taylor, facilitated the process although the presence of a difficult and independent-minded Resident like Birch presented manifest obstacles. The greater part of the opposition, however, emanated from the Sultans, of whom Idris of Perak was very much in the forefront. Details of Malay opposition are discussed in Chapter IV, but so far as Anderson was concerned, there was never any question of retreat in the face of this challenge. As a dedicated and professional British administrator, the most important aspect of the High Commissioner's task was to make sure that a streamlined and efficient governmental system was created. He was determined not to allow the whims and fancies, real or imagined, of the traditional Rulers to put the spanner in the works. The assured economic value of the Malay States made them an integral and significant part of wider British commercial interests.

Just how important the Malay States had become, economically, can be gauged from the fact that Federal revenues increased from $8,434,083 in 1896 to $25,246,863 in 1909. Although the major portion of this, $7,155,124, represented the duty on tin, there were signs that the importance of rubber was assured.[142] The problems arising out of a shortage of labour were being overcome and the population increased from 551,407 to 965,318, the bulk being made up of immigrants.

The stage was thus set for the next phase of British activities in the Federated Malay States. It was an era that was to see an intensification of the centralization process, the outbreak of the First World War in Europe, and the continuing and rapid development of the territory's two major economic assets, tin and rubber.

1. Swettenham was in the forefront of this group and the view found support in R. O. Winstedt, *A History of Malaya*, London, 1962, p. 239, but Sadka asserts that Swettenham exaggerated this point and cites various instances where the Governor lost little time in making decisions. See Sadka, *The Protected Malay States*, pp. 139–40.

2. In August 1876 it was decided that the Lieutenant-Governors of Penang and Malacca, in normal circumstances, had to communicate with the Residents in the Malay States only through the Colonial Secretary. In circumstances where immediate action was called for without reference to Singapore, the Lieutenant-Governors, as officers nearest the States of Perak, Negri Sembilan, and Selangor, were authorized to assist, in every way within their power, in the conduct of business between the Residents and the Governor. Col. Sec. to Acting Resident, Selangor, 24 August 1876, SGR, 1876.

3. The first appointee to this position was Swettenham who acted in this capacity from 1876 to 1881.

4. F. A. Swettenham, 'Malay Problems, 1926', *British Malaya*, May 1926, pp. 7–9.

5. C. P. Lucas, a permanent official in the Colonial Office, advocated British expansion in the Malay States. He was a close friend and supporter of Swettenham and favoured a flexible policy in the Peninsula. He believed that matters of discipline were best left to Residents and, on this issue, had a number of disagreements with one of his colleagues, E. F. Fairfield, who wanted greater control over their activities.

6. Swettenham, *British Malaya*, pp. 363–4.

7. Swettenham, *Footprints in Malaya*, p. 104.

8. These departments included the police, public works, and posts and telegraphs.

9. Memorandum by Lucas, undated, enclosed in Ripon to Smith, Confidential Desp., 19 May 1893, on Smith to Ripon, 29 November 1892, CO 273/1893.

10. He was also critical of the independence of individual Residents, see F. A. Swettenham, *About Perak*, Singapore, 1893, pp. 76–8.

11. C. B. H. Mitchell was Governor from 1894 to 1899 and before taking up his appointment, had been an officer of the Royal Marines having served in the Crimean War. He had the rare distinction amongst Governors of having been a popular economist. He died while serving in Singapore.

12. Governor to CO, Confidential Desp., 1 May 1895, CO 273/1895.

13. Ibid.

14. Draft Instructions to Swettenham, Resident of Perak, enclosure No. 3 in Governor to CO, Confidential Desp., 1 May 1895, CO 273/1895.

15. Quoted in Confidential Notes of a Policy in Respect of the Unfederated

Malay States, by W. G. Maxwell, 15 October 1920, Colonial Office, March 1921, CO 717/1921.

16. Draft Instructions to Swettenham in Confidential Desp. of 1 May 1895, CO 273/1895.

17. The Perak succession, in theory, rotated among three royal lines; on the death of a Sultan his son became Raja Bendahara, while the Raja Bendahara became Raja Muda and the Raja Muda was installed as the new Sultan. But there were variations, as happened when Sultan Abdullah Mohammed Shah died in 1857: his son Yusuf should have become Raja Bendahara but was passed over by the Perak chiefs because he was 'obstinate, tyrannical, and vindictive. . . . The real objection to him was that if they gave him power he would have had the will to wield it and that they, therefore, preferred a weaker man.' So, an outsider, Ismail, was made Bendahara but on Sultan Jaafar's death in 1865, he was not promoted and Abdullah became Raja Muda instead. The situation was further confused in 1871 when Sultan Ali died because both Abdullah and Yusuf were ignored and Ismail was proclaimed Sultan. The Perak genealogical table was thus:

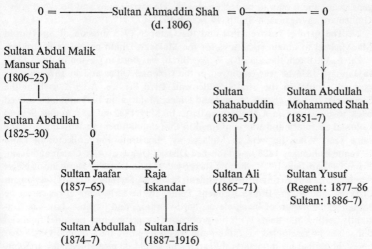

For more details, see Sadka, *The Protected Malay States*, p. 33; Gullick, *Indigenous Political Systems*, pp. 54–7.

18. H. Clifford, *Bushwhacking and other Asiatic Tales and Memories*, London, 1929, pp. 216–22.

19. Confidential Notes by Maxwell, 15 October 1920, CO 717/1921.

20. The early Sultans of Pahang were descended from the rulers of Malacca and established themselves in the fifteenth century. After the Portuguese capture of Malacca, the Pahang Sultans acknowledged the suzerainty of the Johor Sultanate and were installed by them. The overlordship of Johor was interrupted by the Achinese invasion of Johor in the seventeenth century but on the withdrawal of the invaders in 1641 Pahang again accepted Johor control. In the eighteenth century a line of Bendaharas descended from Johor established them-

selves in Pahang but ruled independently. In 1863 Ahmad, the brother of the ruling Bendahara, usurped the throne and was proclaimed Bendahara by his own chiefs. For details see W. Linehan, 'A History of Pahang', *JMBRAS*, Vol. XIV, Part 2, 1936, pp. 1–257.

21. A group of Pahang chiefs led by Dato Bahaman and Mat Kilau rebelled against British rule, and British forces from Perak, Selangor, and Singapore had to be rushed to the scene. See Sadka, *The Protected Malay States*, p. 247; Khoo Kay Kim, *Glimpses of Malaysian History*, p. 62.

22. Confidential Notes by Maxwell, 15 October 1920, CO 717/1921.

23. For a character sketch of Abdul Samad, see note 126 in Chapter I.

24. Confidential Notes by Maxwell, 15 October 1920, CO 717/1921.

25. This happened on 29 April 1898 when an agreement was signed between the Yang-di-Pertuan Besar, Sri Menanti, and the four Lawgivers. For details see Maxwell and Gibson, *Treaties and Engagements*, pp. 65–6.

26. Confidential notes by Maxwell, 15 October 1920, CO 717/1921. The significant personality was Tunku Muhammad, later elected Yang-di-Pertuan Besar, who in the course of years was regarded as a 'Malay of Malays, a great gentleman, and a man to be reckoned with. He carries guns and his word goes'. Guillemard to Masterton-Smith, 19 March 1923, CO 717/1923.

27. The parallel between this and the October 1945 mission of Sir Harold MacMichael to obtain signatures for the Malayan Union proposals is striking.

28. E. W. Birch, the son of J. W. W. Birch, was born in Ceylon in April 1857. In January 1876 he was employed in the Colonial Office and in 1878 was appointed a cadet in the Straits Settlements Civil Service. After a spell at the Secretariat he took charge of the Land Office, Malacca, in 1881 and later moved back to Singapore in a similar capacity. In May 1882 he was Acting Second Colonial Secretary and was confirmed in that appointment in November of the same year. When he went to Malacca as Magistrate and Collector of Land Revenue in January 1888 he established District Offices at Alor Gajah and Jasin. From 1892 to June 1897, when he succeeded Martin Lister as Resident of Negri Sembilan, he was Acting British Resident, Selangor, Secretary to the Government of Perak, and Acting British Resident, Perak. In the early years of his career he earned a reputation of being clever, hard-working, and likeable, but was constantly getting into debt. With his propensity for getting into personal financial difficulties he resembled his father, and was warned by the Colonial Office that unless he settled his monetary obligations he would be passed over for appointment to important posts (for details see Minute by Lucas, 22 April 1896, CO 273/1896; Lucas to Selbourne, 29 May 1897, on Governor to CO, Confidential Desp., 2 May 1897, CO 273/1897. As Resident of Negri Sembilan he did nothing meritorious or blameworthy; he bungled the negotiations with the Sungei Ujong Railway Company but this was attributed to his failure to grasp the implications of his actions. In July 1899, for example, he pledged the Government to pay the entire cost for the improvements of a pier. This action cost the administration $39,000 (for details see OAG to CO, Confidential Desp., 10 January 1901, CO 278/1901). From 1901 to 1903 he was Governor of North Borneo before being sacked for advocating the transfer of the British North Borneo Company's territories to the British Government (see K. G. Tregonning, *Under Chartered Company Rule*, Singapore, 1958, pp. 59–62). In 1904, against the wishes of Anderson, he was appointed Resident of Perak (see Stubbs to Fiddes, 4 January

1908, on HC to CO, Confidential Desp., 27 November 1907, CO 273/1907).

29. Resident, Perak, to RG, 27 December 1905, on HC to CO, Confidential Desp., 10 February 1906, CO 273/1906.

30. Confidential Notes by Maxwell, 15 October 1920, CO 717/1921.

31. Maxwell and Gibson, *Treaties and Engagements*, p. 71.

32. Ibid., p. 71.

33. K. C. Wheare, 'What Federal Government Is', *Federal Tracts*, No. 4, London, 1941, p. 9.

34. Memorandum by W. S. Gibson On the Constitutional History of the Malay States, in Malay States Papers (1931 to 1933) Relating to the Policy of Decentralisation and Constitutional Reorganisation, Cmd. 72483/30 (No. 6A), CO 882, Vol. 12.

35. K. C. Wheare, *Federal Government*, London, 1953, pp. 16–19.

36. R. Braddell, *The Legal Status of the Malay States*, Singapore, 1931.

37. For details of the Imperial federal idea, see J. E. Kendle, *The Colonial and Imperial Conferences, 1887–1911*, London, 1967, pp. 1–20.

38. J. L. Garvin, *The Life of Joseph Chamberlain*, Vol. III, 1895–1900, London, 1934.

39. Swettenham, *British Malaya*, May 1926, p. 9.

40. Scheme for the Administration of the Protected Malay States by F. A. Swettenham, Appendix in T. K. Sabapathy, 'The Federal Council in Malayan Affairs, 1909–27', unpublished B.A. (Hons.) Academic Exercise, University of Singapore, 1961.

41. Sabapathy, 'The Federal Council in Malayan Affairs, 1909–27', Appendix.

42. Ibid.

43. Ibid.

44. Lucas, on the choice of a Resident-General, stated, 'Mr. Swettenham would be the obvious man.' Minute of 30 June 1893 on Governor to CO, Confidential Desp., 4 May 1892, CO 273/1893.

45. Governor to CO, Confidential Desp., 7 December 1902, CO 273/1902.

46. HC to CO, Desp. No. 328, 4 September 1902, CO 273/1902.

47. Governor to CO, Confidential Desp., 7 December 1902, CO 273/1902.

48. *FMS Annual Report*, 1903. Reports on the FMS for 1903, Cmd. 2243, *Parliamentary Papers*, Vol. LIV, 1905. The first of the Conferences was held in June 1898 and this was followed by meetings at irregular intervals. During the era of the Resident-General a total of fifteen such conferences took place, chaired by the Resident-General.

49. Born in 1857, the Hon. Martin Lister was the second son of the third Baron Ribblesdale. After working for a while in the Bank of England he went to work on a coffee estate in Ceylon. He came to Malaya in 1879 and, with T. H. Hill and A. Rathbone, opened coffee plantations in Sungei Ujong and Selangor. He joined the Perak government service in 1884 as Secretary to the Resident, became Collector and Magistrate, Ulu Selangor, in 1885, and two years later was appointed Superintendent of the Sri Menanti States. In 1889 he was made British Resident of Negri Sembilan and occupied this position until his death in 1897.

50. Hugh Clifford was born in March 1866 and came to Malaya in 1883 as a cadet in the Residency of Low in Perak. His accomplishments as a Malay linguist recommended him to lead a special mission to Pahang in 1887 and on the conclusion of a treaty of protection with that State was appointed Political Agent

with consular powers in Pahang. Between 1890 and 1895 he acted on various occasions as Resident of Pahang. He was Resident, Pahang, from 1896 to 1899 when he was nominated Governor of North Borneo by the Colonial Office. He resigned in 1901 and was reappointed Resident of Pahang. In 1903 he was transferred to Trinidad as Colonial Secretary; Colonial Secretary, Ceylon, 1907; Governor of the Gold Coast, 1912; Governor of Nigeria, 1919; Governor of Ceylon, 1925; and Governor of the Straits Settlements, High Commissioner for the Malay States, and British Agent for Borneo, 1927. He resigned in 1929 and died in 1941. He was a prolific writer; for a list of his major works, see W. R. Roff, *Stories by Sir Hugh Clifford*, Kuala Lumpur, 1966.

51. Arthur Butler was acting Resident from April to December 1899 and Resident from January 1900 to April 1901, when he died at Pekan.

52. Lucas to Mitchell, 24 March 1896, and Treacher to Lucas, 17 December 1895, CO 273/1895.

53. Observations on Details of Scheme; F. A. Swettenham to CO, 13 January 1896, CO 273/1896.

54. *Resident-General Office Circular*, No. 64, 1902.

55. L. C. Jackson's father was a Judge of the Supreme Court at Calcutta and he himself was a practising barrister. He was highly recommended to the Colonial Office by the Attorney-General, by Sir Richard Crouch of the Judicial Committee of the Privy Council, and by the leader of his circuit, Mr. Jelf, Q.C. (CO to Governor, Desp. No. 215, 29 May 1896, CO 273/1896).

56. R. F. S. Walker was born in 1850 and educated at the Military Academy, Sandhurst. He joined the 28th Foot in 1871, saw service in Perak in 1876 and in 1879 was attached to the Perak Armed Police. He became Deputy Commissioner in 1880, and Commissioner in 1882. While Commandant of the Malay States Guides he acted as Resident of Perak on occasions when the Resident was on leave. He retired in 1910.

57. H. C. Syers, born in 1852, was appointed Superintendent of Police, Selangor, in 1876. Although not very well educated he was fluent in Malay and Chinese and was very interested in Malaya and its people. He died in a hunting accident in 1897.

58. H. C. Belfield came to Malaya in 1884 as Magistrate and Collector of Land Revenue, Kuala Lumpur, and was later appointed Inspector of Schools, Selangor. In 1891 he was Senior Magistrate, Perak, became Resident of Negri Sembilan in 1901, and Resident of Selangor in 1902. He was an authority on Malay matters and was for a while Chief Examiner in Malay Language.

59. G. T. Hare, before his appointment in the Federation, was Assistant Protector of Chinese, Singapore. He was familiar with Chinese characters and a number of Chinese dialects.

60. For details see J. D. Legge, *Britain in Fiji 1858–1880*, London, 1958, pp. 202–30.

61. Governor to CO, Confidential Desp., 1 May 1895, CO 273/1895.

62. Editorial, *The Malay Mail*, 31 October 1925.

63. Swettenham to Crewe, 3 June 1910, CO 273/1910.

64. The Conference was held in Kuala Kangsar from 14 to 17 July 1897. There are no minutes or verbatim reports of the proceedings, but an account of the Conference may be found in *Colonial Office Eastern Pamphlet* 24A, in the Colonial Office Library.

65. *FMS Annual Report, 1900*, Kuala Lumpur, 1901, CO 576.

66. RG to CO, 13 March 1898, CO 273/1898.

67. Ibid.

68. Swettenham to CO, 17 February 1896, CO 273/1896. Also see Chai Hon Chan, *The Development of British Malaya*, pp. 66, 117, and 183–4; Swettenham, *British Malaya*, pp. 239–41, 278–84; Anon., 'Railways', Wright and Cartwright (eds.), *Twentieth Century Impressions of British Malaya*, pp. 303–13; Anon., 'Railway Road and Shipping Facilities in the Malay Peninsula', *Malayan Series* (British Empire Exhibition), No. XIV, London, 1924; *Fifty Years of Railways in Malaya, 1885–1935*, Kuala Lumpur, 1935; J. S. Sidhu, 'Railways in Selangor, 1882–86', *JMBRAS*, Vol. XXXVIII, 1965, pp. 6–22.

69. Swettenham to Governor, 7 January 1897, in Governor to CO, Desp. No. 15, 18 January 1897, CO 273/1897.

70. Mitchell did not accept the postulation that railway construction always led to the development of a new country and in defence of his ideas quoted the example of the Natal railway extension from Pietermaritzburg to Ladysmith. This had been decided upon by Sir George Colley on the basis of statistics that were collected by Mitchell. These statistics proved so wrong because of the keen competition of the ox-wagon that in spite of every effort between 1883 and 1886 the total receipts did little more than pay for the working expenses. There had also not been any remarkable development of the country through which the railway passed. Admittedly there was a gradual increase in traffic and land settlement but Mitchell was convinced that the improvement of the rough roads there would have achieved similar results. Governor to CO, Desp. No. 288, 24 June 1896, CO 273/1896.

71. Memorandum by Sir Robert Meade, 27 July 1896, on Governor to CO, 24 June 1896; and Governor to CO, 21 November 1896, CO 273/1896.

72. RG to Governor, 7 January 1897, in Governor to CO, Desp. No. 15, 18 January 1897, CO 273/1897.

73. Sir Montague Ommaney, of the Crown Agents, discounted the Natal Railway experience and stated that the abundance of 1 in 30 gradients and sharp curves, and the high capital and working expenditure were exceptional. His impression was that the railway was constructed less to develop a country whose only local product was Kaffir knobsticks, than to secure as much of the interior traffic as possible. He contrasted this with conditions in the Federated Malay States where a rapid and well-sustained development, growing mineral and agricultural production, seemed to create conditions as nearly as possible the opposite of those in Natal. Minute by Sir Montague Ommaney, 3 April 1897, in Governor to CO, Desp. No. 15, 13 January 1897, CO 273/1897.

74. CO to Governor, Desp. No. 57, 12 May 1897, CO 273/1897.

75. HC to CO, Desp. No. 204, 9 May 1912, CO 273/1912.

76. Governor to CO, Desp. No. 504, 17 November 1896, CO 273/1896.

77. Report for the Secretary of State on the Draft Federal Land Code by the Legal Adviser, FMS, 9 December 1896, in Governor to CO, Desp. No. 563, 15 December 1896, CO 273/1896.

78. CO to Governor, Desp. No. 84, 12 March 1903, CO 273/1903.

79. Clifford, *North American Review*, Vol. 177, 1903, pp. 399–409.

80. OAG, SS, to CO, Secret Desp., 27 October 1901, CO 273/1901.

81. Minute by Lucas, 27 November 1901, on OAG, SS, to CO, Secret Desp., 27 October 1901, CO 273/1901.

82. OAG, SS, to CO, Secret Desp., 27 October 1901, CO 273/1901.

83. Ibid.

84. Within the Colonial Office, A. Fiddian thought it unfair to make Treacher's appointment conditional on his retiring at the age of fifty-five, 25 November 1901; C. W. Johnson disagreed and insisted on the condition being imposed, 27 November 1901; Lucas agreed with Johnson, 27 November 1901; and Ommaney supported Treacher but without much enthusiasm, 28 November 1901. See Minutes on ibid.

85. Swettenham raised this difficulty when discussing the future administration of the Federation and used the instance to support his contention that it would be extremely difficult for a High Commissioner, without substantial personal knowledge and experience of the special conditions that prevailed in Malaya, to set his opinion against the views of the Resident-General and Residents. HC to CO, Desp. No. 328, 4 September 1902, CO 273/1902. So far as Residents' Conferences were concerned, the first was convened in 1906 to consider complex land and mining codes that were finally enacted in 1897 and 1899. Swettenham called only two other such Conferences during his tenure as Resident-General, but under Treacher and his successors the Conferences were used as a device to secure agreement on proposed legislation and they discussed general administrative questions and policy. The meetings had no statutory basis, were convened at the convenience of the Resident-General, and consisted of himself and the four Residents. Departmental heads only attended when issues concerning their departments were considered. Between 1896 and 1910 fifteen such Conferences took place. The principal sources of information on the Conferences are the unpublished abstracts of the meetings bound under the title *Abstract of Proceedings, 1922–31* located in the Singapore National Library, and J. A. Harvey, *Index of Decisions, 1897–1928*, Kuala Lumpur, 1928. See P. L. Burns, 'The Constitutional History of Malaya with special reference to the States of Perak, Selangor, Negri Sembilan and Pahang, 1874–1914', Ph.D. Dissertation, University of London, 1966, pp. 285–8.

86. Fiddian to Lucas, 7 October 1902; and Minute by Johnson, 8 October 1902, on HC to CO, Desp. No. 328, 4 September 1902, CO 273/1902.

87. Perak Annual Report, 1902, Report on the FMS, 1902 (Cmd. 1819), Parliamentary Papers, Vol. LX, 1904.

88. The point was emphasized by Swettenham when he commented, in 1910, on Anderson's proposal to abolish the office of Resident-General and replace it with an officer to be styled the Chief Secretary to the Government, the idea being to increase the involvement of the High Commissioner in Federation affairs. Swettenham, on the other hand, argued that the powers already possessed by the High Commissioner were wide enough and the control exercised by him was as complete as could possibly be required. Swettenham to Harding, 19 September 1910, CO 273/1910.

89. For biographical details, see note 73, Chapter I.

90. HC to CO, Confidential Desp., 3 September 1904, CO 273/1904.

91. Stubbs to Fiddes, 5 October 1904, on ibid.

92. This was all the more necessary when the High Commissioner was also a non-Malay speaker since the Resident-General was supposed to meet Rulers and communicate their views to the High Commissioner. Swettenham to Crewe, 3 June 1910, CO 273/1910.

93. Robson, *Records and Recollections*, p. 104.

94. The disagreements between Anderson and Taylor were admitted by the High Commissioner who blamed the Resident-General's staff for leaking these differences. The incidents resulted in Taylor being held up as a champion of the Federation against a Governor who was only interested in the welfare of the Straits Settlements. Swettenham to Crewe, 3 June 1910, CO 273/1910.

95. Memorandum by Gibson, CO 882, Vol. 12.

96. This contrasted with affairs in the Unfederated States where the British Advisers worked closely and intimately with the Sultans, and any directive which had the Advisers' recommendation and the Rulers' approval, had double weight. The arrangement made Advisers far more powerful officials than Residents. Confidential Notes by Maxwell, 15 October 1920, CO 717/1921.

97. Railways, Police, Forest, Malay States Guides, Chinese Affairs, and Finance were federal departments, whereas Land, Survey, Education, Mines and Public Works were quasi-federal.

98. Resident-General Office Circular, No. 2 of 1896.

99. HC to CO, 15 July 1909, CO 273/1909.

100. C. Wray, born in August 1850, joined the Public Works Department, Perak, as Inspector in 1881 and was later appointed Collector and Magistrate, Batang Padang, and Krian. In 1903 he was District Officer, Kinta; in March 1904 was posted to Pahang as Acting Resident and confirmed in that appointment in September of the same year. He was the brother of L. Wray, the Director of Museums, FMS.

101. Perak Annual Report, 1897, Cmd. 9108, Parliamentary Papers, Vol. LXI, 1899.

102. Selangor Annual Report, 1896, Cmd. 8661, Parliamentary Papers, Vol. LVIII, 1896.

103. Memorandum by Gibson, CO 882, Vol. 12.

104. Ibid.

105. The appointment was suggested by Swettenham who, from his personal knowledge and record of Clifford, considered him eminently qualified to be Resident-General. Swettenham to Crewe, 3 June 1910, CO 273/1910.

106. The High Commissioner wrote, 'For goodness sake don't let them send Clifford here.' Anderson to Collins, 12 May 1910, on ibid.

107. The lands were situated at the junction of Gopeng and Tambun Roads and the grounds in which the house stood were well laid out with a coconut plantation behind them. To arrive at the value of mining land in Kinta, Birch noted that 184 acres had fetched $29/70 an acre at an auction in June 1904. Land inside the auction area was valued between $200 and $500 per acre. Donald was allowed to select his land within the auction area in blocks exceeding ten acres each. British Resident, Perak, to RG, 6 September 1905, on HC to CO, Confidential Desp., 10 February 1906, CO 273/1906.

108. RG to Resident, Perak, 24 November 1905, on Confidential Desp. of 10 February 1906, CO 273/1906.

109. In the earlier years of the administration of the Malay States it was not necessary to consider exchanges of land because all land belonged to the Government, but owing to the indiscriminate giving away of land by District Officers, the inaccuracy of hurried surveys, and the rapid increase of mining activity, the Government was compelled to make exchanges, either to resume land required for public purposes, or to rectify errors, or to allow miners to mine land that was

stanniferous. In Kinta alone such cases were common and scores of them had been dealt with from time to time. Resident, Perak, to RG, 27 December 1905, on ibid.

110. Resident, Perak, to RG, 7 December 1905, on HC to CO, Confidential Desp., 10 February 1906, CO 273/1906.

111. HC to CO, Confidential Desp., 10 February 1906, CO 273/1906.

112. Resident, Perak, to HC, 3 November 1907, on HC to CO, Confidential Desp., 27 November 1907, CO 273/1907.

113. HC to CO, Confidential Desp., 27 November 1907, CO 273/1907.

114. It was also curious that neither the High Commissioner nor the Resident-General had heard anything about the exhibition before the beginning of November although leading articles about it appeared in the newspapers and the event was generally discussed at the end of August. Harding to Antrobus, 3 January 1908, CO 273/1907.

115. Minute by Lord Elgin, 14 February 1908, on ibid.

116. Anonymous minute on ibid.

117. Anderson maintained that it was impossible to trust the discretion of Birch and the latter's continuance in the service was a serious difficulty for the administration. Also the Resident's health was not good, as at different times he had suffered from sprue. HC to CO, Confidential Desp., 13 April 1908, CO 273/1908.

118. The Secretary of State, Lord Crewe, regretted the necessity for dealing thus with a zealous public servant, but could not see any other alternative. Minute by Crewe, 24 July 1908, on Confidential Desp. of 13 April 1908, CO 273/1908.

119. At this meeting Birch defended his actions in the specific cases mentioned by Anderson, and showed Antrobus copies of private letters written to him by the High Commissioner about the mining exhibition and the question of the doctors. These letters made a great impression on the Under-Secretary and showed that impatience and impetuosity were not all on the side of Birch. Minute by Antrobus, 28 July 1908, on ibid.

120. Birch promised not to cause any more trouble and this sentiment was privately communicated to Anderson. Minute by Crewe, 1 August 1908, on ibid.

121. In May 1910 when Clifford was mentioned as a possible Resident-General, Anderson was worried enough to say that he would rather have Birch fill the position. Even Taylor, who loathed Birch, admitted the improvement in the Resident's attitude. Anderson to Collins, 12 May 1910, on Swettenham to Crewe, 3 June 1910, CO 273/1910.

122. The largest number of Indian immigrants was resident in Perak, and there was a body of opinion which thought that an Indian should be appointed to the Council, but nothing came of this. Editorial, *The Malay Mail*, 25 March 1908.

123. Since State Governments had ways and means of ensuring a majority, the proposal was not seen as one that need cause any uneasiness. Editorial, *The Malay Mail*, 25 March 1908.

124. Minutes of the Conference of Chiefs of the FMS held at Kuala Lumpur on 20–23 July 1903, Supplement to *Selangor Govt. Gazette*, 1903. A more detailed analysis of Sultan Idris's speech appears in Chapter IV.

125. HC to CO, Desp. No. 204, 9 May 1912, CO 273/1912.

126. HC to CO, Desp. No. 28, 17 January 1906, CO 273/1906.

127. An exception was Low who was appointed by Whitehall as Resident of Perak in 1877. J. de Vere Allen, 'The Malayan Civil Service 1874–1941: Colonial

Bureaucracy/Malayan Elite', *Comparative Studies in Society and History*, Vol. 12, No. 2, 1970, p. 156.

128. Martin Lister was the younger son of a Lord, Hugh Clifford, a nephew of a Lord, and John Rodger was born in a castle and was educated at Eton and Oxford. On the other side of the coin were officials like Tristan Speedy and Bloomfield Douglas, both of whom were inferior types. Ibid., p. 156.

129. Acting British Resident, Perak, to Col. Sec., 6 January 1896, CO 273/1896.

130. Resident, Selangor, to Col. Sec., 4 January 1896, and Acting British Resident, Perak, to Col. Sec., 6 January 1896, CO 273/1896.

131. Governor to CO, Desp. No. 52, 18 February 1896, CO 273/1896.

132. An excellent example was the case involving the Selangor railway engineer, C. Spence-Moss, who used his position to purchase blocks of land in the name of his brother-in-law, in areas earmarked for development. Maxwell investigated the affair only after he had lost confidence in Spence-Moss and set up a commission of enquiry with himself as chairman. Although Spence-Moss deserved to be sacked, the procedure was most irregular. See Sadka, *The Protected Malay States*, p. 230.

133. As a result of the proposals annual salaries in the FMS were fixed at the following levels: 5 Staff posts, 1 × £2,260, 1 × £1,600, 1 × £1,400, and 2 × £1,300; 6 Class 1 posts, 5 × £1,200, and 1 × £1,020; 10 Class 2 posts, 7 × £900–1,020, and 3 × £780–900; 17 Class 3 posts, 11 × £660–780, and 6 × £660–720; 28 Class 4 posts at £540–600, 24 Class 5 posts at £420–480; and 25 Class 6 posts at £350–400. CO to Governor, Desp. No. 171, 16 June 1905, CO 273/1905.

134. Sir G. Maxwell, 'The Malays and the Malayans', *The Nineteenth Century and After*, Vol. CXXXVII, No. 820, 1945, p. 282.

135. Ibid., p. 282.

136. Swettenham conceded that the travelling allowance was increased from $5 to $10 a day but repeated that his predecessor as Resident, Low, drew salary and allowances amounting to $13,200 per annum as long ago as 1886. Swettenham to CO, 11 January 1896, CO 273/1896.

137. Mitchell to Lucas, 2 March 1896, on Lucas to Mitchell, 24 March 1896, CO 273/1896.

138. Lucas was sorry that Swettenham had written and did not think he had grounds to complain. Moreover, Swettenham was assured that he would be largely engaged in travelling and would not be called upon to entertain many visitors. Lucas to Fairfield, 13 January 1896, on Swettenham to CO, 11 January 1896, CO 273/1896.

139. Minute by Fairfield, 13 January 1896, on Swettenham to CO, 11 January 1896, CO 273/1896.

140. Minute by Fairfield, 30 March 1896, and Lucas to Mitchell, 9 April 1896, on Lucas to Mitchell, 24 March 1896, CO 273/1891.

141. De Vere Allen conjectured that Swettenham's motives in coming to Malaya were a searing ambition and a desire to gamble on the chance of a quick promotion. See Allen, *Comparative Studies in Society and History*, Vol. 12, No. 2, 1970, p. 155.

142. 1906 was the first year when duty on rubber was levied and it yielded a sum of $50,023, but this increased to $360,055 in 1909. FMS General Return of Revenue, Expenditure, Trade, and Population, *FMS Annual Report, 1924*, Kuala Lumpur, 1925.

III

THE FEDERAL COUNCIL, 1909–1920

THE first significant constitutional change in the Federated Malay States took place in December 1909 when the Federal Council met in Kuala Kangsar.[1] It was the brainchild of Sir John Anderson and was his response to the dissatisfactions and disappointments expressed by Malay Rulers and British officials about the manner in which the Malay States were administered. He fully recognized that much real power and control had passed from the individual States to the central government and the Resident-General, prerogatives of State Councils in administration were largely nominal, and the policy of legislative uniformity had reduced them to mere registering bodies. The candid views of personalities like Sultan Idris and Resident Birch were an additional source of worry.

It had not taken an experienced and shrewd administrator like Anderson long to grasp the shortcomings of the system which he regarded as one of the many anomalies that the British loved to work.[2] He was pragmatic enough to acknowledge the material benefit that attended federation but lamented the absence of a central legislative authority to ensure smooth and efficient legislation, and the weakness of not clearly distinguishing federal from state matters. A further drawback was that in spite of vast strides being made in economic development, mining and planting interests were denied the opportunity to influence the government of the States.[3]

To surmount these deficiencies, the High Commissioner submitted to the Colonial Office in December 1907 a series of proposals that formed the basis of the Federal Council Agreement. The principal innovation was the establishment of a Federal Council and the final agreement consisted of a preamble and eleven clauses. The objects of the Council were recited in the preamble which made provision for the joint arrangement of all matters of mutual interest to the Federation, or affecting more than one of the States, and the subsequent enactment of laws that would be applied throughout the territory, or in more than one State. The first clause served to establish the

Council, and clauses 2 to 8 dealt with its membership, the terms of office of unofficial members, and matters of procedure. Clause 9 in the first part was concerned with the division of legislative power, and in its second with the division of administrative subjects between the States and the central government. The consideration of the Draft Estimates of Revenue and Expenditure of each state by the Federal Council and their return to the State Council was provided for in clause 10. The last clause stated that nothing in the Agreement was intended to

... curtail any of the powers or authority now held by any of the above mentioned Rulers in their respective States, nor does it alter the relations now existing between any of the States named and the British Empire as established by previous treaties.[4]

An examination of the document reveals that the most significant of the clauses were 9, 10 and 11. The first part of clause 9 was satisfactory in that it made adequate provision for cases where there was a conflict of laws but was restrictive in that it contained nothing which conferred on the Council power of legislation. To complicate matters no provisions were made for State Councils to pass enactments which could have rectified this apparent oversight. In practice, the Federal Council did exercise unchallenged legislative power but the fact remained that its authority to do so was not really constitutional and, if anything, was only implicit. Since the Council owed its very existence to the Constitution and, theoretically, had no powers except those conferred on it by this Constitution, it was a matter of regret that the sanctity for the administration of one of its cardinal functions should have remained a matter of inference, interpretation, and implication.[5]

The second part of clause 9 and the whole of clause 10 require careful consideration because they represented the grant of sole authority for the assumption of any power other than legislative, to the Federal Council. By specifying that:

... any questions connected with the Mohammedan religion, mosques, political pensions, native chiefs and penghulus and any other questions which in the opinion of the High Commissioner affect the rights and prerogatives of any of the above Rulers or which for other reasons he considers should properly be dealt with only by the State Councils, shall be exclusively reserved to the State Councils.

clause 9 suggested by inference that all other powers of Government were to be entrenched in the Federal Council. This particular form was in contradiction to the general practice in other Federal Constitutions. As mentioned in Chapter II the constitutions of the United

States of America and Australia, for example, defined explicitly those powers delegated to the central government, and those not so transferred were within the control of the State governments. Only in the Canadian Federation did the constitution specifically consign powers to the provinces, the rest being entrenched in the Dominion government.[6] Of greater importance in the Malayan context, and a strong reason against assuming any positive inference, was the type of subject mentioned; so far as Islam was concerned, the British were already bound by treaty not to interfere and to delegate the matter to a Council of which the British Resident was an authoritative adviser, and the inclusion of this particular item was bizarre. Mosques, political pensions, native chiefs, and *penghulu* were all clearly State matters not of common interest and not affecting more than one State. The 'rights and prerogatives of any of the Rulers' can only be interpreted as the rights and prerogatives of the Ruler of the State concerned and cannot be of common interest, although the Sultans' rights and prerogatives as a class could be. It could therefore be surmised that all the subjects that clause 9 allocated to State Councils could never have been within the competence of the Federal Council, and this makes it difficult to assign any meaning to it.

Another interesting feature of clause 9 was that the subjects reserved to the State Councils all called for the expenditure of funds and this contradicted the inference contained in clause 10 that only the Federal Council had full and absolute control over State expenditure. Lastly, the theory of the government, as expressed by the High Commissioner in his confidential despatch of July 1910, was that State Councils were merely advisory institutions with no decisive powers and that Malay Sultans were absolute within their respective states and could act with or without the advice of their Councils. So by allocating certain subjects to State Councils, the Agreement gave them definite powers which they could only acquire at the expense of the Sultans and that in turn was inconsistent with provisions of clause 11.

Clause 10, by giving the Federal Council absolute control of all finances, reversed the terms of the Treaty of Federation which had laid down that each State should, after providing for federal charges, spend its own revenue. The Federal Council Agreement mentioned nothing about federal revenue and expenditure, and the term used with regard to State budgets was 'considered' and not 'approved'. This gave it an air of studied vagueness but the inference that was assumed, and consistently acted upon, was that the Federal Council was the final authority in financial affairs, although financial control with reference to certain specific subjects appeared to be vested in State Councils. Taken together clauses 9 and 10 resulted in the Federal Council being established as the main legislative organ and the only financial authority, and created a division of powers by allocating certain subjects to State Councils.

The last clause of the Agreement, quoted earlier, was in fact identical with the concluding portion of the Treaty of Federation. These provisions might have been logical and had real meaning in 1895 but it was impossible to reconcile them in the 1909 Agreement with clauses 9 and 10 and, indeed, with the actual establishment of the Federal Council. The clause was not so much concerned with the personal rights and prerogatives of the Sultans, which were taken care of in clause 9, but with their powers and authority as Rulers with reference to State rights. Before the establishment of the Federal Council, State laws were enacted by State Councils, or rather by the Rulers on the advice of their councils. The States were free to spend their own revenues after the deduction of federal charges. The Federal Council, however, severely curtailed their legislative powers, completely removed their control of finances, and transferred them to State Councils. Yet the clause maintained that the powers and authority of Sultans were not to be decapitated. The basic contradiction was so manifest that it gave rise to allegations that the clause was designed only as a bait to obtain the acquiescence of the Malay Rulers for the new arrangements.[7]

Technically, the Agreement for the Constitution of a Federal Council, 1909, intended to be a major constitutional document, was, instead, subject to a considerable amount of misapprehension and contained contradictions within almost every provision. It failed to deal adequately with the circumstances outlined by Anderson in his observations of 2 November 1910. These clearly acknowledged that under the conditions created by Federation, a central authority had emerged and the rights of component States were subject to encroachment but the Agreement contained no recognition of this. Instead the Agreement of 1909 was drafted as if the Treaty of Federation had been implemented in the letter and in spirit, and that no central authority had resulted. The Federal Council Agreement deprived the States of the legislative and financial prerogatives that were nominally theirs, but made no attempt to reverse, or even check, the administrative encroachment of central authority on State rights although the tendency was obvious.[8]

6

The proposal to establish the Federal Council was approved, in principle, by the Colonial Office in January 1909 as it was believed that these arrangements would be to the advantage of the Federated Malay States.[9] Anderson was complimented for the manner in which he prepared the Agreement, and as the High Commissioner had been prudent and astute enough to have obtained the concurrence of the four Sultans, no obstacles were anticipated in implementing the proposals. One of the changes advocated by Whitehall related to the composition of the Council, and the Colonial Office believed that the consent of the British Government was necessary before any changes in the membership could be effected. The major bone of contention, however, concerned Anderson's proposal in the draft Agreement to set up an Administrative Council.[10] The clause read:

> The Draft of all laws intended and all resolutions or other business proposed by the Government to be submitted to the Federal Council, shall be considered previous to publication by an Administrative Council, and the draft Federal and State Estimates shall also be considered by this Council before publication.[11]

The Colonial Office saw the Administrative Council as a counterpart to an Executive Council which would have to meet at short intervals. The proposed constitution of this Council consisting of the High Commissioner, the Resident-General, the four Rulers, and the four Residents, seemed to suggest that frequent meetings would be difficult to arrange. If, on the other hand, it was designed to meet only to consider draft measures submitted to the Federal Council, the problems of getting members together were still valid. Another objection was that a Council of ten people would first consider the draft enactments, and then the same ten, with the addition of the four unofficial members, would convert themselves into the Federal Council which would transfer the drafts into laws. As the ten members of the Administrative Council would vote as a block in the Federal Council, the unofficial members would find themselves outnumbered and this would make it difficult to induce the more prominent individuals of the unofficial community to accept nomination to the Federal Council. Moreover, under these arrangements members of the Administrative Council would merely be duplicating, in the company of the four unofficials, work already done in the Administrative Council, and this seemed wasteful and unnecessary.[12]

Anderson sought to justify the formation of the Administrative Council by pointing out the improbability of the Malay Rulers taking a close interest in the proceedings, or being regular in their attendance at these meetings. As their knowledge of English was not good it would be difficult for them to follow proceedings. The High Commissioner's intentions were to restrict the functions of this Council to the consideration of draft measures and proposals for legislation and of the Estimates, in which case it would not be a serious problem to get members to attend. As it was, the Residents held meetings at least once a year with the Resident-General, and if the Administrative Council could be established in place of these meetings, it would be advantageous to the High Commissioner, as it would enable him to be present and assist at those gatherings rather than have the resolutions and proposals sent to him for approval at a later stage. The benefits of hearing all the arguments for and against various measures could not be disputed. In circumstances where officials would, as a rule, have to vote solidly within the Federal Council, it was healthy that they be given adequate opportunities to express their views frankly before their adoption by the Government.[13] Communication facilities, as a result of railway extensions and the rapid growth of motor-car traffic, rendered movement easy and Anderson did not think it would be very difficult to convene such meetings.[14]

Although officials in the Colonial Office were not very impressed by the High Commissioner's arguments,[15] they recognized that it would be useful if Anderson could assist at the periodic meetings of the Resident-General and the Residents, and listened to the arguments at first hand. London, therefore, suggested that rather than create an Administrative Council the High Commissioner should arrange to attend and preside at Residents' Conferences.[16]

The creation of the Federal Council in December 1909 posed a grave theoretical constitutional problem to the Colonial Office bureaucracy. So long as the Council was a consultative body, and all legislation remained under the control of the Sultans, there were no legal dilemmas, but if the Council passed laws on behalf of the four Federated States, binding on every person within those states, then a grim predicament arose. Legally, the States were classified as 'Protected States' in the sense that their foreign policy was conducted, on their behalf, by Great Britain. Jurisdiction of the States was never ceded by the Sultans to the British and the power to enact laws for any of the States was not within the ambits of British control. All laws were made by the Sultans who acted on British advice, and although all the senior civil servants were British nationals, they were in the service of the Sultans and not of the British Government. In constituting the Federal Council as the supreme legislative authority of the Federation then, some power or establishment had to confer on the Council the right to legislate for all the States. The Malay Rulers were not in a position to do this because each had the power to enact laws binding only within his own state. The British sovereign could not do it by an Order in Council because the Sultans had never ceded their jurisdiction to her and no Order in Council could be passed under the Foreign Jurisdiction Act of 1890. The British Parliament could not do it because Parliament did not have the prerogative to enact laws binding on foreigners outside British territory, and the Malay States were, theoretically, foreign territory. The only solution seemed to be to persuade each Sultan to sign a treaty surrendering juridical powers to the British Government which could then, by an Order in Council under the Foreign Jurisdiction Act, set up a Council having powers to make laws for all the States. The consequence of such a move, however, would have practically meant the abdication of the Rulers.[17]

In the discussions that ensued, the Colonial Office and the High Commissioner acknowledged the impossibility of asking the Sultans to cede their jurisdiction to enact laws for the four States. Anderson, however, believed that, in the instance of the Federated Malay States, the cession of jurisdiction by the Rulers and the lawmaking authorities of the States would not be to an individual but to a council. He invoked the precedent set by the formation of the German Empire where the sovereigns of all the component states empowered the Reichstag to validate laws binding on all of them. Anderson maintained that the Federal Council Agreement was a document where the Rulers consented to transfer their prerogatives, by mutual agreement, to the Federal Council. Thus the laws made by the Council would have legitimacy in all four states by virtue of the fact that the Sultans, or lawmakers, had conferred their lawmaking rights for their States on the Council.[18] For want of a better alternative, these sentiments were allowed to predominate and the Colonial Office was satisfied to opt for a wait-and-see attitude.[19]

The first meeting of the Federal Council took place on 11 December 1909. The official element consisted of the High Commissioner, the Resident-General, the four Malay Rulers, and the four British Residents, and four unofficials made up the rest of the membership. The Planters' Association of Malaya, formed by British agricultural interests, had for long expressed the wish to be represented on the highest councils of government, and, when the idea of a Federal Council was first mooted, showed great interest in it. By October 1908 the planting industry was valued at £3,000,000, extended over an area of 125,000 acres, and produced 885 tons of exports annually.[20] The total number of workers involved in the industry was in excess of 58,000. The Association claimed that the figures were indicative of the vital role of planters in the growing economic importance of the Federated Malay States. The concern of the Association was echoed and extensively discussed in the local English language press, public interest among the European community was considerably aroused on the question of a Federal Council, and it was anticipated that pressure would be exerted on the administration to make significant concessions to the business community.[21] The establishment of the Federal Council with its initial complement of four unofficial members represented Government acknowledgement of the increased importance of the commercial sector in the economic life of the country. The first representatives of the unofficial group were Frank Douglas Osborne, a partner in a firm of mining engineers, Osborne and Chappell, located in Ipoh; Richard Walter Harrison, a visiting agent, estate valuer, manager of an estate agents company in Klang, Messrs. Whittall and Company, and Chairman of the Planters' Association of Malaya;[22] John Henry Matthews Robson,[23] land agent and managing director of the Malay Mail Press in Kuala Lumpur; and Towkay Leong Fee[24] of the Chinese mining syndicates.

The initial meeting of the Council provided a forum for debate, saw the passage of the Supply Bill and of other Enactments laid before the members. The extent of participation clearly showed that the unofficials appreciated the opportunity to air their opinions on the legislative proposals of the administration. The Sultans too were pleased and gratified at the prospect of meeting regularly, and being able to express their views.[25]

The most noticeable feature of the membership of the Council was the absence of a representative from the Indian community. In September 1911, there were 172,000 Indians in the Federation of whom 43 per cent were classified as labourers and the remainder were contractors, traders, government and non-government clerks, artisans, and landowners. The first calls for representation came from R. Feavatham, an Indian leader, who drew attention to the fact that the size of the Indian population was significant enough to warrant representation, especially as the number of Indian labourers exceeded that of Chinese workers. The Indian community, it was claimed, played an important part in the life of the country and it would be unfair to neglect it.[26] The issue was also raised in the British House of Commons in August 1911 by a Member of Parliament, Ingleby, but the Secretary of State for the Colonies reported the practical impossibility of nominating a suitable Indian to the Council.[27] He referred to the examples of Mauritius and the West Indies where suitable Indians could not be found to sit on Councils in spite of the fact that, in Mauritius at least, there was an old and established Indian community. The Colonial Office asserted that the majority of Indians in the Malay States belonged to the labouring category or were cart drivers and policemen. There was no one of sufficient stature to be appointed, and even if there were one he would not be a fit representative of the majority. The interests of the labourers were adequately looked after by official members of the Council, and it was undesirable, from the British point of view, to increase the membership of the body unnecessarily. Another curious objection advanced by the Colonial Office and by Anderson was that the Sultans would resent the appointment of a 'black man' to sit with them in Council.[28]

Hand in hand with Anderson's proposals for a Federal Council were his ideas concerning the future of the post of Resident-General since the establishment of the Council represented only a part of his grand design for the Federated Malay States. An essential adjunct was his plan to change the title of Resident-General to that of Chief Secretary to the Government. So long as the then Resident-General, Taylor, was still in the service, the measure would have been embarrassing, but the opportunity arose in July 1910 when it became known that Taylor intended to retire and take up an appointment as Director of the newly created Malay States Development Agency in London. The High Commissioner used the occasion to review the office of Resident-General. He claimed that in the six years preceding 1910 conditions in the Malay States had altered considerably; it was easier for a High Commissioner from Singapore to visit and communicate with almost any part of the Malay States than it was for him to do so with, say, Penang, and in so far as the eastern portion of Pahang was concerned, this was more accessible from Singapore than it was from Kuala Lumpur. The successful construction of new railway lines, the expanded telegraphic system running from Penang to Singapore and the network of roads traversing the western Malay States and joining up with the road systems of Province Wellesley and Malacca, made communications within the Federation speedy. The western portion of the east-coast State of Pahang was accessible by two roads, one from Selangor and the other from Negri Sembilan. Therefore, according to Anderson, one of the principal reasons for the continuance of the Resident-General, that of providing a fast link between the Malay States and the High Commissioner, was no longer valid.[29]

The early years of Federation had also seen the growth of a tendency to regard the High Commissioner as someone who subordinated the interests of the Federated Malay States to those of the Straits Settlements.[30] It was the Resident-General who was considered the guardian and protector of Malay States interests.[31] This view had received much currency during Swettenham's tenure of the post and support for these ideas existed among European capitalists in the Malay States.[32] Anderson was able to see the logic of these sentiments and believed that so long as the High Commissioner was not, technically, the responsible head of the administration of both the territories, that impression was bound to prevail. In practice, therefore, the existence of the Resident-General served to compound rather than decrease the problems of the High Commissioner. If, however, it could somehow be clarified that the High Commissioner, instead of being merely someone vested with a certain amount of control over the administration of the Federation and over the kind of advice given to Malay Rulers, was the real responsible head of the government and that the Residents were his direct representatives in the Malay States, only then would the suspicions and doubts attached to his actions be effectively countered.[33]

It was partly towards establishing this position that Anderson proposed in the Federal Council Agreement that the High Commissioner should usually preside at Council meetings, and that half the cost of the High Commissioner's establishment should be placed on the Federal Estimates. He believed that once the public became aware that the High Commissioner was just as much concerned with the administration of the Federated Malay States as he was with that of the Straits Settlements, then some of the difficulties and scepticisms might be allayed.[34]

Anderson pressed for the precise definition of the position and status of the High Commissioner and the Resident-General and requested that it be made clear that the latter was an officer of the former and was nothing more than the High Commissioner's principal adviser and mouthpiece in the Malay States. The Resident-General was not the quasi-independent head of a separate administration. Without intending to take over any of the powers entrusted to the Resident-General, as defined in Mitchell's despatch of 1 May 1895, Anderson advocated that they should in future be exercised by an officer to be styled the Chief Secretary to the Government.[35]

The most violent objections to the change of title emanated from Swettenham. He saw the control of the Resident-General within the Malay States and his authority to represent and protect the wishes of the Sultans, the Malay population, and the other inhabitants of the States, as well as the general interests of the Federation, as being not only an essential condition for good government but also as something that was in accordance with the letter and spirit of the Treaty of Federation.[36] He alleged that Anderson's proposed change was intended to secure something much more than a mere change of label. It was a move to reverse and modify a policy that was worked out after many years of experience, discussion, and debate. In any case Swettenham was convinced that it was highly imprudent to entrench so much power and authority in a High Commissioner who, in addition to being Governor of the Straits Settlements, was also the Consul-General for Borneo and Director of the Affairs of Kedah, Kelantan, and Trengganu.[37]

Anderson's trump card was that before submitting his plan to the Colonial Office he had sent his proposals, in confidence, to the Malay Rulers and had obtained their unanimous agreement.[38] His case was further strengthened by the favourable response of Residents. The High Commissioner was determined to do his utmost to ensure that he would, unquestionably, be regarded as the person responsible for the entire British interest in the region. Anderson felt that such a position of predominance would give him sufficient scope to determine the policies of the several administrations and successfully co-ordinate developments within them.[39]

The Colonial Office agreed that the division of authority between the Resident-General and the High Commissioner had been the main factor responsible for the former being regarded as the champion of Federal interests resisting all the unnecessary encroachments of the Straits Settlements. Whitehall also acknowledged that, in the prevailing circumstances in the area, there was no longer the need for an officer exercising quasi-independent powers and that the creation of a Chief Secretary would produce a situation where his relationship with the High Commissioner would resemble that of a Colonial Secretary with a Governor. The High Commissioner would thus be able to exert the same degree of supervision over the Chief Secretary as he, as Governor, did over the Colonial Secretary.[40]

Officials in London recognized that so long as the communications system was primitive, a semi-independent officer like the Resident-General had an important function to perform. But it was a necessary evil that had served its purpose. The Resident-General in the Federation possessed more than just the trappings of independent authority; he not only issued instructions in his own name but had also, in practice, often acted in an obstructive and embarrassing fashion. Anderson's intentions, in the opinion of the Colonial Office, had the virtue of taking away the independence of the Federal official and were, therefore, welcome. The Chief Secretary was seen as an officer who would perform his duties in the name, and under the orders, of the High Commissioner. After all, the latter official was, by the Federal Council Agreement, the President of the Council and signed all Federal Enactments. All the important issues were debated in his presence, he took a prominent part in the discussions and arguments, maintained a constant personal relationship with the Sultans, and discussed with them, on an informal basis, matters of mutual interest. The Chief Secretary was to have a large amount of power delegated to him, but would act as the mouthpiece and work under the direction of the High Commissioner.[41]

The above changes concentrated and increased the duties of the High Commissioner but this disadvantage was more than balanced by the belief that the public service of the Federation would increase in efficiency. Anderson's capacity to shoulder the burden was never in doubt but, to safeguard his successors, the High Commissioner was instructed, by the Colonial Office, to organize a system of practical government in such a way as to facilitate the handing over of control.[42] The Chief Secretary (Incorporation) Enactment, 1911, was accordingly passed by the Federal Council in November 1910, and came into effect in 1911.

The Enactment itself was significant for three reasons. First, the preamble clearly stated that the Chief Secretary to the Government would possess and enjoy all and every one of the rights, privileges and powers conferred, and exercise all and every one of the duties imposed upon the Resident-General by the Treaty of Federation and by enactments of the Federal Council. Second, by virtue of these factors it was the Chief Secretary, and not the High Commissioner or any other officer, who sued and was sued in court, acquired property, and entered into contracts, etc. on behalf of the Federation Government. Third, the powers the Resident-General possessed of making rules and regulations under various enactments were continued to the Chief Secretary.[43]

The Federal Council Agreement and the Chief Secretary Enactment represented major constitutional changes in the administration of the Federated Malay States. When the last of the Residents-General, Taylor, retired in September 1910, his successor became the first Chief Secretary. In trying to select the most suitable candidate, four contenders were considered. Of the serving Residents, Birch was the most senior but his claims were discounted on account of his ill-health and his imminent retirement. The Resident of Selangor, Belfield, was able, hard-working, and energetic, with a great sense of loyalty which at times was so close to subservience that Anderson was uncertain whether the opinions expressed by the Resident were his own or an echo of the High Commissioner's ideas. For an office requiring a certain degree of independence of judgement and self-reliance, these qualities were not the ideal recommendation.[44] Clifford's name was briefly linked to this appointment[45] but Anderson's assessment of the ex-Resident was most uncomplimentary.[46] Sir Arthur Young,[47] the Colonial Secretary, was the High Commissioner's personal selection, and according to Anderson, had robust common sense, sound judgement, and much administrative ability and acumen. His love for the outdoor life and his extreme hospitality were further qualifications. E. L. Brockman,[48] the Resident of Negri Sembilan, an officer of high personal character who between 1905 and 1908 had acted on various occasions as Colonial Secretary, Resident-General, and Resident of Perak, was commended to replace Young as Colonial Secretary.[49] The Colonial Office sanctioned these proposals and on 1 February 1911, Young assumed duties as Chief Secretary.[50]

The new arrangements, however, were short-lived because in July 1911, Anderson was appointed Permanent Under-Secretary of State for the Colonies, and in September of the same year, Young became Governor and High Commissioner. Brockman moved on to Kuala Lumpur as Chief Secretary and was replaced as Colonial Secretary by R. J. Wilkinson,[51] the Resident of Negri Sembilan. Thus in the short space of two years the Federation not only experienced a major constitutional overhaul but also saw its affairs being conducted by a new team of British officers at the helm.

In the practical workings of these measures, the tone was set by Anderson at the first meeting of the Federal Council. He told the assembly that the Council was established 'to control the finances and to direct the course of legislation'[52] and it might be assumed from this that the control of finance was the High Commissioner's interpretation of the expression in the preamble, 'the joint arrangement of all matters of common interest to the Federation, or affecting more than one State'.[53] It can be conceded that the preamble lacked vigorous definition but, even so, Anderson's point of view was both too wide and too narrow. Such issues as the general policy to be adopted in the alienation of land, the attraction of foreign capital, the preservation of the local food supply, the importation of labour, the reservation and exploitation of forests, the adoption of a satisfactory educational system, and medical preventive measures were certainly matters of common interest to the Federation, but in fact the Federal Council had no say in them. On the other hand, the details of the Taiping Sanitary Board budget or the expenditure on launches of the Harbour Master at Port Swettenham were not matters of common interest and did not affect more than one State, but were subject to the control of the Federal Council.[54]

The initial reaction of the local English language press was that the Federal Council was a step in the right direction. This represented a significant change of attitude because when the idea was first mooted it was scoffed at on the grounds that it would be a mere dummy, a creature devoid both of individuality and vitality, a constitutional echo of the powers that be, and a sop to political science. When the details were published, however, the press welcomed the Agreement as a blueprint containing a degree of liberality that had until then been missing. The unofficial element, admittedly, was in a decided minority but at least it attained a position where it was entitled to be heard. The Council was also expected to demolish any old barriers of prejudice and unhealthy rivalry, and lead to a smoother working of the Federation as well as hold the scales evenly between the different states, communities, and creeds.[55] It was also regarded as a positive step to the unification of government within the Malayan area and was publicized as a precedent for a larger territorial entity to include those northern Malay States that had formerly been controlled by Thailand, and the Straits Settlements.[56]

From time to time, however, the press was also quick to criticize. For example when, on 13 December 1909, the Council debated subjects not previously announced to the public, it was pointed out that the rules governing the Constitution of the Council required a month's prior notice in the Gazette of all items to be discussed at a meeting, although there was a proviso allowing the President to raise matters as topics of urgency. According to the press, there was no justification to invoke that loophole when the bills concerned were the Federal Coast Chandu Enactment and the General Clauses Enactment.[57]

The public, which in effect meant the English-speaking and English-reading sector, looked to debates in Council for information on such issues as public health, education, and labour. These items were discussed regularly but it was most peculiar that the heads of the departments concerned were not present on those occasions and could not, therefore, participate in the proceedings. Their absence gave an aura of unreality to the statements and pronouncements made on their behalf by the Residents or the Chief Secretary, and increased the impression that such problems were worked out in bureaucratic isolation instead of in close collaboration with leaders of coherent public opinion. What was required was the strengthening of the constitution of the Council to enable it to play a more constructive role.[58]

So far as the position of the Sultans in the Council was concerned, the early promises were not fulfilled. At the inaugural meeting of the Council Anderson had declared:

It was no small sacrifice of individuality on the part of the Rulers to enter on the compact of federation and to complete and crown it by the Agreement in virtue of which we are assembled. They made that sacrifice willingly and gladly because they felt the debt which they owe to the protection and help which has been extended to them by England, and because they felt that the prosperity and progress of their states is bound up with the advancement of British interests in the Malay Peninsula. They have done this in the full confidence, based on the facts of the past, that whatever is done either by the British Government or by this Council, the faith and obligations of the treaties under which they agreed to accept British Advisers will always be scrupulously observed. They are confident that we will never forget that our powers are derived wholly from their gift, and that we are here in a Malay country as advisers and counsellors of its Malay sovereigns. I am sure that everyone of us will bear that in mind and that the Rulers who have so earnestly at heart the real good and advancement of the people subject to them, will never have cause to regret that they agreed to this step.[59]

Of course, the hope had been that the changes would restore to the Rulers and the Residents the fuller powers and responsibilities they had exercised before Federation. But these expectations were not realized. The position of the Rulers within the Federal Council was highly unsatisfactory. They had to sit through long debates carried on in a language with which they were not at all familiar, and although the proceedings were periodically summarized in a translation, the results were extremely tedious for the Sultans. Still they regarded it as their duty to sit through the meetings notwithstanding the custom which had evolved for them not to take part in the debates. Only on rare occasions of peculiar importance was this custom varied. It was impossible not to feel that just as the dignity of the Rulers necessitated their abstention from debate, it would also lead to their withdrawal from the Council. It appeared rather degrading for them to engage in controversy, say, with one of the unofficial members, and equally humiliating for them to be placed in the dormant position of silent members of Council. Growing uneasiness was felt by the Rulers themselves who, while admitting their distaste for the system, were just as uncertain as to what the best solution was.[60]

In the final analysis the responsibility for the implementation of the new constitutional measures lay with the British officials, and the tone and tenor of the administration was set chiefly by the High Commissioner and the Chief Secretary to the Government. One of Anderson's prime aims was to bring the High Commissioner directly into the government of the Federated Malay States. He did this by making himself the President of the Council, and justified it by claiming that the Malay Rulers thought it was derogatory to their status to have their Residents placed under anyone other than the immediate local representative of the British sovereign.[61] He was not concerned with moves towards a policy of decentralization. Throughout his tenure of office, Anderson did nothing that was in accordance with that objective. In this he was supported by the Chief Secretary who was also uninterested in pressing for greater devolution. The Chief Secretary was satisfied to keep and hold any powers that the High Commissioner did not want for himself. The refusal of the Colonial Office to sanction the establishment of an Administrative Council had forced Anderson to agree to the idea of periodic meetings between himself, the Resident-General, and the Residents. The Residents were expected to discuss public questions from the point of view of State and Federal interests, advise the High Commissioner on matters of federal importance, and liaise between him and the Sultans. These Conferences, however, were never utilized by Anderson in spite of his pronouncement about the usefulness of such meetings.[62]

The Chief Secretary had replaced the Resident-General because the latter official was too independent and powerful. At a meeting of the Federal Council on 19 January 1911 he stated that Residents had complained that their initiative and their approaches to the High Commissioner were often blocked by the Resident-General who had the power, and exercised it, to turn down proposals submitted by individual Residents. There were the occasional Residents' Conferences where legislation and other policy issues were discussed, but on many other vital subjects the Residents were not allowed to have their say and their ideas never reached the High Commissioner. At the same time the Residents were kept unaware of important matters until, in most instances, they were already implemented. The Chief Secretary was designed to be the channel of communication between the Residents and the Sultans on the one hand and the High Commissioner on the other. Instead of being the ultimate and supreme authority he was to stand between the two categories. He was also to be the principal, but not the only, adviser of the High Commissioner, as the Residents were expected to give their counsel on subjects of public interest and legislation pertaining to the Federation.[63] In practice, however, the situation was very different. The departure of Anderson, the architect of the scheme, and the appointment of Young as High Commissioner, might have been responsible for the discrepancies between theory and practice, and it is conceivable that had Anderson remained for a further few years he would have been able to transform aspirations into reality. In the prevailing circumstances, however, the office of Chief Secretary symbolized even greater centralization in Kuala Lumpur. The authority and the dignity of the Rulers and their State Councils decreased further. Residents were constantly ignored, and their proposals interfered with.[64]

The constitutional question relating to the respective powers of the High Commissioner and the Chief Secretary led to occasional disputes. As mentioned earlier, the preamble to the Chief Secretary Enactment vested considerable powers in that office and the first occasion these were challenged was in August 1914 when the Federal Council debated the Public Emergency Enactment. A study of the proceedings indicates that in many clauses of the Enactment the words 'Chief Secretary' were replaced in pencil by the words 'High Commissioner'. This apparently hurried alteration was vehemently condemned by the unofficial members of the Council who were against the idea of giving wide emergency powers to the High Commissioner. They regarded it as an attempt to link the Federated Malay States inseparably with the Straits Settlements. The Acting High Commissioner, Wilkinson, insisted that it was essential in great emergencies that dictatorial powers should be vested in one man and that the High Commissioner should be that man. Although, in practice, the working of the law would be left in the hands of local authorities, the responsibility for their actions would lie with the High Commissioner who did not intend to evade, divide, or delegate it. Eventually the Bill was passed with the unofficials abstaining in the vote.[65] The non-government members fully appreciated the constitutional point at issue and the only reason why they did not organize public protests and appeals to the Colonial Office was that they did not want to embarrass the Government in the midst of a grave national crisis.[66]

In 1919 the 'Delegation of Powers Enactment' was passed allowing the High Commissioner to delegate powers to the Chief Secretary. But little practical use was made of this Enactment, one reason being that powers exercised by the High Commissioner were administrative rather than statutory, and also because it was recognized that the functions of the two officers were constitutionally different.[67]

The role of the unofficials was, necessarily, a very limited one. They were glad of the opportunity to express their views and to comment on Government policy in general. They also believed that much scope for improvement existed, especially in the manner in which Council business was conducted. Speaking to the Council in November 1912, E. Macfadyen, a particularly vociferous individual, suggested that in the future the Government should attempt to increase the administrative role of the Council by assigning more and more importance to its deliberations. He did not want the Council to remain an organization exercising a purely consultative function in relation to Government policy. He criticized the lamentable lack of consultation on vital issues between the officials and the unofficials, and, as an example, quoted the passage of the 'Suppression of Gambling Enactment' when the first chance the unofficials had of considering the Bill was at the Council meeting proper. This kind of procedure marked the important difference between the character of the Federal Council and a Legislative Council in a Crown Colony. The distinction was bound to cause constant discontent unless the administration could gradually and steadily extend the spheres of usefulness open to the Federal Council.[68] The Government, however, made no attempt to modify the *modus operandi* of the Council and this apparent insensitivity provoked another outburst from Macfadyen in November 1919. He outlined what he considered were the valid concerns of the unofficials and believed that they should act the part of a constitutional opposition. Young disagreed and was not prepared to regard the unofficials as anything more than the coadjutors of Government.[69]

Outside the Federal Council chamber the business and commercial community also expressed fears that the constitutional reforms initiated and implemented by Anderson were designed in some way to foster the interests of the Straits Settlements, and the British Empire in general, to the detriment of the Federated Malay States. These anxieties first found expression in 1912 when proposals were made to form a Federated Malay States Association on the same lines as the Straits Settlements Association.[70] The main object of such a body was to watch over the integrity of the Federation against official encroachment and against any attempted Parliamentary interference from London. The projected Association was expected to maintain strict surveillance over official acts and policies for which, perhaps, even the High Commissioner might not be personally responsible but which had been decided upon in London. The Association would also ensure that the revenues of the Federation were not diverted for Imperial purposes and check that finances originating in the Malay States were usefully employed in improving the administration and facilitating the economic development of the States.[71]

Credibility was lent to these apprehensions when a draft of 'An Enactment to Provide for Extending to the Federated Malay States the Operation of Acts of the Imperial Parliament' was published in the Federated Malay States Gazette of 30 August 1912. This move was seen as the thrust of yet another tentacle aiming to establish a stronger grip on the liberties of the Malay States and one which represented an insidious policy suggested, even dictated, from London to minimize the status of the Malay States and obtain greater control by a sequence of assumptions and presumptions. Had the Federated Malay States been a colony or had they been acquired as a result of war or settlement, then the British Parliament would have been justified in directing the kind of legislation proposed; but since the Federation was, theoretically at least, a territory whose Rulers, singly or collectively, had accepted British protection, advice, and assistance without abrogating more of their sovereign rights than the abandonment of relations with any foreign power, the proposal was obviously illegal. It was also clear that despite the fact that the majority of the senior civil servants in the States were British, the administration was not strictly a British administration.[72] Thus, any attempt to treat States under British protection as countries under the administration of the British Parliament deserved to be resisted and exposed as a dangerous and vicious precedent. The Draft Enactment, if passed, would have the effect of asking the Federal Council to divest itself of the power to examine, adopt, modify, or reject any legislation passed by Parliament for areas under direct British authority. The proposed Bill substituted for the legislative power of the Federal Council a remarkable sanction expressed in its third clause:

If and so often as the Rulers of Perak, Selangor and Pahang and the Chiefs of Negri Sembilan shall have agreed in writing that it is expedient that the operation of any Imperial Act be extended to the Federated Malay States so as to have effect therein in the same manner as if the said States were part of the dominions of His Britannic Majesty to which such Act applies, it shall be lawful for the High Commissioner, subject to the provisions of section six, by order under his hand published in the Gazette, to direct that the operation of such Imperial Act be extended to the Federated Malay States on and after such date as may be specified in that behalf in such order.[73]

In examining the above clause in detail it has to be borne in mind that the Malay Rulers in 1912, as a consequence of the relative insignificance of their State Councils, were practically deprived of all advice. This state of affairs was not unknown to British authorities in the Federation, the Straits Settlements, and the Colonial Office. The Sultans were, therefore, apparently expected to agree without meeting to agree. It almost seemed as if the Rulers were spontaneously to be seized with the conviction that a certain Act of Parliament was just the thing for their States, intuitively notify the High Commissioner of this desire, and provide the British Officer with the necessary justification to proclaim that law to be the law of the Federated Malay States. The Federal Council would never, if this Enactment of Abdication became legal, be aware of the merits or demerits of foreign legislation and would be in no position even to express any opinion on it. The Enactment, naturally, raised trepidation about the entire future of the Federal Council, and non-government opinion felt that whatever the virtues of an Imperial Act there could be no possible pretext to supersede the functions, powers and privileges of the Council. It was alleged that this furtive coercion of the Malay sovereigns, away from the protection of their Councils and the safeguards of publicity, was the obvious motive behind the measure and such a transgression was despicable and disgraceful.[74]

The Colonial Office was taken aback by the strength of opposition

7

to the Bill and, in order to reinforce its claim that it had no desire to undermine the independence of the Malay States in any way, issued prompt instructions to the High Commissioner to withdraw the proposed Enactment. In private, however, officials in London were convinced that the speed of economic and administrative developments in the Federation would in any case result in the sovereignty of the Malay Rulers becoming increasingly shadowy and unreal. In addition they believed that the Sultans, personally, did not baulk at their loss of influence and were in fact grateful for the efficient and successful manner in which the British were governing the Malay States.[75]

Shortly after this episode, another development occurred which caused a stir among those determined jealously to protect the interests of the Federation. In November 1912, Sultan Idris of Perak announced that he had decided to invite his colleagues, within the Federal Council, to accept and endorse a resolution offering Great Britain a first-class armoured ship. It is difficult to believe that the Sultan's pronouncement was either voluntary or spontaneous and it was suspected, by those outside the administration, that the offer of the gift was the outcome of high official influence making its pleasure known to the Ruler.[76] It might be pertinent to note that just prior to the Sultan's announcement he had visited the Tanjong Pagar Docks in Singapore and, while touring the establishment, had acquired useful information about the naval dock. He was accompanied by Young, the High Commissioner, and it was believed that in the course of private conversation the British official might have made the suggestion.[77] What did happen was that the plan was laid before the Council and the meeting decided that the gift would be in the form of cash, designed for the purchase of an armoured ship valued at $20,000,000, payable over a period of five years.[78] The adoption of the resolution was, of course, a mere formality because throughout the debate, the High Commissioner remained in the chair and every one of the British officials and unofficials was in the chambers. This destroyed the final pretext of spontaneity for the resolution. It would have been better, and more statesmanlike in the circumstances, for Young to have left the session during this particular stage of the proceedings for it was manifestly hypocritical of him to have occupied a position where he was in control of the discussion, as the representative of the Government that stood to benefit. The other British members should also have withdrawn from the meeting because it was not a matter in which they should have any say. It was an issue which should have concerned the Malay

Rulers and their chiefs alone and the final decision ought to have been theirs and theirs alone. The Secretary of State for the Colonies, Lewis Harcourt, denied that the idea of the gift had been suggested by the Colonial Office, and maintained that the news had come as a surprise to him. The conclusion drawn by non-government Malayan opinion was that the hint had been given to Sultan Idris by local British officials and, if this were true, it had been done without Colonial Office authority and was, therefore, unfortunate.[79]

If, on the other hand, the initiative had indeed come from Sultan Idris, a series of questions, with wide and far-reaching implications, presented themselves. What was to happen when the five years had elapsed? Could the Malay sovereigns then channel their revenues for the further development of their own States, and were they empowered to help, financially, the more backward Malay States outside the Federation? Or were they to face what would have been a moral demand for the continuance of what could be best described as an Imperial subsidy? The succeeding years, however, left no doubt that the Sultans did not possess any special rights to decide how the revenues of their States were to be expended. More than ever before, the purse strings were very much the sacred preserve of the High Commissioner and his British advisers, and although the gift of the warship did not represent the forerunner of an annual, or even regular, contribution to the Imperial Government, it did set a precedent for the transfer of £2,000,000 to the British Government for the Singapore Naval Base in 1926.[80] It is important also to view the gift of the armoured vessel in the context of the total revenues of the Federation. Since 1896 these had, no doubt, increased steadily and had grown from $8,434,083 to $42,647,687 in 1912 but this had been accompanied by a corresponding rise in the expenditure from $8,598,147 to $30,990,487.[81] So although the States were in the enviable position of having a reasonable bank balance, they were hardly in a situation where they could afford to hand out $20,000,000 without it making a substantial dent in their credits. Conceivably, that same amount could have been better spent in expanding and improving such facilities as the education, health, sanitary, and welfare needs of the local population.

By far the most important external event of the period 1909–20 was the outbreak of the First World War in Europe in 1914, and although the arena of hostilities was remote enough from southern Asia its global repercussions did not pass the Malay Peninsula by. The years immediately preceding the turmoil were years of unprecedented development in the Federation as the rubber industry approached maturity and the price of tin reached new high levels. In terms of the value of exports the figures increased from $76,273,438 in 1909 to $148,669,498 in 1913.[82] This economic prosperity relegated most political issues to the background. There was little politicking in the Federal Council and the early years of its life were characterized by a contented and friendly atmosphere. The unofficial members were pleased with the courteous and helpful way in which Anderson treated them.[83] Any dissatisfaction that might have existed regarding the development of a highly centralized bureaucracy in Kuala Lumpur was also forgotten.[84]

With the outbreak of war there was an immediate decline in the economic prosperity of the States and the value of exports declined to $122,962,929 in 1914, although partially recovering to $161,838,118 in 1915.[85] In 1916 the demand for Malayan produce increased substantially and the renewed prosperity was evident for the rest of the decade. For the man-in-the-street, the actual hostilities were too remote to cause much concern and the only link between him and the war was the higher prices he paid for almost every essential commodity. The planting and mining enterprises were more enthusiastic about disturbed European conditions, since this meant growing demand for their products and, hence, increased prosperity. Politically, no one raised issues sensitive to the administration for fear of being accused of taking advantage of the crisis and unfairly embarrassing the Government. Within the Federal Council, the war brought home to the members the importance for the country to be self-sufficient in its basic food requirements. To minimize the dangers of starvation, the Federated Malay States administration was urged to adopt policies that would encourage padi planting and introduce a system of subsidies.[86] Until then the only area where the authorities had incurred large-scale expenditure in irrigation works for padi planting was Krian. Attention was drawn to the fact that large areas of land given out on *mukim* extracts were unsuitable for padi cultivation because the country had dried up. The indiscriminate clearing of jungle led to water running off quickly and prevented the accumulation which was so essential for padi.[87] The rice crisis also gave rise to one of the rare instances of a Malay Sultan participating in the discussions within the Federal Council. Sir Alaedin Suleiman Shah, the Sultan of Selangor, highlighted the plight of 10,000 Malays in his state who wanted to plant padi but had no land to do so. He suggested that they might be granted three acres of land each in one locality, in each *mukim* or group of *mukim*, and be instructed to standardize the time fixed for planting. The Sultan was also anxious that they should be given all the assistance they might at any time require.[88] A Rice Lands Enactment was passed by the Federal Council in 1917 reserving land for the specific purpose of rice cultivation. In April 1919, Brockman, the Chief Secretary, announced that the Government would guarantee a price of thirteen cents per *gantang*[89] of padi grown in the Federation, and delivered at a rice mill, for the five years beginning 1 May 1919. This compared with the price of seven or eight cents which had hitherto been paid to the farmers.[90]

The first ten years of the Federal Council, therefore, were not characterized by the discussion of either controversial or acrimonious issues and arguments. The firm control exercised by Anderson and his successor, Young, the massive official majority, the invidious position of the Sultans on the Council, the small number of un-officials and the arbitrary method of their selection, all ensured the functioning of an orderly and generally placid legislative organization. The novelty of the concept, the growing prosperity of the Federated States, and the outbreak of the World War contributed further to the creation of an atmosphere which exuded a feeling, albeit superficial, of peace, well-being, contentment and harmony. The fragility of the situation was, after all, amply demonstrated in the early 1920s when, at the first prospect of an impending economic recession, the Utopian image was rudely shattered, all the old political grumblings over excessive centralization reappeared, and were augmented with some new dissatisfactions. The British authorities in Malaya were persuaded to carry out a detailed reappraisal of the established arrangements and the beginnings of a process that came to be known as 'decentralization' emerged—a phenomenon that remained in the centre of the political stage for much of the next two decades.

In retrospect, the constitutional reforms of Anderson did nothing to alleviate any of the shortcomings enumerated by the High Commissioner when the proposals were first formulated. Throughout the period under review, the State Councils were completely ignored, the Malay Rulers were pushed further into oblivion, the British Residents were stripped of more of their independence and individuality and were seldom in the limelight as characters in their own right, and the division of federal and State matters was conveniently abandoned. The Federal Council Agreement, in fact, ran contrary to the declared intentions of Anderson. The High Commissioner had deplored the 1896 Federation because it had reduced State Councils to mere registering bodies with no vested controls over the central authority. Yet under the 1909 proposals, the State Councils were not permitted to pass any legislation that could be interpreted as being repugnant to the provisions of any law passed by the Federal Council. More serious was the requirement that the revenues of each of the component States would be first considered by the central Council, and only on publication of the final figures would information pertaining to these be transmitted to the State Councils. George Maxwell, the arch-critic of Anderson's measures during the 1920s, wrote that everything the High Commissioner did was opposed to decentralization. Anderson had got rid of the Resident-General only to bring himself directly into the administration of the Federation. Maxwell maintained that although *prima facie* it involved only a substitution of the title by that of Chief Secretary, Anderson had linked the abolition of the Resident-General with increased centralization of power in the person of the High Commissioner.[91] It would be fair, however, to say that Anderson did not remain in the country long enough after the inauguration of his measures effectively to work out the details of his policies. What did happen, when Young took over, was that the process of centralization continued unabated and by 1920 reached its height. Politically, therefore, Anderson's reforms failed to live up to the hopes and aspirations of those sections of the population which had viewed them as a panacea for the abuses that developed between 1896 and 1909.

1. The best published account of the period is R. Emerson, *Malaysia: A Study in Direct and Indirect Rule*, London, 1937; reprinted Kuala Lumpur, 1964, pp. 145–53.

2. Speech by J. Anderson, *Federal Council Proceedings*, 2 November 1910.

3. Ibid., 11 December 1909.

4. Maxwell and Gibson, *Treaties and Engagements*, pp. 71–3.

5. Memorandum by Gibson, CO 882, Vol. 12.

6. For details see Wheare, *Federal Government*, pp. 16–19.

7. Memorandum by Gibson, CO 882, Vol. 12.

8. Ibid.

9. CO to HC, Confidential Desp., 8 January 1909, CO 273/1909.

10. Ibid.

11. HC to CO, Confidential Desp., 7 December 1908, CO 273/1908.

12. It is true that Executive and Legislative Councils in Crown Colonies were framed on the same lines, but in those cases the proportion of the members of the

Legislative Councils who were also members of the Executive Councils was not so pronounced. The presence of the four Malay Rulers in the Federal Council too altered the situation. CO to HC, Confidential Desp., 8 January 1909, CO 273/1909.

13. Anderson considered Residents as men of ability and experience occupying posts of great responsibility who should not be made to vote blindly for a measure which they had no opportunity of considering beforehand. HC to CO, Confidential Desp., 8 February 1909, CO 273/1909.

14. Ibid.

15. Among the officials in this category were Risley, Cox, Stubbs, and Fiddes. See Minutes on HC to CO, Confidential Desp., 8 February 1909, CO 273/1909. The name 'Administrative Council' was also considered a complete misnomer for such a body because it was to administer nothing but might claim these powers by virtue of its name. In Crown Colonies the term 'Executive Council' was strictly correct: its primary object was executive and its secondary function deliberative. The secondary function had no place in the written constitution, corresponding very much to that of the British Cabinet rather than to Anderson's ideas for his Administrative Council. Minute by Fiddes, 16 April 1909, on ibid.

16. The idea of the Administrative Council was shelved by the Colonial Office but if experience indicated that the alternative arrangements were unsatisfactory, Whitehall was willing to reconsider. CO to HC, Confidential Desp., 20 May 1909, CO 273/1909.

17. There was also the possibility that the Sultans would themselves comprehend the implication of such action and might jib. Cox to Hopwood, 16 April 1909, on HC to CO, 8 February 1909, CO 273/1909.

18. In the Colonial Office, this argument impressed Cox who felt that the scheme could work, but because the idea was such a novel one and the subject so important, he wanted the Law officers to comment on it. Cox to Hopwood, 26 April 1909, on HC to CO, Confidential Desp., 8 February 1909, CO 273/1909.

19. As a result of discussions between Cox, Fiddes, and Risley it was agreed not to trouble the Law officers but to let the scheme proceed. It was hoped that it would work out in practice. Cox to Hopwood, 29 April 1909, on ibid.

20. Planters' Association to HC, 21 October 1908, on HC to CO, Confidential Desp., undated October 1908, CO 273/1908.

21. HC to CO, Confidential Desp., 7 December 1908, CO 273/1908.

22. Governor to CO, Telegram, Received 14 October 1909, CO 273/1909.

23. J. H. M. Robson, born in May 1870, went to Ceylon in 1889 as a premium pupil on a tea estate and later in the same year joined the service of the Selangor Government. During the next seven years he was in charge of the sub-districts of Rawang and Sepang, acted as District Officer of Klang and Ulu Langat, and Acting Collector of Land Revenue at Kuala Lumpur, and Registrar of Titles, Selangor. He wrote *Records and Recollections, 1889–1934*, Kuala Lumpur, 1934.

24. Leong Fee began life in Malaya as a clerk and later became a small shopkeeper. After a year he started mining in Ampang on a small scale. He soon gave this up and moved to Tambun in Perak to try his hand at coffee planting. The coffee estate failed, and Leong Fee abandoned the project and decided to prospect for tin. This was a tremendous success and his Tambun Mine was one of the largest in the State. He was appointed a member of the Perak State Council in

1895 and Chinese vice-consul for Penang in 1902. See Wright and Cartwright, *Twentieth Century Impressions*, p. 130.

25. Sultan Idris of Perak spoke on their behalf and referred to the Conferences of 1897 and 1903 which, while interesting, met only too seldom. He welcomed the new arrangements as an important step forward.

26. R. Feavatham to CO, 10 September 1911, CO 273/1911.

27. Question in the House of Commons by Ingleby, 1 August 1911, CO 273/1911.

28. Minute by Stubbs, 1 August 1911, on Ingleby's question in the House of Commons, 1 August 1911, CO 273/1911. The logic of the Colonial Office argument, however, was somewhat weird when one considers that in the early politics of the Malacca Sultanate there was clear evidence that Tamil Muslims from Coromandel occupied high court positions, intermarried with the Malay Royal family, and influenced the policies of the Sultanate. See R. O. Winstedt, *Malaya and its History*, London, n.d.; Winstedt, *The Malays: A Cultural History*.

29. By the end of 1911, Anderson expected the railway to be extended as far as the Pahang River, and the road from Benta on the Kuala Lipis road to Kuantan would also be completed, and this would afford communication with the Coast Districts. The High Commissioner believed that there were few colonies in the Empire which allowed such fine facilities for dialogue. HC to CO, Confidential Desp., 27 July 1910, CO 273/1910.

30. HC to CO, Confidential Desp., 27 July 1910, CO 273/1910.

31. Swettenham to Harding, 19 September 1910, CO 273/1910.

32. HC to CO, Confidential Desp., 27 July 1910, CO 273/1910.

33. Ibid.

34. Anderson equated the situation to the distrust that had existed in the early years of the Straits Settlements when the business community in Penang accused the Governor of treating Singapore as the favourite son. With the passage of time, however, these doubts disappeared. Ibid.

35. Anderson had already ended the system under which the Resident-General corresponded formally with the High Commissioner, and reverted to the original plan of communication by minute. He maintained that this saved valuable time and had the added advantage of giving the High Commissioner the opportunity to see the actual papers instead of, in many cases, having only the Resident-General's summary to go on. According to Anderson all that was needed to effect the change of title was a short Federal Enactment. HC to CO, Confidential Desp., 27 July 1910, CO 273/1910.

36. Swettenham contended that to abolish the post of Resident-General was a step backwards. He believed that Malay Rulers had accepted Federation and the control of British Officers because they wanted a representative who would possess a greater measure of authority than any single Resident. Swettenham to Lord Crewe, 3 June 1910, CO 273/1910.

37. To support his thesis Swettenham quoted Sir Cecil Smith's despatch of 30 June 1893 on the question of Federation, which stated: 'There is no doubt in my mind that the time has arrived for putting the administration of the Native States on a sounder footing and for relieving the Governor of a great deal of work which now devolves upon him. On the latter point I may state that notwithstanding the unusual experience I have had—unusual for the Governor of a a Colony—and the intimate knowledge that I possess of all the details of the

working of the Government machine, both in the Colony and in the Native States, it is only by strenuous exertions that I have kept abreast of the business that has to be transacted. If this had been my lot—it is not difficult to imagine the strain that would fall upon a new Governor who had no knowledge of the Colony and of the Native States.' Swettenham also claimed that the Malays were a peculiar people and required special knowledge to deal with successfully. Swettenham to Harding, 19 September 1910, CO 273/1910.

38. He adopted this course of action because he suspected that his proposals were, to a certain extent, in conflict with the provisions of the Treaty of Federation. HC to CO, Confidential Desp., 27 July 1910, CO 273/1910.

39. The public, according to Anderson, was prepared for the change and he anticipated widespread approval for his measures. Anderson to Collins, 29 July 1910, on HC to CO, 27 July 1910, CO 273/1910.

40. In reaching their conclusions Colonial Office officials were swayed to a large extent by the fact that Anderson had obtained the unanimous concurrence of both the Malay Sultans and the Residents. This disposed of any objections there might have been about the scheme contravening the Treaty of Federation. Robinson to Fiddes, 25 August 1910, on HC to CO, 27 July 1910, CO 273/1910.

41. The taking over of the northern Malay States of Kedah, Perlis, Kelantan, and Trengganu from Thai suzerainty, and the commencement of British administration in Johor, made it more important that the High Commissioner should be the real head of the British administration in Malaya. That the work of Governor and High Commissioner was enormous was not disputed, but it was felt that the work of the High Commissioner was more important than that of Governor. It was realized that Anderson would be difficult to replace but the Colonial Office believed that the amount of work a man could do depended on his power of selecting capable subordinates and using them most profitably. Collins to Fiddes, 27 September 1910, on Swettenham to Harding, 19 September 1910, CO 273/1910.

42. CO to HC, Confidential Desp., 19 October 1910, CO 273/1910.

43. G. Maxwell, 'The Position of the High Commissioner in the Federated Malay States', British Malaya, October 1926, p. 164.

44. HC to CO, Confidential Desp., 12 September 1910, CO 273/1910.

45. As mentioned in Chapter II, Swettenham suggested Clifford as an ideal replacement for Taylor. Swettenham to Crewe, 3 June 1910, CO 273/1910.

46. Again, as stated in Chapter II, Anderson was hostile to this idea and labelled Clifford as vain and scheming. Anderson to Collins, 12 May 1910, on ibid.

47. A. H. Young, born in 1854, entered the Colonial Service in 1878 as Commandant of the Military Police in Cyprus. He spent twenty-seven years there as Assistant Commissioner and later Commissioner at Paphos; Commissioner, Famagusta; Director of Survey and Forest Officer, and Chief Secretary to the Government of Cyprus. He administered the Government of Cyprus for six months in 1895 and more briefly in 1898, 1900, and 1904. In 1902 he was sent on a special mission to St. Vincent in the West Indies and was appointed Colonial Secretary, Straits Settlements, in 1906.

48. E. L. Brockman was appointed a cadet in the Straits Settlements Civil Service in 1886 and was subsequently District Officer, Bukit Mertajam; Acting Collector of Land Revenue, Singapore; Collector of Land Revenue and Officer

in Charge of the Treasury, Malacca; Senior District Officer, Province Wellesley; Commissioner of the Court of Requests, Singapore; and Acting First Magistrate and Inspector of Prisons, Singapore. He also acted as Colonial Secretary in the absence of Taylor and was later appointed Federal Secretary. He became Resident of Negri Sembilan on 1 January 1910.

49. HC to CO, Confidential Desp., 12 September 1910, CO 273/1910.

50. CO to HC, 1 December 1910, CO 273/1910.

51. R. J. Wilkinson, born in 1867, was educated at Trinity College, Cambridge, and came to the Straits Settlements as a cadet in 1889. He passed an examination in Malay in 1891 and in Hokkien in 1895, and in 1903, because of his contributions to the cause of education in the Colony, was appointed Inspector of Schools, Federated Malay States. In 1906 he acted as Secretary to the Government of Perak and was confirmed in that post in 1909. He was promoted to Resident, Negri Sembilan, in 1910, before being appointed Colonial Secretary. In 1916 he went to Sierra Leone as Governor and remained there till his retirement in 1922. He died in December 1941. Throughout his career in Malaya, Wilkinson showed great interest in the Malays and wrote extensively on their language, history, and culture. His interest in lexicography culminated in the publications of his two-volume *A Malay–English Dictionary*, Mytilene, 1932.

52. Speech by Anderson, *Federal Council Proceedings*, 11 December 1909.

53. Maxwell and Gibson, *Treaties and Engagements*, p. 72.

54. Memorandum by Gibson, CO 882, Vol. 12.

55. Editorial, *The Malay Mail*, 10 December 1909.

56. Editorial, *The Straits Times*, 22 October 1909.

57. Editorial, *The Malay Mail*, 14 December 1909.

58. 'Report of the Committee on the Constitution of the Federal Council', *British Malaya*, February 1927, p. 5. The members of this Committee were W. Peel (Chairman), H. W. Thomson, W. S. Gibson, J. H. M. Robson, C. Ritchie, and A. F. Richards (Hon. Secretary).

59. Speech by Anderson, *Federal Council Proceedings*, 11 December 1909.

60. 'Report of Committee on Federal Council', *British Malaya*, February 1927, pp. 6–7.

61. HC to CO, Confidential Desp., 27 July 1910, CO 273/1910.

62. Throughout his seven-and-a-half years as High Commissioner Anderson did not attend a single such meeting. G. Maxwell, 'The "New Policy" for the F.M.S.', *British Malaya*, August 1926, p. 107.

63. Speech by Anderson, *Federal Council Proceedings*, 19 January 1911.

64. Swettenham attributed the reluctance of the non-Federated Malay States to contemplate closer relations with the Federation to these developments. Rulers of Federated States were also tempted to make disadvantageous comparisons with the Sultans of those states outside the Federation, See F. A. Swettenham, 'Malay Problems, 1926', *British Malaya*, May 1926, pp. 10–11.

65. *Federal Council Proceedings*, 11 August 1914.

66. Maxwell, *British Malaya*, October 1926, p. 165.

67. Ibid., p. 165.

68. Macfadyen, while willing to concede that the establishment of the Federal Council might have been somewhat in advance of public opinion, insisted that this in no way affected the validity of his argument. See speech by E. Macfadyen, *Federal Council Proceedings*, 13 November 1912.

69. Speeches by Macfadyen and Young, *Federal Council Proceedings*, 25 November 1919. The successor of Young, Sir Laurence Guillemard, stated that unofficials were '. . . there to co-operate with the Government—to advise, to criticise; if necessary to oppose. . . .' See L. Guillemard, *Trivial Fond Records*, London, 1937, p. 95.

70. This was a small body of Europeans from the business and commercial community. Chinese businessmen belonged to the Straits Chinese British Association. The Straits Settlements Association was formed in London on 31 January 1868 and in Singapore on 20 March 1868. The first chairman of the Singapore branch was W. H. Read and the Association was principally concerned with looking after the interests of the unofficials. The Chinese counterpart was formed on 17 August 1900 to promote intelligent interest in the affairs of the British Empire and to encourage and maintain loyalty to the Queen; discuss the social, intellectual and moral welfare of Chinese British subjects; promote the general welfare of Chinese British subjects in a lawful and constitutional manner; appoint a representative committee in London to watch the interests of the Association, encourage higher and technical education for the Chinese; and take steps to defend the rights and privileges of British subjects. See Song Ong Siang, *One Hundred Years of the Chinese in Singapore*, London, 1922; reprinted Kuala Lumpur, 1967, pp. 319–20.

71. Editorial, *Singapore Free Press*, 5 September 1912. Rumblings of discontent on the use of Federation finances for projects outside the Federated Malay States were felt as early as April 1908 when it was charged that money was being lent to Johor and Brunei to facilitate development there. Editorial, *The Malay Mail*, 11 April 1908.

72. The Union Jack did not fly in the Federation except over the residences of British Residents and the Resident-General.

73. *FMS Government Gazette*, 30 August 1912.

74. It was hoped that the proposed Federated Malay States Association would make sure that the honour of Britain, as a powerful party to treaties with weaker states, would not be vitiated just because the States were weak and depredation was easy. Editorial, *Singapore Free Press*, 5 September 1912.

75. Minute by Collins, 10 May 1913, on MacCallum. Scott (M.P.) to Harcourt, 28 March 1913, CO 273/1913. Anderson, who by this time was back in the Colonial Office, was more outspoken in his criticism of the *Singapore Free Press* and accused the editor of possessing neither constitutional nor any other knowledge. According to Anderson, no one in Malaya took the editor seriously, although he was recognized as a man of much experience in and authority on 'mountain dew'. Minute by Anderson, on ibid.

76. As an advertisement of the overabundant revenues of the FMS this act was expected to attract attention not only in Britain but also throughout the Empire. It was also bound to startle people that a quartet of small Malay principalities were in such a good financial position to be able, at the suggestion of the Sultan of Perak, to provide a first-class naval unit as a reinforcement to the British Navy. Editorial, *Singapore Free Press*, 11 November 1912.

77. If this did happen, and if Young was responsible for even a veiled intimation, this would have been taken by the Sultan as at least a request if not virtually a direction. *Singapore Free Press*, 11 November 1912.

78. *Federal Council Proceedings*, 12 November 1912.

79. Editorial, *Singapore Free Press*, 11 December 1912.

80. *Federal Council Proceedings*, 23 June 1926.

81. FMS General Return, *FMS Annual Report*, 1924.

82. Emerson in his book *Malaysia*, p. 152, quotes the figure $154,974,195 as the value of exports for 1913 but in fact that was the value for 1912.

83. This was despite the fact that non-Malay public opinion was against Anderson's proposals to replace the Resident-General with the Chief Secretary. See Robson, *Records and Recollections*, pp. 104–5.

84. Sir Samuel Wilson, 'Visit to Malaya, 1932', Cmd. 4276, *Parliamentary Papers*, 1933, p. 7.

85. FMS General Return, *FMS Annual Report*, 1924.

86. Speech by Eu Tong Sen, *Federal Council Proceedings*, 18 November 1915.

87. Speech by A. N. Kenion, *Federal Council Proceedings*, 24 July 1917.

88. Speech by Sultan of Selangor, ibid., 17 November 1917.

89. One *gantang* was equal to five *kati*, one *kati* being 1 1/3 lb.

90. Speech by Brockman, *Federal Council Proceedings*, 30 April 1919.

91. G. Maxwell, 'Sir John Anderson and Decentralisation', *British Malaya*, September 1926, pp. 134–5.

IV

THE DIMINUTION OF THE
MALAY ARISTOCRACY

THE loss in status and powers of the Sultans arguably began at the moment when they agreed to accept British Residents, but this process was undoubtedly accelerated after Federation. Certainly by 1922 they had become figureheads in every sense of the word.[1] A major factor contributing towards this was the almost absolute financial dependence on the British. In theory the chiefs, ruling families, and headmen had a right to a share of the revenues derived directly or indirectly from all land; but this right which formerly had amounted to a percentage of the actual receipts was now represented by the payment of a fixed annual sum.[2] These allowances were reviewed from time to time and changes were made[3] but the initiative had to be taken by the Residents who had to justify any proposed increases to the Resident-General who in turn, provided he agreed with the Resident, sent the correspondence to the High Commissioner. The latter studied the recommendations, added his personal comments, and despatched the complete file to the Colonial Office bureaucrats on whom rested the ultimate decision.[4] Officials in London were generally sympathetic to such requests for increased Rulers' allowances but this did not detract from the fact that, in order to have their cases considered, they had to first convince the Residents, the Resident-General, and the High Commissioner. It was, therefore, very much in the Sultans' interests to retain their popularity with important British officials in Malaya and it would be unrealistic to imagine that financial considerations were less significant than their rights to exercise their traditional powers. Their reluctance to indulge in independent thought and action was, to that degree, natural. These unsatisfactory arrangements were recognized by some, and in 1906 *The Malay Mail* advocated that the Sultans should be entitled to higher incomes so as to enable them to maintain greater state. It was further suggested that they should be supplied with good motor cars, experienced chauffeurs, and cadets of at least three years' standing, to keep them 'in daily touch with the administration'.[5] On the other hand, control of the purse strings, from the British point of view, was an excellent, if covert, method of ensuring that the Rulers would be kept on a tight rein.

The declining role of the Sultans in State Councils has been discussed in earlier chapters, but there was a further encroachment on their legislative functions in September 1896 when the Judicial Commissioner for the Federation was appointed. In practical terms this meant that the right of appeal to the Sultan-in-Council, which had hitherto operated in Perak, was transferred to the Judicial Commissioner. The British official was also given the power to make rules, act as a judge of appeal in civil and criminal cases, and exercise the prerogative of revision in criminal cases. There were no provisions for appeals from the Judicial Commissioner's decisions.[6] The Perak State Council discussed the measure on 30 April 1896 and observed that, in the first instance, the appointment was due largely to opinions expressed by the business and commercial community of the Straits Settlements, the English language press, and members of the legal profession, presumably on the assumption that conditions in the Malay States were identical with those in the Colony. The State Council maintained that the people of Perak were happy with the system in existence and that if the change was at all necessary then the final appeal to the State Council had to be preserved. Malay chiefs feared that whoever was appointed Judicial Commissioner would be incapable of appreciating issues from the local point of view until after a few years' residence in the Malay States, and since he would probably be an official of mature age he would scarcely interest himself in studying Malay laws, customs, and ideas.[7] Sultan Idris drew attention to the differences between British and Malay standards of justice and the Dato Sri Adika Raja,[8] a prominent member of Council, regarded the Order as an infringement on the powers of a Malay Ruler.[9] Both Birch, the Acting Resident, and R. G. Watson, the Acting Secretary to the Government of Perak, supported the sentiments of the Malay members, but the Colonial Office was less sympathetic. Officials in London believed that the relative positions of the Resident and the Sultan would be no worse than that of a Governor of a colony in the sense that they would have independent courts at their sides and above them. The principle involved was that it was impossible to continue a system which allowed appeals from a trained judge to an untrained executive.[10] Accordingly, the Order was passed on 28 September 1896 and came into force on 1 October 1896. The objections of the Sultan were somewhat allayed by Swettenham's assurances that all death sentences would be referred to the Ruler and his Council, the Order would not interfere with the rights of the population to petition their sovereign, and that there would be nothing to prevent him from exercising his powers of pardon.[11] On his appointment as Judicial Commissioner, on a salary of $9,600 a year, Jackson took over the British jurisdiction earlier ceded to the Residents, as well as the jurisdiction of the Rulers-in-Council—a measure that was in contradiction to the original pledge that regular British jurisdiction would not be introduced into the Malay States.[12]

So far as general administration of the States was concerned, the Sultans soon discovered that scant respect was accorded to their opinions. The British administration had always functioned on the assumption that in appointing Residents the decision was one for the British and the British alone.[13] A perusal of the Treaties which introduced the Residential system and later brought about the Federation of Perak, Selangor, Negri Sembilan, and Pahang, however, might reasonably give rise to the supposition that a Sultan ought to be consulted whenever an 'Adviser' was to be posted to his State.[14] For years no Sultan had either felt confident or incensed enough to insist on the prerogative, and it was not until 1901 that Sultan Ahmad Maatham Shah of Pahang considered it within his purview to question the reappointment of Clifford as Resident of his State. This particular vacancy had arisen as a result of the death of the previous Resident, Butler, on 18 January 1901.[15] Pending the arrival of Clifford, whose last post had been that of Governor of North Borneo, D. Wise was appointed Acting Resident. Sultan Ahmad was satisfied with Wise and liked him because his 'conduct and ways of administering the Government, which are soft and gentle and patient', were similar to those of Butler, and because Wise's knowledge of the Malays was extensive.[16] Under those circumstances he asked Swettenham to confirm Wise as the substantive Resident. The Resident-General's reaction was swift and to the point. He told the Sultan that Clifford's selection had been ratified by the Secretary of State and, in any case, it was 'neither usual nor possible' to take into account the preferences of a Malay Ruler in the appointment of Residents.[17] Any illusions that the Sultans might have harboured, concerning their rights in this respect, were thus effectively nipped in the bud. Sultan Ahmad's futile gesture of withdrawing from the Government of Pahang and appointing the Tunku Besar as Regent[18] was largely ignored by the British.

Even more direct was the manner in which the British manoeuvred traditional Malay royal appointments. In practice these had been the preserve of the Sultans acting either in conjunction with their Councils of Chiefs, or according to the provisions of traditional Malay law, *adat*, operating within the Malay States.[19] After Federation these considerations were abandoned on a number of occasions but nowhere was this more obvious than in Perak. As mentioned in Chapter II, force of tradition and general practice there had decreed that succession to the Sultanate was to rotate between the members of three of the State's royal families, and at any one time each of them would have a representative who was either the Sultan, the Raja Muda, or the Raja Bendahara. Since 1875, however, the post of Raja Bendahara had been left vacant largely due to the alleged involvement of Malay royalty in the Perak civil war that followed the death of J. W. W. Birch.[20] This situation was rectified in February 1907, when the British installed Raja Abdul Jalil, the elder son of Sultan Idris, as Raja Bendahara. The first moves in this direction had begun as early as May 1903 when Abdul Jalil wrote to Treacher[21] setting out in detail his claims to the office. The question was referred by the Resident-General to Swettenham, who discussed the merits of the case with Sultan Idris. No firm decision was reached at that meeting and the issue was temporarily shelved.[22] It was revived in February 1905, after the retirement of Swettenham, in the form of a memorandum from the chiefs of Perak to the Resident, E. W. Birch. The document extolled the virtues and qualities of Abdul Jalil, and his tact in dealing with other chiefs and the people of the State was praised.[23] The driving force behind the Memorial was probably Sultan Idris, strongly supported by Birch. The Resident-General, Taylor, and the High Commissioner, Anderson, both of whom were relatively new appointees with little experience of the Malay States, were not as enthusiastic, but knew enough of Perak traditional law to realize that such a step contradicted normal practice. Taylor maintained that Abdul Jalil had not displayed qualities that commended him as a suitable heir to the Raja Muda, and suggested that the authorities should not rush into making the appointment.[24]

The death of Raja Musa,[25] the Raja Muda, on 12 March 1906, added greater significance to the Raja Bendaharaship as it meant that whoever succeeded to that post would quickly become the Raja Muda. The Raja Bendahara, therefore, had to be someone acceptable not only to Sultan Idris but, more important, to the British as well. So in spite of the conflict with traditional law, Raja Abdul Jalil was appointed Bendahara on 25 February 1907. The considerations underlying the decision were concerned more with the need to select an individual whose loyalty was to the British advisers and less with the reaction that might arise in the event of *adat* being violated. On 6 April 1908, Abdul Jalil was elevated to Raja Muda in a ceremony held in Kuala Kangsar.[26] Although there were no riots, or even demonstrations of protest, the appointment did not please the Malay population of the State. The objections expressed were not personal, because Abdul Jalil was indeed hard-working and anxious to do right, but on the score that the probability of the son of a ruling Sultan succeeding to the throne contravened traditional law. Much of the criticism centred on the fact that there were alternative candidates who possessed stronger claims to the office. For example, there was Raja Ngah Abubakar bin Raja Omar, the grandson of the twenty-fourth Sultan, Ali; and the sons of ex-Sultan Abdullah, the twenty-sixth Sultan, any of whom would have been more acceptable from the point of view of custom and tradition. The British justified their choice by pointing out that Abdul Jalil's mother, who was also the principal wife of Sultan Idris, was of ancient lineage and was crowned and installed by Low in 1887 at the same time as Sultan Idris, because some doubts existed about the strength of Idris's claims.[27] Raja Abdul Jalil's right to the position was therefore traced through his descent on his mother's side. But, apparently, the British were not convinced by the force of their own arguments because no attempt was made to obtain the consent of the State Council before the decision was announced. The impression created was that Sultan Idris had successfully pressed his son's candidature on a High Commissioner not well versed with Malay customs, and by so doing, had introduced a system of primogeniture foreign and opposed to Perak *adat*.[28] By supporting the Sultan the British could only have disillusioned the average Malay who saw his Sultan as the fountainhead and the preserver of custom and tradition. To many the whole episode represented a distinct and regrettable break with the past and was contrary to the spirit of the treaties whereby the British authorities had promised to respect and uphold the traditions of the Perak Malays. Anderson's personal involvement in the affair surprised the Colonial Office despite the realization that, from the British viewpoint, the individuals with the best claims to the office were 'impossible'.[29]

The elevation of Abdul Jalil to Raja Muda by no means solved the problems that continued to focus the attention of the British on Perak royalty. The office of Bendahara was, after all, now vacant and two strong candidates were in contention. The first was Raja Ngah Abubakar who had earlier lost out to Abdul Jalil, and the other was Raja Chulan, the second son of ex-Sultan Abdullah. Of the two, Raja Chulan was the one who caused great anxiety to both Sultan Idris and the British administration. He was born in 1869 in Tanjong Brombang, near the mouth of the Krian River, and after the banishment of his father to the Seychelles, he and his elder brother, Raja Mansur, were educated at Perak Government expense at the Raffles Institution, Singapore, and later the High School, Malacca. In 1886, Chulan joined the Government service and was posted to the Resident of Perak's office. After a succession of land office appointments he became Assistant District Magistrate, Krian Selama, in 1897. He was later promoted to District Magistrate, Krian and remained in this office until his retirement in 1911.[30] He married Raja Puteh Kamariah, a daughter of Sultan Idris, in 1899, and accompanied the Sultan to England in 1902 for the coronation of King Edward VII. His ability, zeal, and keen intelligence were beyond question, and these qualities were amply demonstrated not only in his capacity as a civil servant but also in his role as a member of the Perak State Council from 1907 onwards, and later of the Federal Council.[31]

On 23 March 1909, a meeting took place between Sultan Idris and Birch, the Resident, where the question of the next Raja Bendahara was discussed. According to Birch, the Sultan clearly preferred Raja Ngah Abubakar, who was married to another of the Sultan's daughters, and was confident that the appointment would be acceptable to every Malay in the state. The only thing that worried Idris was Chulan's possible reaction and this anxiety was reinforced by suspicions that the British favoured Chulan.[32] When assured by Birch that his suspicions were unfounded,[33] Idris asked for a pledge from the Colonial Office that no son of ex-Sultan Abdullah would ever be considered eligible for an appointment that could lead him to the Sultanate. Such a promise, in writing, would clear the path for Raja Ngah Abubakar. Birch himself was impatient to have a Bendahara installed, due to the disturbed state of affairs on the Perak River, and was certain that Ngah Abubakar was just the person to rectify them.[34] Anderson endorsed the recommendation on the grounds that of the other candidates, Mansur was an 'unmitigated blackguard' and Chulan's 'parentage is a matter of considerable doubt and that fact alone is enough to bar him amongst the Malays'.[35] The Colonial Office concurred and in May 1909 it instructed the

High Commissioner that, in the interests of good government, no member of ex-Sultan Abdullah's family would ever be eligible to become Sultan.[36]

If Birch's account is correct, all obstacles to the appointment of Raja Ngah Abubakar should have been effectively removed. It is surprising, therefore, that no further action on the matter was taken for almost five years. When the subject was broached again in March 1914, Sultan Idris seemed to have had second thoughts. Ngah Abubakar was still regarded as a person of unimpeachable integrity, force of character, and admirably suited to rule, but the Sultan was not disposed towards appointing him. Instead, he wanted the British administration to recognize first the claims to succession of the children of his daughters married to Rajas Mansur and Chulan. The High Commissioner, Young, was willing to accede to the Sultan's wishes, and favoured modifying the earlier British decision to recognize the two sons of those marriages as members of the Sultan's own family, in the same fashion as Abdul Jalil had been allowed to represent his mother's branch, the family of Sultan Yusuf. But such a British concession, it was advocated, should be accompanied by the appointment of Ngah Abubakar as Bendahara because the Sultan's reluctance to do so was shutting out the late Sultan Ali's family from their rightful place in the order of succession.[37] The Colonial Office was distinctly embarrassed but agreed to alter the earlier ruling to the extent that the sons of the daughters of Sultan Idris were accepted, for the purposes of succession, as members of the Sultan's family.[38]

The way again seemed clear for the nomination of Raja Ngah Abubakar as Bendahara, but before this could be formalized he died. It was now June 1915 and it was becoming more urgent that the vacancy should be filled. All things being equal, the name of Raja Chulan stood head and shoulders above the other contenders. His appointment would have received the universal support of all the Perak Malay chiefs and he possessed the added advantages of maturity, wisdom, and experience. These factors were not lost on him when he initiated a Memorial from the members of ex-Sultan Abdullah's family to Lewis Harcourt, the Secretary of State for the Colonies, asking for a reconsideration of their status. The petition outlined the good work and the unquestioned loyalty that the children of Abdullah had displayed towards the British by setting out their public service record, but the crux of their argument involved the practice of Perak *adat* law.[39] Any possibilities that Raja

Chulan might have had of success were, however, shattered by the acrid comments of the Colonial Secretary, Wilkinson. Much emphasis was laid on these because they came from someone who was regarded by the Colonial Office as an expert on Malay affairs on account of his length of service in Malaya as well as his knowledge of the history, language, customs, and traditions of the indigenous population. Wilkinson, who claimed to know Raja Chulan well, believed that although he was not anti-British in any political sense, he was interested only in self-aggrandizement and advancement, and would be 'a thorn in the side of the British Government if he became Sultan, because his sense of his own importance and his idea of his own abilities would bring him inevitably into conflict with the Resident.'[40] It was also alleged that Chulan had never shown any special interest in, and had never been identified with movements for Malay progress.[41] The British were afraid that if he ever became Sultan he would rely too much on the letter of the law and insist on Treaty provisions forbidding British interference in Malay religion and custom thereby over-reaching himself with probably serious consequences. Whole-hearted support for these views came from the Chief Secretary, Brockman, and the High Commissioner, Young.[42] On the strength of these opinions the Colonial Office decision to resist any reconsideration came as no surprise.[43]

The virtual rejection of Raja Chulan's claims resulted in attention being focused on Raja Alang Iskandar, the second son of Sultan Idris, who was an Assistant Commissioner in the Police Force.[44] The Data Laksamana, the Dato Panglima, the Dato Sri Adika Raja, and the other Perak chiefs were willing to accept Iskandar as the new Bendahara without showing much enthusiasm. Even the British were quick to concede that notwithstanding his pleasant personality, Sultan Idris's second son was neither very able nor strong in character.[45] For a time the name of Raja Abdul Aziz, the second son of the last Raja Muda, Musa, was mentioned as an alternative candidate, but his youth and comparative inexperience were to his disadvantage.

Before the question could be resolved Sultan Idris fell ill and died on 14 January 1916. He was succeeded as Sultan by Raja Abdul Jalil who assumed the style and title of Paduka Sri Sultan Abdul Jalil Nasruddin Makutaram Shah. The accession had the blessing of the British because, despite the fact that Abdul Jalil was considered 'stupid and was for a time an excessive opium smoker', his loyalty and honesty were beyond question.[46] This meant that the offices of

Raja Muda and Raja Bendahara were now vacant. On 29 March 1916 Sultan Abdul Jalil, the High Commissioner, the Chief Secretary, and the Resident of Perak conferred, and the British proposal to appoint Raja Alang Iskandar to the post of Raja Bendahara received the Sultan's acquiescence. The decision was officially announced at the close of the Perak State Council meeting of 17 April 1916. The tactic of making Iskandar the Bendahara rather than Raja Muda was a calculated one and was designed to leave open the option to appoint someone else Raja Muda if Iskandar proved unfit. This consideration, although logical and practical from the British viewpoint, put an end to another long-standing local Malay tradition of automatic succession from Raja Bendahara to Raja Muda. The latter post was left unfilled for over two years during which Iskandar lived at Telok Anson, serving his 'apprenticeship', and assisted the District Officer in matters relating to the Malays.[47] It was not till August 1918 that the decision to promote Iskandar to Raja Muda was taken. At the same time Raja Abdul Aziz was made Raja Bendahara and Raja Yusuf, the eldest son of Sultan Abdul Jalil, was appointed Raja di Hilir.[48] The claims of Raja Chulan were again ignored.

Sultan Abdul Jalil died of influenza on 26 October 1918 and was succeeded as Sultan by Raja Alang Iskandar with Raja Abdul Aziz being appointed Raja Muda in December 1918.[49] The passing of an era was completed with the arrival in 1920 of a new High Commissioner, Sir Laurence Guillemard (1920–7), and a new aura of enlightened thinking found its way into British attitudes towards Malaya. More credence was given to the opinions of Malay Rulers and one of the earliest indications of this departure from established practice involved Raja Chulan. In June 1920 Sultan Iskandar was anxious to elevate Raja Yusuf to Bendahara and appoint Raja Chulan, Raja di Hilir. He was supported by the Orang Kaya Setia Bijaya di Raja, a prominent member of the State Council, who told the Resident that Chulan's selection would be welcomed by members of the State Council and by all the other Malay chiefs. This in itself was not a new phenomenon but the British response was. The Resident, the Chief Secretary, and the High Commissioner were unanimously agreed that the British ban on the descendants of ex-Sultan Abdullah should be completely lifted.[50] The bipartisanship of official British opinion in Malaya surprised officials in London and the reluctance of the Colonial Office to approve the proposal, so soon after the arrival of Guillemard in Malaya, was understandable.[51] The

High Commissioner, however, pressed strongly the need to change ideas and emphasized that the situation was different from what i had been when Wilkinson wrote of Raja Chulan in 1915. In the intervening period Chulan had grown older and this had mellowed him considerably. Also, it was most unlikely that Chulan could progress from Raja di Hilir to Sultan in the ordinary course of events when one took into account that he was over fifty years of age, the Sultan being just over forty and both the Raja Muda and the Raja Bendahara were in their thirties. Even in the unlikely circumstance of those above him dying unexpectedly there was no sacred obligation on the part of the British to appoint him Sultan if he were considered unsuitable. The High Commissioner laid great stress on Sultan Iskandar's desire to recognize Chulan's claims. He believed that there was a need to allay the fears of the Malay aristocracy about the hopelessness of their position and some sort of a gesture was called for which might help to regain some of their confidence and trust.[5] The High Commissioner's views were strongly echoed by his chief Secretary, W. G. Maxwell,[53] who observed that the Malays had never really understood the reasons for the imposition of the ban on the family of ex-Sultan Abdullah—an act which had, for several years puzzled and wounded the feelings of Rajas and chiefs.[54] Faced by these compulsive arguments, the Colonial Office in December 1920 relented, the ban on the family was lifted, and Chulan's appointment as Raja di Hilir was approved.[55]

This ended one of the more bizarre episodes involving Malay royalty and the British administration. Successive incidents represented a gradual stripping of their prerogatives from the Sultans, a corresponding increase of British involvement in affairs from which they had previously abstained, and an increasing disregard for the traditional laws of the Malays. Nowhere was this more obvious than in the selection of candidates to fill the more important traditional appointments in the Malay States. On a strict interpretation of the Treaties, concluded between the Malays and the British, these subjects were meant to be within the purview of the Malays but with the growing economic and political commitment of the British in the area, the perils that could arise from the solemn observance of the provisions were considered too hazardous. In the choice of these dignitaries, therefore, stress was laid on their loyalty to the British and their willingness to play second fiddle rather than on the strength of their claims in accordance with Malay *adat* law. It was considered more important to have a safe, albeit incompetent, ruler than an independent and intelligent personality like Raja Chulan on the throne. What made the procedure somewhat incomprehensible was that it did not take Malay royalty very long to recognize the façade and to realize that the occupation of what were supposed to be the premier offices in the States did not imply the right to exercise real power. The disregard for *adat* law was significant for the effects this had on the average Malay citizens. For as long as they could remember, *adat* had been sacrosanct and the Sultans were regarded as duty-bound to preserve and safeguard traditional institutions. So confronted, as they were, with the systematic and unbridled destruction of these rituals they were overwhelmed at the inability and, in some cases, the lack of interest of their Rulers to perform satisfactorily the functions for which they were designed. So far as the Malay *raiat* was concerned the Sultanate had forfeited one of its principal duties and Sultans were no longer entitled to the respect in which they had been held.[56]

Even at lower levels of the administration the British did not hesitate to intervene in and reverse decisions taken by Rulers. In Negri Sembilan, for instance, the intentions of the Yamtuan Besar were summarily overruled in 1905, when the Resident, D. G. Campbell,[57] refused to accept the Ruler's choice of a new Dato Penghulu for Rembau. In justifying his decision, Campbell alleged that the official selected was not deserving and did not enjoy the confidence of the people. The Resident, therefore, invoked clause 3 of the Rembau Treaty, concluded on 31 March 1883, and installed a supposedly more acceptable candidate.[58] The treaty provision referred to stated:

> Whenever there is trouble or dissension in the country of Rembau, the Penghulu and Datohs and other inhabitants of Rembau desire to make reference to His Excellency the Governor of the Straits Settlements and whatever decision may be given by the Governor, all the persons who have signed their names at the end of this Agreement will accept and obey.[59]

In the case under discussion, however, no evidence of trouble or dissension was advanced, Campbell interfered without any reference to either the Penghulu, the Datohs, or the people of Rembau, and seemed unconcerned with the disparaging effects it might have had on the status of the Yamtuan Besar.

The British interfered again in September 1908 on the occasion of the election of the Orang Kaya Bongsu of Ulu Muar. The affair originated in 1907 when the holder of the title resigned and died soon after. There were three claimants to the position, Rasip, Kamah, and Ujang, and in September 1907 the Dato Johol and his fellow electors announced the unanimous election of Rasip. On further investigation the Yamtuan Besar discovered that the Dato Johol had some doubts about Rasip, and that one of the three other electors favoured Kamah. The Yamtuan Besar suggested reconsideration and in the discussion that ensued the Dato Johol agreed to support any candidate favoured by the Ruler. This resulted in the selection of Kamah and a public announcement to this effect was made. At this point the British Resident stepped in and insisted that Rasip's election had been unanimous and that this had been confirmed by an inquiry at which the Ruler was not present. R. C. Grey, the Acting Resident, took great care to draw the Ruler's attention to the obligations of the British to observe the customs of the country and to their treaty commitments for, after all, the Government was the servant of the Treaty. The authorities said that it was impossible to set aside the customs of the country just to satisfy the personal wishes of the Yamtuan Besar.[60] This example demonstrated clearly that whenever it suited their intentions the British were not averse to quoting treaty provisions which to all other intents and purposes were not worth the paper they were written on.

The public reversal of the Ruler's actions, however justified it might have been, was a severe blow to the very foundations of Malay royalty. The colonial administration seemed bent on humiliating the Sultans and this certainly was the case in the dispute, in 1905, between Tungku Mohammed and Campbell. The controversy centred on the desire of the Yamtuan Besar to use the title 'Sultan'. The Resident argued that the term 'Sultan' indicated an assumption of powers in excess of those vested in the Ruler, whereas Tungku Mohammed asserted that up to the time of Yang di Pertuan Janggut (also known as Yang di Pertuan Imam), the fifth Yamtuan Besar (1861–9), seals bearing the title 'Sultan' were in constant use. For example, the first Yamtuan Besar, Raja Melewar (1773–95), had two seals, one designed on the lines of the seal of the Menangkabau Sultans and the other resembling the seal of the Sultans of Johor. A third seal bearing the title 'Sultan' was used by Tungku Antah (Tungku Mohammed's father) after the civil war. But Tungku Mohammed's strongest weapon was a royal seal made for him by Birch, when he was Resident, and paid for out of Government funds, which bore the title 'Sultan'. Faced by this irrefutable evidence the decision by Anderson, not to allow the Ruler to use the title, was strange. The High Commissioner pointed out that the Ruler's position as Yamtuan Besar had been arranged after consultations with the other chiefs of Negri Sembilan and implemented by the Agreement of 1898.[61] Any modifications, therefore, would require the sanction of the King of England as well as the other signatories of the document. More important was Anderson's impression that the term 'Sultan' implied absolute power within the State whereas 'Yang di Pertuan' had some reservations attached to it.[62] The High Commissioner refused to reopen the question despite the fact that the change would not have been accompanied by an increase in the exercise of real power by Tungku Mohammed. But considerable doubt exists as to the accuracy of Anderson's definition of the two terms. As mentioned by Tungku Mohammed the expression, Yang di Pertuan, was used in all four cases of Perak, Selangor, Pahang, and Negri Sembilan in the Treaty of Federation which Swettenham had taken round for signature. It was also used in 1895 by the Resident, Lister, because according to him 'fifteen years ago the title Sultan was scarcely known to Malays in these states. It is supposed that the Dutch and then the English styled the Rajas of Malay States as Sultan—not knowing what their actual titles were.'[63] The whole affair was clearly one where the ignorance of British administrators resulted in the unfair victimization of a Malay Ruler.

Changes in the administrative machinery of government, discussed in earlier chapters, also helped to weaken the Malay sovereigns. In formulating and implementing the Federation scheme no attempts were made to assess whether or not the Sultans or the people of the four states wanted the new arrangements. The virtual *fait accompli* served to isolate the Rulers more and more from the centre of power which moved rapidly to the Federal capital of Kuala Lumpur. A salutary protest against their loss of power and the whole process of centralization was delivered by Sultan Idris of Perak at the Second Durbar of Rulers held at Kuala Lumpur in July 1903. On that occasion he acknowledged the economic benefits and the material advantages that had accrued to the Malay States as a consequence of British rule, was fulsome in his praise of Swettenham, but expressed dissatisfaction with the political repercussions. Idris confessed his inability to understand clearly the meaning of union, or *persekutuan*, as applied to the four states, saying:

... if, however, the four states were amalgamated into one, would it be right to say that one state assisted the other, because assistance implies something more than one, for if there is only one, which is the helper and which the helped? A Malay proverb says that there cannot be two masters to one vessel; neither can there be four Rulers over one country.[64]

He declared himself to be against the tendencies for over-centralization and advanced an almost forlorn hope that affairs of the states might be managed by their own officers and that the government of each of the states might retain its separate identity.[65] Swettenham attempted to minimize the significance of the Sultan's very forthright speech by attributing Idris's unease to the fact that a new High Commissioner, whose identity was at that time unknown, was due to assume control over the administration of the region.[66] The Colonial Office was, despite these assurances, concerned enough to promise that the Secretary of State would always be prepared to give full and sympathetic consideration to any representations the Sultans might wish to make.[67]

The dislike of, and opposition to, centralization continued unabated and in 1905, at a meeting of the Perak State Council, Sultan Idris made a long speech in which he accused the British of seriously changing the position and authority of Residents and, in doing so, contravening the provisions of the Treaty of Federation.[68] Again, in 1907, the Sultan of Perak openly aired his differences with the conduct of British administration and on several occasions threatened the Resident-General, Taylor, that he would communicate his displeasure on the failure of the government to honour treaty obligations to the Secretary of State and even to the King of England.[69]

In 1910 Anderson told the Federal Council that it was designed to act as a body that would curb central authority because 'both the Rulers and the Residents felt more and more keenly that matters which are to them of the greatest importance were removed entirely from their control'.[70] The loss of authority and effective power of control had created the impression among the Rulers of Kelantan, Trengganu, and Perlis (states that before 1909 were under Thai suzerainty) that the Sultans and Residents in the Federation were 'mere marionettes who worked on wires pulled by an Under-Secretary in Kuala Lumpur' and that the Federation far from being a true federation was a conglomerate instead.[71] But however genuine and altruistic Anderson's sentiments might have been the results did not match up to them. The Rulers in the Federal Council remained nonentities and centralization increased. Then why, it might be asked, did the Sultans agree to the proposals in the first place? The reality of the situation was that the Malays were left with little choice to do otherwise. The Rulers recognized that their comforts and incomes, and those of their children and relatives, depended substantially on the good impression that they created on the High

Commissioner. Thus, a proposal emanating, as it did, from Anderson, and strongly recommended by the Residents, could hardly have been critically received by the Sultans.[72]

The practical demise of the Malay sovereigns was completed in ways which were more subtle. For instance, there was the manner in which their allowances were referred to in official correspondence. In this, and in the Annual Estimates of Revenue and Expenditure, they were frequently described as 'salaries'.[73] Issue was taken on this point by Sir Roper Lethbridge, the editor of the *Golden Book of India and Ceylon*, who interpreted the term as being grossly insulting and implying that the Rulers occupied the status of officials. The 1903 Estimates for Perak, approved by the High Commissioner, came in for much criticism from Sir Roper because at the head of the Expenditure Accounts, in the most prominent position, were the 'Personal Emoluments' of the Resident. This was followed by a list of all the Secretaries, their clerks, and so on, and after many pages, among and parallel to the salaries of all manner of underlings, came the 'salary' of the Sultan. It was considered astounding that a British Civil Servant of the standing of Swettenham, with his long experience and close acquaintance with the intense sensitivity of the Malay minds to seemingly trivial matters, should have allowed such a thing to happen. The 1905 Estimates, at the instigation of the new High Commissioner, Anderson, substituted 'Personal Emoluments' for 'Salary' but the position of the Sultan remained much the same as it was in 1903—at the top of a page which contained an entry specifying the salary of a scavenger.[74] The Colonial Office flurried with embarrassment but was anxious not to give further publicity to the question. The feeble excuse proffered was that none of the Sultans, who alone were concerned, had raised any objections either to the word 'Salaries' or to the manner in which the Estimates were framed.[75]

A more deliberate manipulation of the status of Sultans was revealed in their relationship with the Resident-General. The first Conference of Rulers at Kuala Kangsar in July 1897 was largely informal and dignified but throughout the minutes of the meeting it was made clear that the Resident-General enjoyed a distinct precedence over the Sultans. The record of the proceedings, for example, stated, in order of importance, the participants at the Conference and the first persons mentioned were the High Commissioner and the Resident-General. After these British officials came the Sultan of Perak and the Perak State representatives, the Sultan of Selangor and the Selangor State representatives, and so on. On the second day, when the High Commissioner did not attend, the Resident-General was accorded pride of place.[76]

The minutes of the Second Rulers' Conference held in Kuala Lumpur in July 1903 emphasized the precedence in even stronger terms. They opened thus, 'The first of the Conferences of H.E. the High Commissioner, the Resident-General, and the Rulers, Residents and Members of the Council of the Federated Malay States was held in Kuala Kangsar, Perak, in July 1897.'[77] Paragraph 3 of the same set of minutes stated that the High Commissioner was 'met by the Resident-General, the Rulers of Perak, Selangor, and Negri Sembilan, the Residents, Heads of Departments, and a large assemblage of the public'.[78] Paragraphs 6 and 7 recorded the arrival at the Conference Hall of the Rulers in an order of ascending importance and stated that after they were all assembled, the High Commissioner, accompanied by the Resident-General and escorted by the Perak troopers, reached the hall.[79] The priority, thus established, was maintained in the Agreement for the Constitution of the Federal Council of 20 October 1909. Paragraph 2 gave the order of antecedence as the High Commissioner, the Resident-General, the four Rulers, the four Residents, and the four unofficials.[80] At the formal openings of meetings of the Federal Council the Chief Secretary retained the precedence of the Resident-General over the Sultans.

The period 1896–1920, representing as it did the second phase of British imperialism in Malaya, therefore saw the stature of Malay royalty reach a new nadir. Their belittlement was related not only to the amount of money put at their disposal but also to their traditional role in Malay society. From the economic standpoint the era had been one of unprecedented prosperity. The introduction of rubber, the expansion of tin mining, and the extension of road and railway communication had resulted in an increase in revenue from $8,481,007 in 1896 to $72,277,146 in 1920.[81] The relegation of the Sultans to the position of salaried individuals, however, effectively excluded the possibilities of their obtaining a fair share of this increased well-being. The plight of those on the fringes of the Sultans was even more tragic. In 1907, for example, the Raja Muda of Selangor lived in as much state and in about the same class of house as a young British official of six or seven years' service.[82] The financial dependence and impoverishment of the Malay aristocracy was a formidable barrier to the proper maintenance of the pomp and dignity in keeping with their social prestige. This led to humiliation and a tendency towards withdrawal and introversion.[83] For the Malay population it was particularly agonizing to see the High Commissioner and the Resident-General—later the Chief Secretary —being able to summon reserves of ostentation that were denied to their traditional Rulers.

The dilution of the legislative functions of the Sultans added to the confusion created in the minds of both the Rulers and their subjects. The resistance provided by Sultan Idris and his colleagues on the Perak State Council to the removal of his appellate powers was genuine enough, and aptly indicated the concern for the retention of a rite that constituted an integral element of the Sultanate.[84] But all these protestations were dismissed brusquely and the innate lack of understanding demonstrated by the British officers remained a hall-mark of Malay–British relations throughout the period. British authorities did not fully comprehend the fact that, to the average Malay, the complexities of an alien jurisprudence were as foreign and remote as could be imagined. The social life of the Malays was guided, to a large extent, by the tenets of Islam within which Islamic law occupied a prominent position.[85] In those circumstances the Sultan was regarded as the fountainhead of all power and the final arbiter of all disputes. Although the vacuum in Malay society created by the removal of the Rulers was eventually filled by British-type institutions, the effects this process had on the prestige of the Sultanate were devastating.

By assuming responsibility for administrative and royal appointments of any consequence the British further damaged the Sultans' positions. The incident in Pahang when the request of Sultan Ahmad, to have Wise appointed Resident, was summarily rejected caused much dismay to the Ruler and prompted him to dissociate himself from the British-controlled administration, by appointing a Regent. It might have been a gesture which injected some sense of realism to the charade but was not significant enough to initiate a reappraisal of British policy. In the area of royal appointments the stratagems of the administration in Perak, geared as it was towards ensuring that only the weak and the incompetent succeeded to the Sultanate, had an almost farcical touch about them. All established laws of succession were ignored and were replaced by a tragi-comic predicament where the British found themselves at sixes and sevens. As puppeteers they often discovered that they had tugged at the wrong strings and were forced into predicaments where they were compelled to reverse their decisions. The Raja Chulan scenario was a prime example of the pitfalls the British experienced. The public humiliation of the Yamtuan Besar of Negri Sembilan arising out of the *Orang Kaya Bongsu* incident was yet another consequence of British interference. Taken together these events clearly demonstrated the massive decline in the status of the Sultans.

Occasional fits of resistance against centralization of power, by Sultan Idris in particular, while significant in themselves, had as much effect on the practical course of events as a pea-shooter might have had on an advancing Centurion tank. Both Swettenham and Anderson, who were the principal architects of British policy in the Malay States, were too preoccupied with the exploitation of the economic potential of the country and the creation of a smooth functioning administrative system. As such they did not find the time even to consider modifying their plans to make them acceptable to the Sultans.

So far as the Colonial Office was concerned, the officials were inclined to be guided wholly by the authorities on the spot. The absence, until the return of Anderson to Whitehall, of a personality familiar with the ways of the Malays and conditions in the country might have dictated this eventuality.[86] This, however, did not prevent periodic announcements aimed at maintaining the fiction that British administration in Malaya was a form of indirect rule although even in London there was no doubt where power really rested.

A distressing by-product of relations between the Malay aristocracy and the British authorities was the gulf that developed between the Sultans and their Malay citizens.[87] The Rulers, stung by the huge loss of their traditional powers, were content to stay in the background while the Malay masses grew more aware of their sovereigns' powerlessness. By 1920 few could deny that the final vestiges of indirect rule had been trampled on and the Sultans were reduced to little more than glorified idols with feet of clay and the rest of the Malay aristocracy was converted, at best, into a minor Civil Service.

1. This view is supported by W. R. Roff, *The Origins of Malay Nationalism*, Yale, 1967, p. 93; Sadka, *The Protected Malay States*, pp. 156, 196 and 392; Emerson, *Malaysia*, pp. 124, 139 and 155.

2. Returns on Land Matters, Enclosure No. 11 in HC to CO, 9 August 1911, *Parliamentary Papers*, Vol. LX, 1912–13, pp. 372–3.

3. In 1887 Sultan Idris of Perak received an annual salary of $18,000 but this was increased to $36,000 in 1891. Further increases were approved in November 1902 when the sum for the Sultan of Perak was $40,000, the Sultan of Selangor had his salary increased from $18,000 to $20,000, and the Ruler of Negri Sembilan from $9,000 to $12,000. In the case of the Sultan of Pahang his emoluments were increased in 1899 from $24,000 to $36,000. RG to HC, 26 September 1902, in Governor to CO, Confidential Desp., 22 October 1902, CO 273/1902.

4. HC to CO, Desp. No. 175, 1 June 1909, CO 273/1909.

5. Editorial, *The Malay Mail*, 4 August 1906.

6. Report of the Legal Adviser, T. H. Kershaw, on the Perak Order in Council No. 6 of 1896, 'The Judicial Commissioner's Order in Council, 1896', 13 August 1896, in Governor to CO, Desp. No. 394, 29 August 1896, CO 273/1896.

7. Moreover, the Judical Commissioner would not go out of his way to look after Malay interests because such considerations were not likely to affect his promotion prospects, whereas in the case of a Resident, failure in his post would have been disastrous to his career. The argument that followed was that apart from the question of local knowledge it would safeguard the population more if the Sultan were to receive final advice on legal, as well as other, issues from the Resident. Acting Resident, Perak, to Col. Sec., 1 May 1896, in Governor to CO, Confidential Desp., 5 May 1896, CO 273/1896.

8. The Dato Sri Adika Raja was Wan Muhammad Saleh who was born in 1861 and entered government service as a Malay writer in 1881. He was made Sri Adika Raja in 1892 when he was Superintendent of Penghulu in the Ulu Kuala Kangsar district. In late 1892 he was appointed Assistant Collector of Land Revenue, Kuala Kangsar.

9. The Malay chiefs were unanimously agreed on this and argued 'rapidly and vehemently' to get their views accepted. Acting Resident, Perak, to Col. Sec., 1 May 1896, in Governor to CO, 5 May 1896, CO 273/1896.

10. Fairfield to Wingfield, 28 May 1896, on ibid. It was also suggested that the whole opposition to the scheme arose not from the Sultan and his Malay Chiefs but from the Acting British Resident. Johnson to Wingfield, 28 May 1896, on ibid. The only Colonial Office official who harboured some doubts was Lucas, who felt that it was unwise to assume that the convictions of the Malays were superficial and believed that Malay Rulers were very tenacious in their attempts to safeguard their rights and privileges. Memorandum by Lucas, 28 May 1896, on ibid.

11. RG to Col. Sec., 13 June 1896, in Governor to CO, Desp. No. 283, 21 June 1896, CO 273/1896. Swettenham's tactics led Lucas to comment that the Resident-General 'manages the Natives very well'. Lucas to Fairfield, 21 July 1896, on Governor to CO, 5 May 1896, CO 273/1896.

12. Jackson to RG, 20 November 1896, in Governor to CO, Confidential Desp., 22 November 1896, CO 273/1896.

13. They were appointed by the Governor with the sanction of the Secretary of State who determined their salaries and other allowances. See Sadka, *The Protected Malay States*, pp. 226–7.

14. Clause V of the Pangkor Engagement stated 'That all Revenues be collected and all appointments made in the name of the Sultan', and Clause VI 'That the Sultan receive and provide a suitable residence for a British Officer to be called

Resident—who shall be accredited to his court and whose advice must be asked and acted upon on all questions other than those touching Malay Religion and Custom.' In the Federation Treaty the relevant clause was the fourth which repeated much of what was in clause VI of the Pangkor Engagement. See Maxwell and Gibson, *Treaties and Engagements*, pp. 28–9 and 71.

15. T. C. Fleming (DO, Pekan) to HC, 21 January 1901, in OAG to CO, Desp. No. 41, 1 February 1901, CO 273/1901.

16. The Sultan also mentioned that the Malays of Pahang were especially ignorant and rude, and as such it was vital that the British Resident should be an understanding person. Sultan of Pahang to OAG, 12 March 1901, in OAG to CO, Confidential Desp., 18 April 1901, CO 273/1901. The opposition of the Sultan to Clifford might have been a consequence of the Resident's years in Pahang when, during the outbreak of the Pahang rebellion, he showed himself to be a formidable opponent of 'riotous' Malays. Clifford, known in Pahang as Tuan Sa'lipat, had a reputation of being quite abrupt in his dealings. See Anonymous, 'Early Days in Pahang', *British Malaya*, November 1929, p. 219.

17. HC to Sultan of Pahang, 18 April 1901, in OAG to CO, Confidential Desp., 18 April 1901, CO 273/1901.

18. Stubbs to Hopwood, 23 February 1909, in HC to CO, Desp. No. 27, 27 January 1909, CO 273/1909.

19. For details of the Malay Ruling class, see Gullick, *Indigenous Political Systems of Western Malaya*, pp. 65–94.

20. The Commission of Enquiry found that there had been a conspiracy to kill Birch, and that Sultan Abdullah, Sultan Ismail, and various chiefs of Upper and Lower Perak were involved. See Sadka, *The Protected Malay States*, p. 92.

21. Abdul Jalil was then the Raja di Hilir, or head of the 'downriver' group of chiefs, having been appointed to the post on 15 January 1898.

22. Swettenham wrote to Treacher: 'I agree with you about the Raja di Hilir: he has done his best to qualify himself for the post to which he may fairly aspire, but there is no hurry. The Sultan's view is that when, in his opinion, the right time comes, he will take action and until the Sultan moves, we may very well be satisfied. I think you should tell the Raja di Hilir that in matters of this kind the Government can only take action on the Sultan's initiative and that it is wiser for him not to try to hurry matters.' Quoted in Resident, Perak, to RG, 18 February 1905, in Governor to CO, Desp. No. 110, 16 March 1905, CO 273/1905.

23. His performance as Raja di Hilir was considered satisfactory and it was said that he had never given any offence in the course of his duties. The memorialists hoped that the title of Raja di Hilir would be maintained and that a Raja, who was a fitting person, would be appointed at the discretion of the Sultan and the Resident. Translation of Memorial from the Chiefs of Perak to Resident, Perak, 14 February 1905, in ibid.

24. The fact that the post had been vacant for thirty years was used to justify a further postponement. RG to HC, 7 March 1905, in Governor to CO, Desp. No. 110, 16 March 1905, CO 273/1905.

25. Raja Musa was the son of the twenty-third Sultan, Jaafar, and the nephew of Sultan Idris. He was appointed to the State Council in June 1894 and installed as Raja Muda on 12 January 1899. OAG to CO, Desp. No. 116, 15 March 1906, CO 273/1906.

26. Editorial, *The Straits Times*, 9 April 1908.

27. Idris was not, according to the system of rotation, in the direct line of succession but was considered eligible as great-grandson of one Sultan, nephew of another, and son of a Bendahara. The factor in his favour was that he had been prominent in his support of British policies. See Sadka, *The Protected Malay States*, p. 164. Sultan Idris's lineage can best be illustrated by the following table:

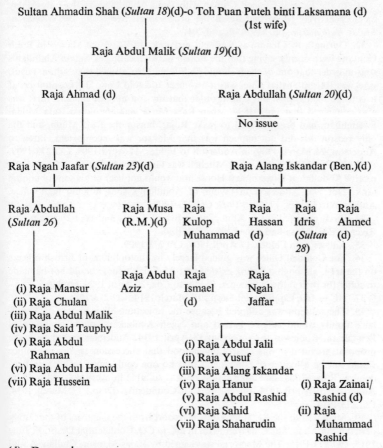

Sultan Ahmadin Shah (*Sultan 18*)(d)-o Toh Puan Puteh binti Laksamana (d)
(1st wife)

Raja Abdul Malik (*Sultan 19*)(d)

Raja Ahmad (d)   Raja Abdullah (*Sultan 20*)(d)

No issue

Raja Ngah Jaafar (*Sultan 23*)(d)   Raja Alang Iskandar (Ben.)(d)

Raja Abdullah (*Sultan 26*)   Raja Musa (R.M.)(d)   Raja Kulop Muhammad   Raja Hassan (d)   Raja Idris (*Sultan 28*)   Raja Ahmed (d)

Raja Abdul Aziz   Raja Ismael (d)   Raja Ngah Jaffar

(i) Raja Mansur
(ii) Raja Chulan
(iii) Raja Abdul Malik
(iv) Raja Said Tauphy
(v) Raja Abdul Rahman
(vi) Raja Abdul Hamid
(vii) Raja Hussein

(i) Raja Abdul Jalil
(ii) Raja Yusuf
(iii) Raja Alang Iskandar
(iv) Raja Hanur
(v) Raja Abdul Rashid
(vi) Raja Sahid
(vii) Raja Shaharudin

(i) Raja Zainai/ Rashid (d)
(ii) Raja Muhammad Rashid

(d)   Deceased
(Ben.)   Bendahara died in that appointment.
(R.M.)   Raja Muda died in that appointment.

28. Editorial, *The Straits Budget*, 23 April 1908.

29. The Colonial Office believed that Anderson should have informed Whitehall of his intentions especially because there was no doubt that Malay custom had not been observed. Stubbs to Antrobus, 22 May 1908, on OAG to CO, Desp. No. 116, 15 March 1906, CO 273/1906.

30. Raja Chulan retired prematurely because the service had by then become a cadet one and promotion was determined by qualifications rather than length

of service. As a Malay chief much of his time was taken up with receiving people and he was unable to do his official work satisfactorily. Financially too his salary and political allowance were insufficient to maintain his large family because he was not allowed to hold land and had no private means. HC to CO, Confidential Desp., 10 January 1911, CO 273/1911.

31. In the Federal Council Chulan with Dato Abdullah was the only Malay member actively to participate in the proceedings. See Roff, *The Origins of Malay Nationalism*, pp. 119, 199, and 201.

32. During Low's tenure as Resident in Perak (1877–89) the Malays in Bukit Gantang were openly saying that the British were educating ex-Sultan Abdullah's sons in order that one of them should be Sultan. Idris alleged that Sultan Yusuf, who was Regent at that time, was most upset and told Low, 'This cannot be. If it is to be then I must kill you in order that my son may be Sultan.' Idris was also convinced that until 1899, when Raja Musa was appointed Raja Muda, Swettenham had been inclined to make Raja Mansur the Raja Muda, and the only reason this did not happen was that Mansur was incompetent. Birch to Anderson, 24 March 1909, in Anderson to Fiddes, 17 April 1909, CO 273/1909.

33. Birch told Idris that when Mitchell was Governor he had pledged never to receive Abdullah at Government House and would not hear of his sons obtaining rank. Nor was Anderson in favour of Abdullah's sons holding high office. Anderson to Fiddes, 17 April 1909, CO 273/1909.

34. Birch expected Ngah Abubakar to live at Tepus and take charge of the River as Raja Musa had done before him. Ibid.

35. Anderson to Fiddes, 17 April 1909, CO 273/1909.

36. The Colonial Office was guided largely by the opinions of British officers on the spot, although a feeling existed that Abdullah's sons should not be made to suffer for their father's offences. Fiddes to Cox, 20 April 1909, on ibid.

37. HC to CO, Confidential Desp., 17 March 1914, CO 273/1914.

38. The solution was adopted because the objectionable members of Abdullah's family would still be barred and Ngah Abubakar would be appointed Bendahara. Robinson to Anderson, 18 April 1914. Anderson agreed with the proposal provided it was clearly understood that succession to any one office would not be a matter of course and that no one could hope to become Bendahara, Raja Muda, or Sultan unless he was suitable in every way. Minute by Anderson, 19 April 1914, on HC to CO, Confidential Desp., 17 March 1914, CO 273/1914.

39. Memorial to the Rt. Hon. Lewis Harcourt from the members of the family of ex-Sultan Abdullah, 31 March 1915, in HC to CO, Confidential Desp., 17 June 1915, CO 273/1915. The Memorial was signed by Rajas Mansur, Chulan, Abdul Malik, Said Tauphy, Abdul Hamid, and Kamarazaman. When the First World War started and the European staff in Perak was seriously depleted, Chulan volunteered his services for court work and functioned as a magistrate of the First Class. On anniversaries of the commencement of the War he took the lead in publicly expressing his desire, and that of the Malays, for a British victory. HC to CO, Confidential Desp., 13 October 1920, CO 717/1920.

40. Quoted in HC to CO, Confidential Desp., 17 June 1915, CO 273/1915.

41. Raja Chulan was president of the Kastam Zaria Club in Kuala Kangsar in 1915 but this was a prestigious organization composed of the local Malay aristocracy and government servants and involved in such activities as football

tennis, croquet, chess, and cards. On issues such as Malay education he believed that English education for the Malays should be restricted in the interests of peasant agriculture. On the other hand, however, he pressed for greater attempts to employ Malays in government technical and clerical services. See Roff, *The Origins of Malay Nationalism*, pp. 184 and 201.

42. British officials in Malaya did not regard the events of 1875, i.e. the killing of J. W. W. Birch and the subsequent turmoil in Perak, as matters of the past, and felt that the time had not come for the removal of all restrictions on Abdullah's family. HC to CO, Confidential Desp., 17 June 1915, CO 273/1915.

43. Anderson attributed the Memorial to Chulan and advised that it was best for the High Commissioner not to argue unduly but simply tell the petitioners that the Secretary of State was unable to reconsider his predecessor's decision. Minute by Anderson, 31 July 1915, on ibid.

44. Iskandar was educated in England and on his return to Malaya in early 1900 was attached to the Secretariat in Taiping. On 1 August 1905 he was appointed Assistant Commissioner of Police on an annual salary of £300. Although his mother was not of royal descent she was acceptable as a member of one of the leading families in Kampar. Resident, Perak to Chief Secretary, 15 April 1915, in HC to CO, Confidential Desp., 17 June 1915, CO 273/1915.

45. Ibid.

46. The British also believed that Abdul Jalil was not so much under the influence of Raja Chulan and his mother-in-law as Idris had been. Minute by Anderson, 20 January 1916, on Telegram HC to CO, Received 15 January 1916, CO 273/1916.

47. British reasons for appointing Iskandar Bendahara and not Raja Muda were: (a) it was the wish of Sultan Idris; (b) although as a rule the Bendahara became Raja Muda this was not absolutely necessary; (c) if a Bendahara was found, after appointment as such, to be unfit for the post, another member of the Royal family could be selected as Raja Muda; and (d) in this particular case it was desirable to prove Iskandar before definitely appointing him Raja Muda. HC to CO, Confidential Desp., 18 May 1916, CO 273/1916.

48. The proposals originated from the British and were agreed to by Abdul Jalil who was convinced that they would be welcomed by the major chiefs of the state. HC to CO, Confidential Desp., 20 August 1918, CO 273/1918.

49. These arrangements were expected to stop a lot of intrigue because the Perak succession would then be definitely stabilized. Minute by Finn, 20 December 1918, on Telegram HC to CO, 18 December 1918, CO 273/1918.

50. The moving force behind the proposal was, obviously, Guillemard who believed that it was advisable to be guided by the wishes of the Sultan supported by the State Council and chiefs. The High Commissioner suggested that the announcement of the two appointments be made in the State Council and be accompanied with a statement that the bar against the descendants of Abdullah was wholly removed. HC to CO, Confidential Desp., 10 June 1920, CO 717/1920.

51. Colonial Office personnel seemed to retain a nagging distrust of Chulan and went so far as to attribute the wishes of the Sultan and his chiefs to the constant pressure from Chulan and his mother-in-law ('a very masterly woman who used to henpeck her husband, Idris'). London wanted Guillemard to give further consideration to the matter at a later date. Minute by Collins, 24 July 1920, on HC to CO, Confidential Desp., 10 June 1920, CO 717/1920.

52. Sultan Iskandar's personal stock in the eyes of the British had risen considerably since he ascended the throne. He had developed from a pleasure-seeking youth to an eminently satisfactory and enlightened ruler who was able to solve the problem of reconciling loyalty to Britain and appreciation of Western ideas with allegiance to Malaya and sympathy with the aspirations of his subjects. HC to CO, Confidential Desp., 13 October 1920, CO 717/1920.

53. W. G. Maxwell, born in 1871, was the eldest son of W. E. Maxwell. He was appointed a junior officer in Perak in 1891 but was transferred to the Straits Settlements Civil Service in 1904. He was appointed Solicitor-General in 1906 and Acting Attorney-General in 1908. When Kedah was transferred from Thai suzerainty in 1909 he was sent there as British Adviser. He acted as Colonial Secretary in 1914, 1916, 1918, and 1919; Secretary to the High Commissioner in 1915 and 1917; British Resident, Perak in 1916. In 1918 he was appointed General Adviser, Johor, and in 1920 became Chief Secretary. He was the compiler of *The Perak Laws, 1877–1903*, Kuala Lumpur, 1905, 2 Vols. See W. Makepeace, G. E. Brooke and R. St. J. Braddell, *One Hundred Years of Singapore*, London, 1921, Vol. II, pp. 440–1.

54. Maxwell had a high personal regard for Chulan's character and loyalty and noted the esteem in which he was held by Europeans, Malays, and Chinese alike. The Chief Secretary was confident that Chulan would fill the appointment of Raja di Hilir with distinction. Maxwell to Collins, 3 December 1920, CO 717/1920.

55. The Colonial Office admitted that in 1909 there might have been a misunderstanding as to what Sultan Idris really wanted because 'the Malays wrap up their meanings to such an extent that it requires high powers of divination to get at them accurately'. Maxwell's advice was considered crucial as his ability to discover what the Malays really wanted was fully recognized. Minute by Collins, 25 November 1920, on HC to CO, Confidential Desp., 13 October 1920, CO 717/1920.

56. These attitudes were later reflected in the formation of organizations such as the *Kesatuan Melayu Muda* and the *Belia Malaya* which opposed the 'bourgeois-feudalist' leadership of the traditional élite. For details see Roff, *The Origins of Malay Nationalism*, pp. 222 and 233.

57. D. G. Campbell, born in 1866, joined the Selangor Government as second Surveyor in the Public Works Department. He was transferred to the land office in 1885 and later was appointed Assistant District Officer, Rawang. He was promoted to District Officer, Kuala Langat, and acted in a similar capacity in Ulu Selangor and Klang. He was appointed Resident of Negri Sembilan in February 1904 and remained there till December 1909.

58. HC to CO, Confidential Desp., 2 September 1909, CO 273/1909.

59. Maxwell and Gibson, *Treaties and Engagements*, p. 50.

60. To cushion the affront to Tengku Mohammed, the Yamtuan Besar, Anderson blamed the Dato Johol for the whole mix-up. It was suggested that the Dato should be severely reprimanded because he made it appear that 'You [the Yang di Pertuan] were in opposition to the Government in the matter'. Campbell also made arrangements for the Dato and his followers to go to the Ruler's Palace to apologize formally but Tungku Mohammed was not interested in any penitence and wanted his nomination of Kamah to stand. Notes of meeting held at Kuala Kangsar on Saturday, 14 August 1909, at which Sir John Anderson,

Tungku Mohammed, E. W. Birch, R. J. Wilkinson, D. G. Campbell, the Tungku Besar, and the Tungku Laksamana were present, enclosure in HC to CO, Confidential Desp., 2 September 1909, CO 273/1909.

61. For details of the Agreement, see Maxwell and Gibson, *Treaties and Engagements*, pp. 65–6.

62. Notes of Meeting at Kuala Kangsar, 14 August 1909, in HC to CO, Confidential Desp., 2 September 1909, CO 273/1909.

63. Negri Sembilan Annual Report, 1895, Cmd. 8257, *Parliamentary Papers*, Vol. LVIII, 1896.

64. Minutes of the session of the Conference of Chiefs of the FMS held at the Conference Hall, Kuala Lumpur, on 21 to 23 July 1903, Supplement to the *Selangor Government Gazette*, October 1903.

65. Minutes of the Session of the Conference of Chiefs of the FMS held at the Conference Hall, Kuala Lumpur, on 21 to 23 July 1903, Supplement to the *Selangor Government Gazette*, October 1903.

66. Governor to CO, Confidential Desp., 25 September 1903, CO 273/1903.

67. CO to Governor, Confidential Desp., 20 November 1903, CO 273/1903.

68. Anderson believed that Birch, the Resident, was behind the Sultan's protests and was encouraging Idris to voice dissatisfaction because he did not want the status of Residents eroded further. HC to RC, 16 December 1905, in HC to CO, Confidential Desp., 10 February 1906, CO 273/1906.

69. The Colonial Office regarded Idris as a troublesome Ruler but again Birch was made out to be the real villain who was manipulating the Sultan. Stubbs to Fiddes, 4 January 1908, on HC to CO, Confidential Desp., 27 November 1907, CO 273/1907.

70. Memorandum on Constitutional History by Gibson in CO 882, Vol. 12.

71. HC to CO, Received 14 March 1932, Cmd. 92300/32 [No. 25], No. 23 in Eastern No. 163, CO 882, Vol. 12.

72. In asking the Secretary of State to assess the importance of the Malay Rulers' unanimous agreement to the Federal Council proposals, Swettenham pointed out that the changes had not emanated from the Sultans. Swettenham to Harding, 19 September 1910, CO 273/1910.

73. The Colonial Office admitted that the use of the term 'salaries' was, no doubt, open to criticism but, according to Whitehall, it was used only to differentiate the personal income of the Sultans derived from the annual revenues of the States from 'Privy Purse Expenses' and other allowances for their palaces and staff. Lucas to Lethbridge, 2 March 1905, in Lethbridge to Lyttelton, Secretary of State, undated March 1905, CO 273/1905.

74. Sir Roper Lethbridge, who had served for several years in India, compared the Malayan situation with the unchivalrous insolence sometimes shown to Indian feudatory Princes. The main difference, however, was that the insolence in India was chiefly from newcomers from England but the civil service, as a rule, was scrupulously correct in all its dealings and assumed a role of the defender of the helpless. Lethbridge to Lucas, 4 March 1905, CO 273/1905.

75. The Colonial Office defended Swettenham by saying that he had the full confidence of Malay Rulers and would never have knowingly countenanced anything which would have wounded their feelings. Lucas to Lethbridge, 9 March 1905, CO 273/1905.

76. *Colonial Office Eastern Pamphlet* 24A.

77. Minutes of the Conference of July 1903, *Selangor Government Gazette*, October 1903.

78. The Sultan of Pahang did not attend and was represented by his son, the Regent, who arrived a day late.

79. Minutes of the Conference of July 1903, *Selangor Government Gazette*, October 1903.

80. See Maxwell and Gibson, *Treaties and Engagements*, p. 72.

81. FMS General Returns, 1895–1920, *FMS Annual Report*, 1920.

82. The Raja Muda lived in the capital almost unknown and there was a body of unofficial opinion which felt that he ought to be supplied with as fine a house as that occupied by the Resident, good furniture, gardeners, carriages, and a motor-car. Editorial, *The Malay Mail*, 4 November 1907.

83. The Sultans were galled to realize the extent to which their influence had decreased in direct ratio to the influence exercised by British officials in the Malay States. As a façade, some Rulers assumed an attitude of dignified reserve. Editorial, *The Malay Mail*, 4 August 1906.

84. See Gullick, *Indigenous Political Systems*, pp. 114–20.

85. Ibid., p. 114.

86. In June 1910 an official in the Colonial Office referring to advice coming from Swettenham wrote, 'In the past we have not always been sufficiently alive to the danger of guiding ourselves by advice of ex-Governors who have got out of touch with local conditions and developments.' Minute by Fiddes, 9 June 1910, on Swettenham to Crewe, 3 June 1910, CO 273/1910.

87. It was suggested that the population would have welcomed a situation where Sultans made more public appearances. The more interest the Rulers took in public and social functions, the more homage they would receive. Editorial, *The Malay Mail*, 4 August 1906.

V

THE MALAY UNDER BRITISH RULE

THE main priority of the British administration in the Federated Malay States was to establish an effective and efficient system of government so as to create stable conditions conducive to the successful economic exploitation of the country. Therefore it was not surprising that social, educational and other questions of social welfare received only secondary consideration in the early years of the Federation. The effects of these policies, so far as the Malays were concerned, were disastrous and adversely affected their economic, political, and social status within the community.

As mentioned in Chapter I, most of the Malays had, before British intervention, lived along river banks and on the coast at the river estuaries. As stated there the population in 1835–6 was estimated for Perak at 35,000; Selangor, 12,000; Rembau, 9,000; Sungei Ujong, 3,600; Johol, 3,000; Jampol, 2,000; Jelebu, 2,000; Sri Menanti, 8,000; and Pahang, 40,000.[1] In addition there were approximately 9,000 aborigines scattered about the country.[2] There were also other assessments of population, before and during the British period, for each of the States and the variation in numbers was at times significant and difficult to explain. In 1861 the Governor, Sir Orfeur Cavenagh (1859–67),[3] put the population of Perak at 50,000[4] whereas Major J. F. A. McNair writing in 1878 estimated the Malay population in 1870 at 30,000;[5] in 1879 a count for poll tax purposes, conducted by Malay penghulu, numbered the Malay population inclusive of slaves at 59,682.[6] The population of Selangor was believed to be 6,000 in 1824,[7] but fifty years later, in 1874, it had reduced to 5,000; in 1875 it increased again to 6,000, by 1878 to 10,000, and a rough census of 1884 showed it as 17,097.[8] The Malays in Sungei Ujong totalled 2,000 in 1878 and those in the rest of Negri Sembilan (apart from Jelebu) aggregated 30,000 in 1888.[9] The unstable character of the population can, to a large extent, be explained by its sensitivity to political events, and a common reaction to oppression, invasion, and civil war was escape to another region.[10]

Also the steady flow of people from Sumatra and the Thai-controlled States in the north resulted in the opening up of new districts; the lower Krian and Kurau valleys of Perak were cultivated by Malays from Province Wellesley, Kedah, and Petani; Cheras, Semenyih, and Beranang in Selangor were settled mainly by people from Sungei Ujong. From abroad, Abdul Karim bin Ibrahim, a Sumatran, came to Selama in Perak in the 1870s and established a community there. The multitude of foreign Malay immigrants can be gauged from the fact that in 1879 they numbered 9,274 in Perak alone. Selangor had its share of Bugis and Sumatrans, while Negri Sembilan attracted Menangkabaus and Achinese from Sumatra and settlers from Java.[11]

In 1891 two population censuses were conducted, one exclusively for Perak and the other for the Straits Settlements and the Protected Malay States.[12] In the case of Perak there was some disagreement between the two documents as to the size of the Malay population; the former put the figure at 96,719 while the latter estimated it to be 99,069. Selangor had 26,578 Malays; Negri Sembilan, 48,480; and Pahang, 53,104.[13] Further counts were carried out in 1901, 1911, and 1921, and according to them the Malays in Perak increased from 142,168 to 199,034 and 239,128 respectively: in Selangor from 40,640 to 64,952 and 91,787; in Negri Sembilan from 56,935 to 69,745 and 77,648; and in Pahang from 73,462 to 87,109 and 102,258.[14] Most of the Malays in this period continued to live in their traditional environments and in 1911 they constituted 11.5 per cent of the urban population in Perak, 10.7 per cent in Selangor, 14.4 per cent in Negri Sembilan, and 23.3 per cent in Pahang. This percentage fell in 1921 to 10.4 per cent, 9.0 per cent, 9.1 per cent, 16.3 per cent respectively.[15] More specifically in 1911 the Malay proportion was 9.0 per cent in Kuala Lumpur, 10.1 per cent in Ipoh, 7.5 per cent in Taiping, 3.4 per cent in Kampar, 12.4 per cent in Seremban, 20.6 per cent in Klang, and 25.7 per cent in Teluk Anson.[16]

So far as Malay relations with the British were concerned, the introduction of the Residential system was the consequence arising out of decisions made by the Rulers and chiefs of Perak, Selangor, Negri Sembilan, and Pahang. The ordinary Malays were not considered and all they knew about the Europeans was that over the course of past centuries they had come as traders but had either left of their own accord, or had been driven away by Malay warriors. It was in this context that early British administrators found themselves faced with the task of devising a workable system of government. To begin with, it was necessary to secure the trust and sympathy of the indigenous population and to make Western forms of administration, ways of life, and outlook 'acceptable to the mysterious, the dignified, the suspicious, the high-spirited Malay'.[17] Despite the best intentions this process, which brought Christian administrators face to face with Muslim beliefs, created certain tensions. The most serious incident was the assassination of Birch who, to the Malays, signified the dislocation of traditional life and the transfer of power from the hereditary ruler to an alien stranger.[18] Much of this bitterness disappeared with the consolidation of the Residential System and the tendency of officials to pay more regard to the opinions, feelings, and susceptibilities of the Malays. What replaced it was a paternalistic British attitude which implied that Malays were incapable of wise or just government.[19]

Although the Federation of 1896 gave the economy of the country a boost it had little material effect on the condition of the Malays. Their overall position in 1900 was summed up in the *Annual Report* for that year which stated that the British had provided the indigenous population with security for life and property; permanent land titles; road and rail communications; a local market for its labour and produce; free education, hospital treatment and medicine; and banks where they could deposit their small earnings at interest. They had abolished slavery and piracy; partially eliminated the scourges of cholera and smallpox; established the rule of law and equity, and made the peasant equal to his prince before the law. The British contributed financially to mosque construction, created opportunities for Government service at fixed salaries and pensions, and liberated the Malays from the ardours of arbitrary taxation, forced levies, and the system of *kerah* or compulsory labour. In return the Malays, if landowners, paid a small amount of quit rent but were not taxed on their tobacco or clothing or on the export of padi. From the British point of view, the only complaint the local population could have had was they had not been forced to work as the Indonesians had been by the Dutch administration.[20]

This picture of a thoroughly and justly contented Malay population, however, was seriously challenged in 1902. The Resident-General, Treacher, changed his opinions and expressed disappointment that the Malays had not shared fully in the general prosperity that a growing alien population had brought to the Federation. He noted that labour for roads, railways, irrigation, and other public works was almost entirely South Indian, working under the superintendence of British and Eurasian engineers and managers. The

Malays therefore had no share of the wages paid for these projects and most of the savings and pensions were taken out of the country.[21] Foreign traders and shopkeepers also monopolized the supply of essential commodities and most of the food consumed, clothing, and other consumer goods were imported. The situation was aggravated by European and Chinese capitalists employing aliens on agricultural plantations and tin mines with the prospect of both employers and employees eventually retiring with their wealth to the countries of their origin.[22] Finally, Government officials were largely foreigners whose 'Personal Emoluments' in 1902 amounted to over $3,000,000. Like the other categories mentioned, these officers intended to retire in their own countries, obtained most of their supplies from abroad, and made regular remittances to their families at home.[23]

Criticisms of British policy were strongly expressed by *The Malay Mail* which was the most influential of the English language newspapers in the Federation. It accused the administration of losing the close rapport it had formerly enjoyed with the Malay population. Increased correspondence, improved communications, and the shortage of trained staff tended to keep the District Officer at his desk, devoting more time to his duties as treasurer, land officer, magistrate, and Sanitary Board Chairman, rather than touring his district.[24] Government officials became 'office-red-tape-machines' who knew little of the lives of the population and were no longer looked upon as friends.[25] The average Englishman resident in Malaya considered it a waste of time to bother with 'native prejudices',[26] and it was left to exceptions like Wilkinson to plead that racial dominion depended on character rather than wealth or even intelligence. He was sorry that the Malays' patriotism, self-respect, reverence for the law, loyalty to their rulers, courtesy, and love for study for its own sake were constantly criticized as not being 'business'. Wilkinson believed that 'no economic prosperity need altogether blind us to the element of truth in the criticism passed by Socrates on certain admired types of statesmanship: "they have filled the city with markets, docks and suchlike trash, instead of soberness of thought and strength of character" '.[27]

An essential element of mutual understanding is, of course, language, and on this subject Maxwell, when Colonial Secretary, stated that 'Malay being the language of the state, Government servants are expected to be acquainted with it; no bonus will, therefore, in future be granted by Government to officers in the service passing in it'.[28] This meant that all British officers who joined the administration as cadets were required to pass a difficult examination in Malay but ignored the fact that for every one who joined as a cadet there were a dozen who were appointed in a different capacity. For the vast majority, therefore, there was no kind of compulsion to study the language and, since no cash incentive existed, a large proportion of the British administrators did not bother to acquire even a working knowledge of Malay and the presence of English-speaking Jaffna Tamil subordinates allowed them, superficially at least, to function normally. This bond of sympathy created by earlier British officials had meant a great deal to the Malays and it was unfortunate that this should be considerably weakened as a result of the language policy.[29]

According to *The Malay Mail* the practical consequences of Maxwell's instruction was that 75 per cent of British officials could not carry on a conversation with a Malay 'to save their lives' and, in 1897, it was said that there were over a hundred officers in Kuala Lumpur alone to whom the lives of the Malay population were practically a sealed book.[30] The bureaucrats knew little and cared less about the Malays and their predicament,[31] and those with an intimate understanding of the Malays decreased sharply in the early years of the twentieth century. The few who were genuinely interested faced the further handicap of a shortage of suitable textbooks on the subject. In May 1906 the Resident-General, Taylor, realized this and consulted the Residents with the purpose of remedying the situation. This gave Birch, Resident of Perak, the opportunity to attack general British policy towards the Malays. He was convinced that it was unproductive to go on categorizing the Malays as being 'devoid of usefulness'. This attitude had sprung from the circumstances of British intervention and the implementation of a policy which refused to treat the Malays as a privileged group. To overcome these difficulties Birch believed that a more positive approach, showing real concern for their past history and culture, was necessary. He pointed out that under rapidly changing conditions, which had changed the conduct of administration radically, British officers interested in the Malays had to create these opportunities themselves, whereas in the early years of British rule the same knowledge was forced on them by virtue of their positions.[32] A Conference of Residents, meeting in December 1906, decided to take urgent action[33] and in January 1907 it was proposed to issue a series of pamphlets on Malay questions. They were to be based on materials contained in government records and on the contributions of British officials. The entire project was put under the charge of Wilkinson who expected each booklet to comprise an introductory essay of a general character, followed by appendices on the technicalities of the subject. The intention was to produce a textbook as well that could be used for the examination of civil service cadets.[34] Between 1907 and 1911 seventeen such papers were published, ten of which were written by Wilkinson, four by R. O. Winstedt,[35] and one each by C. W. Harrison, G. E. Shaw, and J. Rigby. The subjects discussed ranged from Malay Literature, Law, History, Life and Customs, to Industries. A second series was planned and was meant to include more detailed studies but between 1912 and 1927 only seven such works were produced; two each by Wilkinson and C. C. Brown, one by A. Caldecott, one by J. E. Nathan and Winstedt, and one by a Dutch scholar, G. A. Wilken, translated by G. Hunt.[36]

The fact that the country was being exploited for the benefit of the more materialistic aliens was noticed also by a few enlightened Malays. They realized, in 1903, that although their traditional ways of life were left intact they had almost nothing to show in the way of economic and educational progress. There was no one, in the shape of a 'Protector' or 'Immigration Agent', to look after their interests, and the establishment of a Malay settlement in Kuala Lumpur had not resulted in any significant improvement.[37] An editorial in *The Malay Mail*, comparing the position of Malays in Klang with those in Bandar Maharani in Johor, concluded that the latter were better off and happier than the former. At least those living in a state ruled by a Sultan did not have to face the harassment and competition which an energetic alien population provided. All that the British government had provided the Federation Malays with were beautiful laws in a language they did not understand, hospitals with Chinese cooks, vernacular schools with inspectors who could neither read nor write Malay, a system of surveys which required a wait of a year or so for a grant of land, post offices that did not cater for rural deliveries, a savings bank they had probably never heard of, and a system of waterworks incapable of supplying sufficient water.[38]

The Malays also believed that expatriates by their government, mines, and railways had made it difficult for the indigenous population to live as they had. Their fishing grounds were interfered with, padi fields appropriated for sago and sugar, forests cleared indiscriminately, and rivers polluted by unrefined mining techniques. The Malays did not seek any special privileges but felt that they needed a certain amount of protection from those who came to the

Federated Malay States and worked to the detriment of the indigenous population. They could not become miners, railwaymen, clerks, or rubber planters overnight, but unless they were given land and encouraged by the government, they could never hope to make any progress. It was alleged that the administration had taken away the Malays' means of livelihood[39] and implemented policies which put them at the mercies of Chinese miners, European rubber planters, and Chettyar money-lenders.[40] British rule had not brought any permanent benefits to the Malays who were further handicapped because the prices of essential commodities in the Federation had soared with increased prosperity and in real terms the people in the British protected states were worse off than, say, their counterparts in Kelantan.[41]

In response to all the diverse but significant views and opinions discussed above, the administration of the Federated Malay States initiated a number of measures which sought to correct the imbalances that had been created as a result of hastily formulated government policies. The most relevant of these ranged from education to employment, agricultural settlement, land reservation, and irrigation schemes designed to increase rice production.

When the British first intervened in the affairs of the Malay States there had been no organized system of education. Passages of the Koran, in Arabic, were taught by rote in classes conducted by Islamic priests and *hajis* many of whom were themselves wholly illiterate.[42] The administration inaugurated vernacular Malay schools and, between 1883 and 1885, two or three schools were opened where elements of English were imparted to the children of a few European officials, Eurasians, a sprinkling of Chinese, and sometimes a Malay or two. Malay vernacular schools, started in the 1880s, continued to increase in number annually and in 1890 an Inspector of Schools was appointed in Perak. Education Codes for vernacular and English schools were formulated in some of the states but no attempt was made, before Federation, to standardize these principles.[43] The whole question of education posed great difficulties to British officials. Swettenham, for example, believed that nothing but good could result from teaching the 3 R's in the Malay language but was convinced that habits of orderliness and punctuality, and the duties inculcated by teachers in the hope of making good citizens of their pupils, were more valuable. He thought it unfortunate that as soon as an Easterner had been taught to read and write English very indifferently he got the impression that the government was responsible for his future employment. The result was bound to be an over-crowding of the market for that kind of labour while many other profitable trades suffered from a shortage of workmen because of the bias against manual labour.[44] The British did not aim to give the Malays the kind of higher education that was provided by the Government of India to Indians, and preferred to see the establishment of classes where useful trades would be taught. The policy was aptly expressed in 1920 thus:

> The aim of the Government is not to turn out a few well educated youths, nor a number of less well educated boys: rather it is to improve the bulk of the people, and to make the son of the fisherman or peasant a more intelligent fisherman or peasant than his father had been, and a man whose education will enable him to understand how his lot in life fits in with the scheme of life around him.[45]

In the years preceding the Federation Agreement little progress was made in the field of Malay education. In 1896 the Resident of Perak, Treacher, reviewed the achievements of vernacular Malay schools since 1874. From his inquiry it emerged that of all the past pupils of schools in Perak, 59 were employed as teachers, 57 as clerks, 61 as orderlies, 8 as domestic servants, 1724 as padi planters, 346 as gardeners, 75 as syces, 15 as sailors, 43 as constables, 142 as fishermen, 103 as labourers, 57 as boatmen, 146 as traders, 2 as *penghulu*, 2177 were variously employed as shopkeepers, miners, etc. Fifty were learning English, 138 were dead, 982 had moved out of the state, and 1000 were unaccounted for.[46] As a proportion of the total Malay population the figures represented 6706 pupils out of a total of over 100,000.[47] It was clear that the established schools were backward and that the administration lacked interest in the progress of these schools. Until 1896 there were no inducements for Malay boys to continue schooling after the age of twelve and many of them preferred to leave and go into such jobs as driving bullock carts.[48] Many parents were also unwilling to send their sons to government schools because they were afraid that their children would be influenced by Christianity.[49]

With Federation a fresh look was taken at the subject of education. The administration was still convinced that Malay education had to remain rudimentary in character and confined to very narrow limits.[50] In 1898, on Swettenham's initiative, a school to train Malay teachers was established at Taiping, Perak,[51] but the arrangements were not very satisfactory. The institution was financed jointly by Perak and Selangor but was only able to admit ten students in a two-year course chosen from students who had passed the fourth standard in a Malay vernacular school. The instruction provided was poor in quality and was handicapped by the lack of suitable books.[52] In 1900, on Wilkinson's urging, the government established a larger and more ambitious college at Malacca to cater for the entire Federation and the Straits Settlements. The college at Taiping was closed and it was left to Malacca to supply thirty trained teachers a year for the 227 schools in the territories.[53] When Wilkinson became Federal Inspector of Schools (1903–6), he took the lead in trying to publish, with government funds, the more popular Malay folk tales and encouraged the production of books suitable for use in Malay schools. The results, however, were not impressive and few proper books appeared. The amalgamation of educational organization in the Federation and the Straits Settlements in 1906 was a further blow to Malay education. The new Director of Education, I. B. Elcum, was resident in Singapore and concerned himself largely with the development of English education. Malay vernacular education was largely allowed to look after itself.[54] There were also in every Malay state hundreds of square miles of uncultivated swamp and jungle land where communications were still primitive. In such districts the spread of education was seriously hampered, and experience showed that vernacular schools under Malay teachers, if not constantly supervised, often inculcated habits that were contrary to those of diligence, punctuality, cleanliness, and care.[55] Even in areas where vernacular education was properly introduced, several difficulties persisted. The question of efficient teachers continued to plague the system. The 171 schools in Perak in 1909, for example, possessed only eighteen trained teachers in all and it was not surprising that standards were low.[56] Another cause of worry was that among the ranks of trained teachers were some who could not themselves read or write proficiently.[57] The administration itself readily conceded, in 1913, that results were highly unsatisfactory and no advantages could accrue by simply increasing the number of schools so long as the supply of well-trained teachers remained inadequate.[58] To remedy the situation the Perak state government, strongly supported by Sultan Idris, expressed its dissatisfaction by breaking away from the Malacca college and setting up its own vernacular teacher-training college, at Matang in 1913. It was hoped that the training establishment would produce about twenty-seven teachers annually but the number never exceeded fifteen.[59]

In 1915, R. H. Kenion, an unofficial member of the Federal Council, criticized the system of Malay vernacular education and suggested the appointment of a commission of inquiry.[60] The initial reaction of the Chief Secretary, Brockman, was cautious, but in 1916 the government appointed an Assistant Director of Education with the express object of superintending Malay vernacular education in the Federation and the Colony.[61] The first occupant of the post was Winstedt who, on taking up his appointment in the middle of 1916, was asked to carry out a thorough inquiry into Malay vernacular education. In this connexion he visited Java and the Philippines to find out at first hand the systems of vernacular and industrial education in force there and, on his return in 1917, prepared a report[62] that led to the introduction of a new educational system for Malay schools.

Winstedt's report determined the course of Malay education for the next twenty-five years or so. It ensured that Malay peasants did not get too grandiose ideas and had a distinctly rural slant. He regarded the schools as institutions that would provide the most elementary instruction and give a strong manual and agricultural bias.[63] He recommended that the Fifth Standard in Malay schools be abolished and that emphasis should be placed on subjects like drawing, horticulture, and other industrial arts. He wanted the government to scrap unsuitable textbooks and prepare a new series of Malay readers and textbooks dealing with hygiene, physiology, geography, arithmetic, and agricultural science. So far as administration was concerned, Winstedt recommended the creation of a separate and distinct Malay schools inspectorate staffed largely by Malays familiar with vernacular needs and standards. Taken together these proposals helped to make Malay education more efficient and a better instrument of policy than it had been.[64]

An ancillary problem facing Malay vernacular schools was one of attendance. In 1916 only 18,044 out of a total population of 472,291 went to school and represented a percentage of 3.8. In 1912 it was estimated that 38 per cent of the boys and 8 per cent of the girls of school-going age attended Malay schools in Perak, and the proportion did not improve over the next four years. The situation in Selangor and Negri Sembilan was better but only because in 1891 and 1900 respectively, laws were enacted that compelled Malay boys between the ages of seven and fourteen, living within a radius of two miles of a government school, to attend classes. The success of these measures persuaded the state of Perak, in 1916, to adopt a similar enactment in an effort to improve attendance.[65] Even then attendance throughout the Federated Malay States was irregular, and in the circumstances of the pre-war rubber boom, many of the boys left school to work on estates or small holdings.[66]

So far as the organization of an English schools system was concerned, it was hoped that with the appointment, in early 1897, of a Federal Inspector of Schools greater progress would take place. An early issue that arose concerned the wisdom of providing Malays with an education which did not groom them for manual labour and gave them a smattering of knowledge that would only make them discontented by not providing them with careers or even qualify them to compete successfully for subordinate Government jobs. On his arrival, J. Driver, the Inspector of Schools, started work on a new Education Code. He envisaged a few English language institutions which would turn out boys whose knowledge of the language would equip them for employment in positions where a command of English was essential.[67] This Education Code, in its final form, was implemented in 1899. It gave prominence to grants-in-aid being made dependent on general efficiency rather than individual passes; improvements in teaching methods; encouraging missionary and other philanthropic bodies to engage in education by providing them with liberal examination grants, salary grants, building grants, and so on; and training pupil teachers. In English schools education was to commence at the infant level and conclude with the seventh standard, the curriculum approximating to that of an elementary school in England.[68]

The British were struck by the fact that Malays were not too keen to avail themselves of the advantages of industrial training. Where such facilities did exist, for example at the Malay Settlement in Kuala Lumpur, the response was dismal. On the whole Driver's tenure of office was not remarkable for progress and achievement in the field of education. An obvious reason, of course, was the fact that his ideas could not be fully implemented due to his death in April 1903. The more important consideration, nevertheless, was that he did not possess even an elementary knowledge of the country and its people, and did not speak any Malay. He was recruited from the island of Mauritius and, on arrival in the Malay States, was required to undergo a programme of orientation designed to familiarize him with his new surroundings. In the circumstances, it was a luxury the Federation could scarcely afford, and a more prudent course of action would have been to select a candidate who was acquainted with the region. The value of this experience was appreciated when a successor to Driver was chosen. The appointee was, as mentioned

10

earlier, Wilkinson, whose selection was seen by Treacher as a forerunner of a new era for the Malays. The Resident-General was convinced that, if the administration was generous in its support and provided the necessary encouragement for Wilkinson's efforts, there would, in the course of time, emerge a generation of young Malays trained, confident, and capable of holding their own in competition with Europeans, Chinese, and Indians who had virtually monopolized the commercial, industrial, and administrative activities of the country.[69]

In February 1904, after a careful study of the situation, Wilkinson compiled a detailed and definitive memorandum aimed at establishing, in a suitable place within the Federated Malay States, a special residential school for the education of Malays from good families. It was hoped that this institution would train Malay boys for admission to certain sectors of the government service. According to Wilkinson, the failure of Malay boys to take full advantage of the educational opportunities open to them was due to the effects of economic considerations of their character and opinions. To begin with, they lived in country districts while the better English schools were all located in the towns. In addition, they had few literary traditions that taught them to prize education, they were accustomed to varied and intermittent employment and had not quite learnt the virtues of punctual and steady work; they had no problems in earning a living and considered their vocations less important than family matters and the incidents of village life. As a result, they were often improvident and laid great store on issues that the average European might consider trivial. The Malays would, for instance, cheerfully abandon lucrative employment to attend some festival or to look after a distant relative who might be ill. They were over-indulgent towards their families and were more likely to deny their sons an education than annoy their wives by sending the boys away from home. They were usually too illiterate to appreciate that a boy's occasional absences from school represented important gaps in what was meant to be a continuous course of instruction, and materially damaged the result of a whole year's efforts.[70]

To overcome the problems Wilkinson planned to found a special school for Malays in a country environment and in conditions that would be familiar to the pupils. To ensure regular attendance and to institute facilities for character building, the school had to be residential. Exceptional efficiency was a prerequisite so as to ensure that a large percentage of the boys would successfully complete their educational course requirements. Boys would not normally be admitted unless they were at an age which would enable them to complete their course. It was expected that the school would consist partly of boys from prominent families, whom it was desirable to educate because of the influence they were likely to exert, and partly of boys of exceptional ability who were likely to serve the state well and contribute to the material and spiritual advancement of their countrymen. An important feature was that the school was to be staffed by British teachers.[71]

Initially, an annual intake of twenty-five boys was conceived of whom twenty were to be scholarship-holders selected on merit and five were to be sons of good families. They would, ordinarily, enrol at the age of ten and follow a primary course extending over five years. It was hoped that such a background would qualify them to pass the seventh standard examination creditably and secure employment either as clerks or interpreters. The best students would form the nucleus of a proposed lower division of the Civil Service after three more years of advanced instruction in English language, law, history, and literature. Provided there was sufficient individual attention there was no real reason to doubt that they would be successful. Wilkinson estimated that, once organized, the school would be capable of turning out about twenty clerks and interpreters and four officers per annum capable of performing duties requiring greater responsibility.[72]

The Inspector of Schools was convinced that if a special school for Malays was established in a Malay capital with the full support and encouragement of a Malay sovereign it would, with the general backing of the Government, be an object lesson to the Malays, demonstrate the importance of education, and exhibit the sincere desire of the administration to improve the position of the indigenous population. Wilkinson hoped that the school would retain a distinctive Malay character, disseminate Malay literature, teach English, and help to improve the Kuala Kangsar Art School[73] and any other Malay technical schools that might be established. He was confident that the school would, in time, create an educated higher class among the Malays that would be beneficial to, and play an influential role among, the masses. He did not favour compulsion and, in his planning, catered for only a small number of special admissions under the category of 'sons of native chiefs' because he expected that a large number of boys from good families would be selected on merit and awarded scholarships.[74]

Wilkinson's ideas and arguments were powerful and compelling and influenced Treacher to modify his earlier opinions. The Resident-General's previous attitude had been formulated as a reaction to a suggestion by the Resident of Perak, Rodger, in August 1903, advocating the foundation of a special school in the Federation for the sons and relations of Rajas and chiefs.[75] Treacher opposed the proposal on the grounds that it would be to the advantage of the sons of Rajas and chiefs to mix freely with boys of other races and social classes rather than be cocooned in a separate institution. He believed that the Central School, Taiping, and the Victoria Institution, Kuala Lumpur, were quite capable of providing a good general education and that it would be preferable for the few Malays likely to benefit by it to complete their education at the Raffles Institution, Singapore, founded with the object, among others, of providing a good education to the sons of Malay aristocrats.[76] These sentiments were shared by the High Commissioner, Swettenham, who claimed that the only strong argument for a special school for the children of Malays of good families was that they might receive more attention than in a general school; but this could easily be achieved by having a special class for them. He cited the Malacca School as an excellent place to train intelligent Malay boys and suggested that some scholarships should be provided by the Government for deserving Malays to enable them to take advantage of the facilities in Malacca.[77]

Treacher's conversion to the idea of a special school for the Malays was bolstered by the Residents who supported the proposal at the Conference of Residents in March 1904. Both Sultan Idris and the Dato Adika Raja of Perak welcomed the suggestion with delight, referring to it as the 'germ of an Oxford'[78] for the Federation. The Sultan was confident that it would be a success and was certain that the other Rulers, Rajas, and chiefs would support the idea. According to Wilkinson, there were a number of Malay boys who were eligible for admission to the Malacca School but he was convinced that a scheme for an institution located in the Malay States had a greater chance of success than one for sending the lads to Malacca. Accordingly, the advantages of Kuala Kangsar as the site, with the presence there of Sultan Idris, the existence of the Malay Art School, and the absence of any considerable township, were obvious.[79]

The only element of discord was sounded by Taylor who, as the officer administering the Government, expressed scepticism and believed that the earlier objections of Treacher and Swettenham were still valid. He feared that the pupils for the new school would be obtained by taking away from the existing institutions their most promising Malay students.[80] Wilkinson admitted that English schools in the Straits Settlements and in the Federation did have a few Malay students but they had failed to produce significant results due to the racial idiosyncracies of the Malays and the deficiencies of the schools themselves. The Raffles Institution, the Penang Free School, and other leading schools in the Colony and the Federation were elementary schools which, though occupying the position of the Board Schools in London, were inferior to their counterparts both in terms of staff and equipment. A limited number of intelligent pupils did distinguish themselves at these schools but if the Cambridge Senior Local Certificate was taken as the minimum of literary knowledge expected of a boy who might be called upon to interpret English law, the Penang Free School, with its total enrolment of about 900, produced two Senior Local boys a year and, until 1904, the Malacca High School had groomed only one pupil, who migrated to the Raffles Institution and ended up with a Junior Local Certificate.[81] There were no reasons, therefore, to presume that Malay boys sent to the existing schools would transcend the enormous percentage of comparative failure.[82] Efficiency could have been increased by insisting on smaller classes and recruiting better teachers but, if operated on a grand scale, the expenditure would have been prohibitive. The other alternative was for the Government to do for one institution what it could not afford to do for every school in the Malay States. Wilkinson made it clear that the preference for an exclusive school was not due to any belief in the educational value of isolation or in the aristocratic principle recognized in the schools of Java. The notion of sending Malay boys to study in England was not favoured by Sultan Idris because, apart from the expense involved, it would tend to denationalize the youths and lessen their knowledge of their own language, religion, and country.[83]

In July 1904 the High Commissioner, the Resident-General, and the Inspector of Schools met and agreed to establish a special school for Malay boys. It was to start on a modest scale with three classes of from twenty to thirty boys each and was sanctioned on the understanding that W. Hargreaves, from the Penang Free School, would agree to become the first headmaster.[84] The final arrangements were completed at the end of 1904 and classes began in January 1905.[85]

From the beginning, social distinctions were an essential part of the school despite Wilkinson's democratic aspirations. Of the seventy-nine pupils enrolled in the first year only a handful were from commoner families. Royalty and nobility predominated and twenty-six of the fifty-four boarders were directly descended from royal houses. The school was organized and managed on the same lines as an English public school and was often referred to as 'The Malay Eton'.[86] At the end of the first two years the results exceeded all expectations. Twenty-one of the eighty boys passed a stiff seventh standard examination and, according to Wilkinson, showed that a few good schools could soon supply the administration with every clerk it needed and thus make it independent of the Jaffna Tamils.[87] In May 1909 the school moved to new premises and changed its name to the 'Malay College'. By 1913 the enrolment rose to 138 and remained more or less constant until the 1930s.[88]

In general, however, Malays were not fairly represented in the English schools of the Federated Malay States. The main reason for this, as mentioned earlier, was that English schools were town schools while most of the Malays continued to live in the rural areas. No real effort was made by the authorities to take English education into the villages although there was sufficient evidence to indicate that the desire to attend such schools did exist and was manifested in the large number of applications received for admission to the Kuala Kangsar school. A significant feature of Malay students was their readiness to continue, or resume, their studies after leaving school. The Training College in Malacca, for example, often had pupils who had actually resigned government teacherships to study on the subsistence allowances given to such students. One of the first students to enrol when the College opened in 1900 had, since leaving the institution, continued to study in an English school during his spare time, and in 1904 applied for admission to the Kuala Kangsar school. There were also several young Malays, in good positions, who applied for admission to the new school at the cost of their salaries. The attitude was in striking contrast to the aversion that the average Chinese or Indian clerk showed to academic pursuits of any sort.

On the question of vernacular and English education for the Malays the British administration in the Malay States cared little for Malay schools. This was principally because they catered for a section of the population that was practically voiceless and whose members in the government service were paid less than the humblest clerks.[89] They did their work in silence and were exposed to a great deal of misrepresentation by those who were often not in a position to appreciate what they did.[90]

From a teacher's point of view Malay boys were highly unsatis-factory pupils. The economic conditions under which they lived and the variety of their sources of livelihood might have made them versatile, but did not make them either persistent or punctual.[91] According to Wilkinson the average British teacher was unable to appreciate Asian ideals and tended to ridicule Malay books and writings because he could not understand them: handed out to his pupils an unpalatable diet of dull scientific names, or introduced fables and stories about foxes and other animals that the local children had never even seen. The bewildered schoolboys were not allowed to think for themselves; they were not encouraged to observe; they were put off with slovenly and inaccurate explanations like the statement that the fox was a kind of a civet cat or *musang* and they were severely reprimanded if they dared to inquire why the English should hunt inedible animals with horses and dogs. The Malays were taught to calculate in pounds, shillings, and pence to save their teachers the task of preparing new books dealing with dollars and cents. The entire atmosphere of public instruction was deadening to literary taste. A private inquiry revealed that few of the vernacular schoolteachers had ever read a single book outside the textbooks and prayer-books they were forced to study. The situation was a sad consequence of the change that enveloped Malay literary traditions under British guidance.[92]

In some respects, however, education was useful to the Malays. They seemed more intelligent and less liable to be exploited by falsification of accounts or be swindled because they lacked know-ledge. A number of petty officials were able to read and write and this enabled them to perform their functions more efficiently. Un-fortunately the progress achieved was not without its disappointing features. No highly educated class of Malays emerged to spearhead any movement towards further improvement. The talent for observa-tion possessed by older Malays perished through disuse and names of common animals and plants were forgotten by the book-educated Malays. Also the ability to read and write was seldom accompanied by the desire to do so. The appreciation of traditional literature, the great bulk of which was oral in character,[93] was no longer prevalent and nothing of value replaced it. Old superstitious beliefs still predominated in the villages, and imposters continued to trade suc-cessfully on popular naïvety in matters of magic and sorcery. British methods of instruction also failed to take racial distinctions into account. The books used were identical with those used by English school children and Malay pupils living two degrees north of the equator were asked to read tales of Christmas trees, and robins frolicking in the snow. The waste of time and effort under such circumstances was enormous, and, at best, the system could only hope to create an Asian governing class rather than Asians capable of self-government.[94]

Closely linked with the efforts to establish an educational system was the problem of employing Malays in the government as well as commercial sectors. As mentioned in Chapter 1, the Malays, descended as they were from a race of fishermen and cultivators, possessed the resourcefulness and a knowledge of the land that enabled them to lead comfortable lives without much physical labour. In agriculture, for example, clever labour-saving techniques were employed through the use of automatic water-wheels, while the traps for fishing were imaginative and indicated a knowledge of the habits of fish, as well as manual dexterity in rattan work. In the collection of jungle produce they were more efficient than even the industrious Chinese, and in piracy the old Malays had used to tremendous advantage natural features such as channels, shallows, and swamps along the coast.[95]

When the British assumed control of the government of the Malay States, they did not find an indigenous civil service and thus lacked the advantage of reforming and disciplining, as for example in Egypt, something already in existence. They were forced to create a civil service essentially British in character and the only Malays employed in responsible administrative work were the *penghulu* in charge of agricultural districts. These local officials who had occupied vital positions in traditional Malay society usually belonged to the lower ranks of the aristocracy, and were responsible for district subdivisions or *mukim*. Their principal duties were to maintain law and order, act as arbiters in small cases, report on the general progress of the *mukim* and enforce Government regulations.[96] *Penghulu* were nearly always married men and worked for some years on a salary that varied from $15 to $30 a month. On this allowance they kept, more or less, an open house for the people and were called upon to meet various other financial obligations. This was unfortunate because the Federation was by no means an impoverished territory and could well have afforded to pay higher salaries.[97] Appointments for the Malays of higher rank were few and far between. The authorities believed that the Malay upper class had failed to cope with events within the States and thus could not act as a reservoir for District Officer and Head of Department material. In view of the great amount of economic and governmental activity the British felt that they just could not afford the time to train Malays for administrative duties. On rare occasions, however, some members of the aristocracy were given posts such as 'Judges of the Supreme Court' and 'Native Magistrates'.[98] Again, in 1900, the Orang Kaya Mentri of Perak, the Sri Adika Raja, and the Sri Maharaja Lela were appointed superintendents of *penghulu*.[99] So, because it was vital to organize the day-to-day business of ruling, Englishmen were recruited for all the higher appointments, and Eurasians and Chinese from the Straits Settlements, together with candidates from Ceylon and India, were given the less important jobs. But it was hoped that, in the future, educated Malays would replace Indians and Ceylonese in the subordinate appointments although this expectation was somehow contradicted by the belief, among some British administrators, that as Malay vernacular schools did not teach English their products would not be suitable for the majority of government functions.[100]

The declared policy of the administration thus was to encourage, so far as possible, the entry of Malays into the government service. Birch, for instance, considered the Malays to be the heirs to the country and believed that the object of British rule should be to preserve the best of their cultural traditions and assimilate them into the modern world. He was also convinced that the neglect of the Malays had been due to the preoccupations of the authorities with governing a country where large financial interests were at stake.[101] Both Swettenham and Treacher blamed Malay failure on their lack of energy and ambition to take part in the country's prosperity. Others suggested more complicated causes, advocated a more positive approach, and believed that British protection implied a tacit moral obligation to protect Malay ambitions.[102]

Despite the pronouncements, until the close of the nineteenth century, little or no serious attention was paid to the subject of Malay employment. Even subordinate posts such as peons and railway porters were filled by foreigners. Only a very small proportion of the European officers came into close contact with the people of the country and this created the impression that the majority of them knew little and cared less about the Malays. It was widely acknowledged that it was nobody's duty in particular to find employment for the Malays and it was said that it was difficult to obtain Malays for vacant appointments. The British officials failed to recognize that the better class of Malays were to be found not in the towns but in the villages or *kampong*.[103] The fact remained that far too little was done for the Malays in their own country. Granted that it was not practical to offer them influential jobs for which they were unfitted, there was no reason why they could not have filled a far greater number of minor appointments like peons, policemen, railway guards, and ticket collectors.[104]

In 1902 the Resident-General, Treacher, reiterated the intention that it was the desire of the administration to encourage as much as possible the entry of Malays into government service. He noted that a few members of the Perak aristocracy had shown an aptitude for official work and that some Malays were being employed as Settlement officers, demarcators, and forest rangers.[105] Rodger, the Resident of Perak, however, was convinced that the authorities had not made sufficient use of the services of Malay officials and that this was the main reason, in contrast with India and Ceylon, why the administration was compelled to appoint a relatively large proportion of Europeans. He, therefore, called for the greater employment of Malays; the development of their capacity by means of education when young, and later by means of official practical life; and an increase in their sense of responsiblity by entrusting them, more and more, with important posts and enlarging, rather than restricting, the scope of their powers as they grew in confidence.[106]

Swettenham stated that the Government should appoint as many Malays as were qualified to any posts in the administrative service, but regretted that Malays capable of wielding authority, with justice and intelligence, were all too rare. In a more practical vein, to induce the best Malays into the administration, he suggested that the status and salaries of *penghulu* should be raised to more realistic levels. Salaries of between $100 and $200 a month were proposed instead of the $20 or $40 being paid to them and the High Commissioner was confident that, with a fair education, Malays could replace a number of Europeans employed in settlement work, mine inspecting, revenue collection, and other such duties.[107]

In June 1903 a group of Malay clerks in Perak sent a Memorial to the Acting State Engineer, drawing attention to the problems of Malays trying to obtain employment. They argued that, under the aegis of British protection, not a single middle-class Malay had occupied a government position other than that of orderly, punkah-puller, and police constable. The Malays regarded themselves as being in a disadvantageous position, when compared with their co-clerks of other nationalities educated in India or Ceylon, because education in the Federation terminated at the seventh standard and did not provide the required academic background to pass the Senior Grade Clerical Examinations. The indigenous population was hopelessly outclassed by Chinese and Indian rivals, at every qualifying and competitive examination, because it lacked sufficient practical knowledge of spoken and written English. In the circumstances the petitioners asked for preferential treatment over the other nationalities and for exemption from having to pass the Senior Grade Clerical Examinations.[108] Their hopes, however, were dashed when the Conference of Residents of March 1904 considered the matter, and decided that it would be inadvisable to give in to the demands.[109]

The subject of Malay employment next appeared at the Second Conference of Rulers held in Kuala Lumpur in July 1903. At that meeting it was revealed that, in 1903, the number of Malays in the police force totalled 1,175; there were 587 *penghulu* and Malay magistrates, and 874 were engaged in general office duties in government departments. Treacher pointed out two difficulties with regard to the higher appointments in the regular civil service, the first being that the jobs were filled as a result of a stiff competitive examination held by the Civil Service Commissioners in England, and secondly that no one could become a satisfactory magistrate unless he possessed a good knowledge of the principal laws of the country, including the law of Evidence, and of the Government General Orders and Rules.[110]

Rodger, speaking at the request of Sultan Idris of Perak, emphasized that the protected Malay States were not British colonies and that British officials were there to assist, but not to replace, the Rulers in the administration of their States. He hoped that it would be possible to extend the employment of Malays even if this meant the exclusive reservation of certain jobs in the government service, and to differentiate between the qualifications required from Malays and those from other races.[111]

The hypothetical backing for the Malays and the sympathy felt by most British officials for them was not, however, translated into practice. In the aftermath of the Second Conference of Rulers there was little improvement in the number of Malays employed by the Government. In June 1906 the Government of Perak, recognizing the unsatisfactory state of affairs, issued a proclamation in the form of advice, from the Sultan to his subjects. It drew the attention of

Malays in the State to the vast number of job opportunities that had arisen, as a consequence of expanding rubber plantations, and urged them to take full advantage of the chances. The only drawback was that the proclamation failed to take into account the strong disinclination on the part of many employers, in the rubber industry, to recruit Malays. It was hoped, nevertheless, that in view of the unique appeal, planters would give Malays the opportunity to prove themselves. While acknowledging that it was too much to expect money-making enterprises to turn themselves overnight into philanthropic organizations, *The Malay Mail* suggested that, with a little patience, the Malays might prove useful in some aspects of estate work and thus reduce the dependence on a precarious immigrant labour market. If the experiment turned out to be a failure then there was no more to be said, but the planters would have the satisfaction of knowing that they had tried to do something for the people in whose country they were making their fortunes.[112]

The initiative met with only moderate success and a number of Malays did find employment on rubber plantations but as a proportion of the total workforce the figures were unimpressive. According to the 1911 Census, Malays constituted only 14 per cent of the estate population compared with the 25 per cent Chinese and 60 per cent Indians.[113]

Towards the end of 1909 some non-government quarters believed that it was time for the authorities not to force Malays into occupations they detested and for which they were not fitted, but to educate them in such a way that they would be induced to work.[114] Early in the following year the government finally decided to launch a co-ordinated plan for establishing a core of Malay administrators in the Federation. The 'Scheme for the Employment of Malays (Higher Subordinate Class)' was designed to create a special service of administrative officers from among the better pupils of the Malay College. Under the scheme, the four Residents, on the advice of the headmaster, nominated annually from among those who had passed the seventh standard examination, candidates considered suitable for the administrative service. Final selection was the prerogative of the Resident-General and those chosen were admitted as probationers for a further three-year course at the College.[115] During this time they were instructed in subjects leading to the Junior Cambridge Certificate with special training related to official correspondence, Treasury work, and other prescribed subjects.[116] After completing the course successfully the graduates were appointed as Malay Assistants, Class III, to a separate Malay Administrative Service (MAS).

The new Malay officers did not share in the work attached to the central bureaucracy and their duties were confined to district administration in areas where the Malays predominated. They assisted the European district officers as Settlement officers, attached to Land Offices, were sometimes appointed Malay Assistant Secretaries in the State Secretariats and were also involved in several minor routine clerical duties. Promotion in the service was agonizingly slow and prospects were further reduced by the fact that, as a rule, they served only in their own States. In terms of actual numbers, Malays serving in the administration and earning more than $200 a month never reached sizeable proportions.[117]

Towards the end of the First World War the first moves towards a reorganization of the Malay Administrative Service began. The idea was to make it more attractive and more responsible. It was recognized that the 1910 Scheme had produced a sense of dissatisfaction and even a distaste for further service in the Government among the Malay officers.[118] The new scheme implemented in July 1917 made a number of nominal concessions that raised the status of Malay officials, but did not radically alter the character of Malay participation in the administration. The officers were now known as 'Malay Officers', their salaries were increased marginally, and promotion was made less cumbersome.[119]

The reorganization did not, however, solve all the outstanding problems. The most significant of these concerned two or three Malays who were at the top of the Special Grade, had been acting in responsible positions during the war, and now expected promotion to the Malayan Civil Service. At the Conference of Residents held in February 1917 it was decided that the principle of promotion could be best effected by the appointment of Malays to the Civil Service as supernumeraries on Class V of the salary scale £400 × 15 – £460 × 20 – £500 per annum. Class V was the lowest grade in the Civil Service and although subsequent promotion to higher grades was not ruled out it was made clear that Malay officers would remain in the category of supernumeraries and could not rank with cadets for seniority.[120] The first to be appointed was Raja Said Tauphy[121] but the selection did not affect the principle of employing Malays as assistants in rural areas.

Further measures designed to employ more Malays were introduced in September 1917 when a Scheme for Malay Inspectors of Police was forwarded to the Colonial Office.[122] This was followed in

October of the same year by a scheme for Malay officers in the Department of Agriculture which, it was hoped, would provide careers for a number of educated Malays whose work would benefit the country.[123]

Although all the above employment proposals were intended to benefit the Malays the policies were rather belated and in effect condemned the Malays, for years to come, to a position of inferiority. In 1919 the proportion of Malays in the General Clerical Service was 10.5 per cent compared with the 19.5 per cent Chinese and the 55 per cent Indian element.[124] The lack of adequate publicity was one of the reasons but the scarcity of training facilities, both technical and literary, also accounted for the failure of the Malays to take on technical and professional jobs. In spite of statements to the contrary there was, too, the absence of sympathy and understanding from some European officials who made no attempts to study the Malay temperament and were accustomed only to handling English educated subordinates. The Malays, on their part, were prone to lay aside their education the moment they left their offices, and reverted quickly to the conditions prevailing in their *kampong*. The number who consciously sought to improve their efficiency at home was small and the inability to make adequate progress within their professions could frequently be attributed to this. The paucity of Malay textbooks and the necessity to think persistently in a foreign language was another excessive strain on Malay minds.[125] The Malay Administrative Service has been labelled as 'fraudulent as a device for sharing real power with Malays'[126] but had far-reaching repercussions. Since it was largely state-based, the initial opposition of the Malays to British rule was a local rather than a national phenomenon and real Malay power was first exerted through State Governments.[127]

Turning next to another aspect of British policy towards the Malays we come to the establishment of a Malay Agricultural Settlement on the fringes of Kuala Lumpur. The project was initiated in 1899 on the recommendation of the Resident-General and the Resident of Selangor for the purpose of educating the Malays to take a more active part in the administration and thereby share in some of the advantages that had accrued from the growing prosperity of the Federated Malay States. To carry out these intentions it was decided to give Malay youths a Malay–English education, teach them a trade, and provide them with the means to acquire the arts of the country as well as revive and perpetuate traditional industries.[128] A block of land 224 acres in area, situated between the Klang River and Batu

Road,[129] was reserved for the settlement. It was divided into small lots and on them were to be settled, free of rent, respectable Malays willing to obey the rules drafted for the guidance of the settlement. Classes, covering a wide range of industrial subjects, conducted by specially qualified Malay teachers, recruited from different parts of the Peninsula, were to be organized and instruction in animal husbandry, silver work, weaving, embroidery, mat-making, and other related cottage industries was to be arranged. A Board of Management,[130] nominated by the Resident of Selangor, was to administer the Settlement, direct the education of the children, and generally look after its welfare and progress. In 1899 a total of thirty families settled on what was considered to be a splendidly situated reserve. The settlers could not alienate their holdings on any account, and rules and regulations were framed regarding the planting and upkeep of trees.[131]

The experiment was a unique one and by the close of 1900 two hundred half-acre allotments were occupied by respectable Malays and approved by the Board of Management. Fruit trees were planted, holdings were adequately fenced, and seventy houses were erected wholly at the cost of the occupiers. The total resident population was 235 of whom thirty-eight were children of school-going age. The Board took pains to organize a large and convenient recreation ground, build a boarding house for Malay scholars attending the Victoria Institution, construct three houses for Malay teachers, and lay a number of necessary roads. A wood carver, from Negri Sembilan, and a silversmith were recruited as instructors and, although they began without any regular pupils, their work was much appreciated by the European community which bought objects at prices which realized a profit of over $100 to the Board.[132] In 1901 a temporary building was utilized as a Malay vernacular school and houses were built for a blacksmith and a tailor. A proper survey was conducted, the holdings resettled by T. W. Clayton, and the number of occupation permits increased from thirty-one in 1900 to seventy-five. It was also decided to grow rice on the settlement and towards this end an English plough costing £5 and four waterwheels for irrigation, each costing £55, were ordered from England. The general progress of the settlement was, however, somewhat delayed by the lack of road communications with Kuala Lumpur although a road connecting Batu and Ampang Roads was started towards the end of the year.[133]

Although the settlement clearly benefited a class of Malays the

Government was anxious to assist, the aims of the architects of the Scheme, which included the spread and encouragement of technical education, and the resuscitation of certain Malay handicrafts and ornamental workmanship in danger of dying out, had not been achieved and could only be accomplished by extreme patience and infinite tact. Many respectable Malay families did lead their natural village lives almost within the precincts of a city, the neighbourhood attracted the best class of Malays, and many who would otherwise have preferred to live in less populous areas were tempted to move into the settlement. What was questionable was whether this in itself warranted the scale of expenditure contemplated. On the issue of technical education and the encouragement of traditional artistic crafts the expected response of the young Malays did not emerge, and little use was made of the facilities placed at their disposal. The authorities acknowledged that it was a superhuman task to persuade the Malays to take an interest in any project they did not fancy. They might, as a favour to their British advisers, go along for a while but their compliance often ended with the cessation of personal incitement. This was precisely what happened with the young people of the settlement. They were not particularly attracted to the work and refused to be bound by it. The obstacle to progress, according to the British, was the Malays' temperament and it was recognized that advance could only be made at their rate and not with the rapidity the authorities were keen to infuse.[134] Inside the Board of Management too the initial euphoria gave way to disillusionment and the Secretary complained, in 1902, that only one of the three European members[135] took any interest in the settlement and at the meeting of 15 November 1902 only three out of the eight members were present. Things were in a mess, the Board did not keep its records in order and the Secretary was unable to disentangle the difficulties. The padi scheme had failed miserably and it emerged that it had been undertaken against the advice of the Malay members and had resulted in a loss of $1,000.[136]

Towards the end of 1903 affairs of the settlement looked very bleak. The silversmith's apprentice was dismissed for laziness and incompetence, the services of the tailor and his apprentices were dispensed with, and it was discovered that the land earmarked for padi and subject to flooding was abandoned by the rice farmers. The imported irrigation wheels broke down and, since repairs would have had to be carried out in England and the cost was prohibitive, the authorities chose to build a dam instead. After two and a half years the school building, which had already cost $2,000, was still un-completed. The silversmith, whose work had markedly deteriorated and who needed constant supervision, absconded and left on a pilgrimage to Mecca. To make matters worse the poverty-stricken villages were warned that, unless they contributed more to the Mosque Fund, they would not be provided with a place of worship.[137] So far as management of the settlement was concerned the Secretary of the Board was given a free hand, in February 1903, to make all except the most important decisions.[138]

In succeeding years the situation got worse. It became increasingly difficult to induce boys and girls to attend school regularly and to persuade occupants to maintain their holdings in a proper state of cultivation.[139] In 1909 the Resident of Selangor, Belfield, acknow-ledged that a number of lots in the settlement remained unoccupied. The initial novelty associated with the project had worn off and only an unprecedented amount of frenzied activity on the part of the Board of Management could have overcome the indifference of those for whose needs the settlement was designed to cater.[140] Unfor-tunately, the enthusiasm did not materialize and in 1918 several of the lots were resumed by the Board in accordance with the rules because the registered occupiers did not reside in the settlement.[141] The engineers of the project had hoped that, once established, the scheme would have formed the nucleus of similar experiments throughout the Federation.[142] The Malays would thus be put on their mettle and provided with the opportunities to show that, when they cared to do so, they could hold their own against anybody else. Instead, the Malay Agricultural Settlement limped on through the years and, despite the expenditure of large sums of money, it stag-nated as kind of a shanty town while, all around it, the town of Kuala Lumpur developed and blossomed both in size and in im-portance.

The future of traditional Malay land holdings was another prob-lem that came sharply into focus during the twentieth century. The rapid economic development threatened to disrupt forever the land-based Malay way of life, and the calamity was first recognized by Belfield, the Resident of Selangor. To put the subject into proper perspective it is necessary to look back to the early years of Fed-eration when European agricultural enterprise was wallowing in a state of uncertainty and stagnation. The authorities of that period did all in their power to encourage the permanent settlement of Malay agriculturalists and put every facility available at their dis-

11

posal. They were granted agricultural lands freely and were given lots adjacent to main roads so as to ensure proper accessibility as well as ease the problems of transport. A situation was thus created where Malay allotments stretched along most of the frontages of the older roads. The experiment was not as successful as hoped and most of the holdings remained unkempt and semi-abandoned. Worse, they wholly or partially blocked access to extensive areas of land and, overgrown as they were with *lalang* and weeds, they harboured a variety of vermin which were a danger and a source of nuisance to the owners of adjacent estates. To alleviate the situation the Government took steps to repossess such blocks of land as were subject to that penalty for abandonment, and some estate proprietors bought out intervening Malay lands and secured road frontages wherever possible. Many important properties, however, remained isolated and Belfield was convinced that it was highly improper to let Malays settle in such localities. He accordingly instructed all District Officers in Selangor not to alienate to Malays any land adjacent to a government road without the Resident's previous sanction. Belfield wanted to concentrate Malay gardeners in designated areas and was not in favour of their occupying any land that could conceivably be used for scientific planting.[143]

In 1906 there were distinct signs that Malay owners of agricultural land in Selangor began to realize that their holdings were of high marketable value and were, therefore, worth looking after. This was especially noticeable in the case of lands in the neighbourhood of rubber estates. The owners of these allotments found themselves in a position where they could negotiate profitable terms with big planters for whom the acquisition of the small holdings was often vital. The price of land was further enhanced by the optimistic forecasts for both planting and mining organizations. All classes of the community were affected by this, there was more money in the pockets of businessmen, and this, combined with a policy that discouraged the alienation of land along main thoroughfares to Malays, created and boosted the demand for advantageously sited lands and fostered the tendency among landowners to await a further advance in values. In the meantime rents on all such plots were punctually paid and there was a general willingness to conform to all the provisions of tenure, thus obviating any risk of losing the land for non-compliance with the obligations thereby imposed on them.[144]

Nevertheless the increasing premiums on land resulted in constant approaches being made to Malays to purchase their lands, whether ancestral or recently acquired and cultivated.[145] The prices offered were so attractive that it was commonly believed that the majority of the Malays would find it difficult to resist the carrot dangled before them. At the same time the authorities were reluctant to be a party to a situation where the bulk of land held by the Malays would leave their possession and become the property of foreign commercial interests.[146] The Federal administration appraised the state of affairs in 1907 but the various complexities of the problem prevented the emergence of definite legislative proposals. At a Conference of Residents in October 1908 Birch, the Resident of Perak, suggested that a certain amount of land should be set aside specifically for occupation by Malays, but again no steps were taken to legalize the proposition.[147] Birch continued to show great enthusiasm over the problem and conducted a census of Malay holdings which revealed that nine-tenths of the land originally owned by the Malays had been sold or transferred to persons who were not Malays. He believed that since the Malays were not in the habit of making provision for their children and grandchildren, it was the duty of the Government to make sure that they did so. Birch discovered that at the death of a Malay head of family what often happened was that all the land owned by him was sold, and his heirs were soon reduced to poverty. There was the example of the wealthy Malay gentleman in Perak who had nine children. On his death his surviving family decided that the property should be divided according to the precepts of Islamic law. The eldest son, however, successfully induced his brothers and sisters to sell the entire property instead, with the result that they were all reduced to destitution.[148]

In the period 1 July 1909 to 31 December 1910, the sale of land by Malays to aliens in Perak, exclusive of the districts of Krian and Kinta for which no figures are available, amounted to 996 lots, in Selangor to 1,416 lots, and in Negri Sembilan to 225 lots.[149] These figures lent strength to the argument that as land increased in value the first category of the population to sell out were the Malays. It was postulated, therefore, that it would be in the best interests of the indigenous population if the Government could reserve lands, at selected locations, for it. One suggestion was that an area of about 2,500 acres, cut up into lots of about 5 acres each, should be set aside. Each of the holdings could be made subject to conditions that a strict cultivation clause was complied with, that no individual could own more than one lot, and that the land could only be sold to, or bought by, a genuine Malay cultivator. It was considered that it would be a reproach to British administration if Malays, even through their own foolishness, ceased to be the owners of land in large areas of their own country. As poor people it was necessary for them to be protected against a natural desire to conform to the legitimate ideas of capitalists whenever land appreciated in value.[150] Government action still did not materialize and in 1911 in Perak Malays bought 213 lots of land from non-Malays but sold 754 lots, a net reduction of 541 holdings. In a large number of cases the Malays became divorced from the land-owning class and became agricultural labourers on lands belonging to others, or found other jobs.[151] The next year the gap widened to 741, being the result of 961 sales and 220 purchases,[152] and in 1913 the difference was 1,337.[153] It became clear that, unless urgent protective measures were introduced, the ultimate decimation of the Malays as land-owners was only a matter of years away.

To save, or rather salvage, Malay landed interests the Government finally formulated the Malay Reservations Enactment of 1913. In doing so the authorities were aware of the fact that the proposals contained in the Bill were unusual and advocated measures which interfered with the vested interests of individuals. The justification advanced was that the Enactment appeared to afford the only means to the end which was desired. The end was considered to be of paramount importance and the British felt that if any feelings of resentment should emerge from individuals affected by the Bill, it had to be remembered that the Sultans had agreed, in principle, to the measure and supported its introduction.[154]

The Malay Reservations Enactment was introduced entirely in the interests of the Malays and was designed to benefit the community rather than the individual who might be tempted to dispose of his holdings by the high prices being offered for land. The aim was to protect what was known amongst the Malays as *kampong* lands as opposed to what were called *kebun*. In other words the emphasis was on land handed down from generation to generation of Malays. It would have been tragic if these ancestral lands were to pass out of their hands into the control of foreign speculators. It was common knowledge that in the few years preceding the Enactment men were scouring the country endeavouring to persuade Malays to sell their land, not for the purpose of taking it over and working it, but to speculate, float companies, obtain profits, and then, possibly, clear out. The danger was a very real one and Brockman, the Chief Secretary, claimed that in 1911 alone a prospectus was contemplated where no less than 645 Malay holdings appeared to be in the hands of option holders. The capitalists tried to acquire these lands in order to float a company and although that particular prospectus did not actually materialize, there was no doubt that people were busy trying to procure an increasing number of Malay holdings.[155]

The Federal Council passed the Enactment[156] on 25 November 1913 and the measure came into force on 1 January 1914. The Bill did interfere with the existing rights of those Malays whose holdings might be included in Malay reservations but this was inevitable in any effective scheme for the protection of Malays against themselves so far as disposal of their lands was concerned.[157] Some preliminary steps were taken to implement the intentions of the Enactment in 1914 but no definite proceedings were instituted till 1915. Areas in Perak and Selangor were designated as Reservations but only in Perak was any progress recorded in the enforcement of the provisions to the letter. Over the years it became clear to the British administration that the Bill was not successful in entirely preventing the Chinese and Indians from discovering loopholes in the law. The most common tactic used by immigrants was to employ Malay nominees to hold foreclosed land on their behalf.[158]

In the practical economic sphere the only preserve which retained a distinctly Malay character was rice planting but unfortunately this was the sector which least interested and concerned the administration. The great stress laid on tin mining and on western-type agricultural enterprises worked to the detriment of the Malay padi planters who found themselves deprived of their lands and pushed more and more into oblivion. Rice harvests fell and the country began to depend increasingly on the import of the grain from Java, Thailand, and Burma. Until the implementation of the Federation Agreement the serious problems that faced the Malays and their traditional economic existence did not attract significant British concern. The first administrator impressed with the necessity to keep padi planters in business and to lure more of them to come and settle in the protected States, was E. W. Birch. He observed that the Malays who planted rice in the district of Krian were not natives of Perak but had come from States not under British protection. These sojourners were not very interested in remaining in Krian permanently and were prepared, if their expectations were not realized, to seek their fortunes elsewhere. They were, therefore, not settlers in the strict sense of the word and were unlikely to settle permanently unless the Government were willing to do something to assure them of regular crops and a supply of drinking water.[159]

The general British attitude was that padi planting had to be looked at from the standpoint of sound economic principles, the first condition of successful agriculture being that it had to be profitable. Several reasons were advanced for the non-cultivation of tracts of land available for rice growing along the coasts of the Peninsula. One factor was the lack of population; whole districts were uninhabited and men could choose their occupations without being forced into agriculture by competition. The presence of the mining industry contributed to this shortage because if an agriculturalist could earn twice as much as a labourer as the cultivation of his fields would have brought him, he would abandon agriculture and live on imported rice. Apart from labour paid for by wages there were, sometimes, fields of enterprise open to Malays which led to whole communities of agriculturalists leaving a particular State. The *gutta percha* industry was one of these and there was an occasion when padi planters of Muar, Padang, and Batu Pahat, in Johor, abandoned their lands to collect *gutta* and their descendants, after two or three generations, grew up entirely ignorant of agriculture. The authorities also believed that the modern Malay of the Straits Settlements and the Peninsula, except in the remote inland districts, was not satisfied with leading a purely agricultural existence. Since rice planting required the cultivator to be satisfied with poor fare and a simple, modest, and economical style of living, only the inhabitants of Negri Sembilan were considered ideal peasant material. Lastly, the price of rice had kept pace with the increase in wages and people found that the price of imported rice was less than what it would have cost to grow it domestically.[160]

Birch, however, remained convinced about the wisdom of a policy which would encourage Malays to devote more time and energy to rice planting. He believed that a start could be made by initiating a scheme of irrigation canals to ensure sufficient water, good drainage, and a substantial amount of drinking water as well. The Krian district was the leading candidate for such a programme and in June 1889, Wellman, the Acting Magistrate of that district, submitted a set of proposals dealing with the problem. On 30 April 1892 the State Engineer Perak, Caulfield, despatched another report to the Governor, Clementi Smith, who, while recognizing the obvious advantages of the project, decided that it could not, at that juncture, be implemented. This was followed by a detailed report on the plans to Swettenham, the Resident, by the Public Works Department and in June 1892 a useful memorandum on irrigation was drawn up by Sir Frederick Dickson, the Colonial Secretary (1885–92).[161]

In 1893 the idea was resuscitated by Birch who persuaded Swettenham to approach the Governor again. On this occasion Smith decided to consult the Government of India and, in consequence, an officer from the Indian Public Works Department, Claude Vincent, came to Perak to study the proposed scheme. His findings, completed in 1894, with the exception of a few suggested amendments, were very similar to the conclusions reached earlier by Caulfield. The report was considered significant enough to merit further investigation and in June 1897 a qualified irrigation engineer from India, R. G. O'Shaughnessy, arrived in Malaya to conduct a more detailed study. His estimate of the cost for the whole project was $859,000 as compared to Vincent's $300,000. The State Engineer, however, disagreed with these estimates and feared that the ultimate cost would be nearer $1,000,000. Caulfield, accordingly, prepared a new 'inundation scheme' estimated to cost a modest $450,000.[162]

The financial implications of the whole operation worried the Governor, C. B. H. Mitchell, who suggested that it should be temporarily abandoned until the main railway line was completed. Mitchell was also dubious about whether the landowners, who were the proprietors of a large portion of the district it was proposed to irrigate, would be prepared to pay a water rate that would return even a small interest on the large outlay. In the Governor's opinion, the landowners might be ready to pay in years of drought but these years were exceptional and amounted to, perhaps, one in about four or five.[163] The reluctance of the authorities to commit any money was strange because it was clear by then that the venture would guarantee regular rents, regular crops, a settled population, and an indirect revenue to the district and the railways.

The Colonial Office, however, was more enthusiastic and favoured starting the project immediately provided, of course, that the finance for it could somehow be found. Mitchell's doubts about income were hardly considered an obstacle to commencement because the uncertainty could, in any case, never be resolved until the works were completed and postponement did not necessarily remove it. The consensus was that a start should be made even if the total sum required was not available. It was conceded that in these circumstances progress would be slower, establishment charges would be increased, and the commencement of revenue postponed; but against this it was hoped that the work would be of better quality because it was less hastily done and greater economy would be exercised than if a large annual vote were available. Whitehall deprecated any delay unless the enterprise was to be entirely abandoned.[164]

Swettenhan continued to campaign for the scheme and drew attentiom to the large quantities of rice being imported into the Malay States. He highlighted the dangers of famine, extreme distress, and possible trouble if anything were to interfere with this importation. The Resident-General recalled that Krian depended for its very existence on an uncertain rainfall and a system of ditches and sluice gates to retain the water and, if necessary, prevent flooding. These arrangements were unsatisfactory and the water so obtained and stored was not, especially during a period of prolonged drought, either sufficient or suitable for drinking purposes. As a result harvests were uncertain and a large proportion of the population was a transient one. Swettenham therefore urged that the scheme be carried out and asked for it to be put under the direction of an experienced engineer capable of completing it successfully.[165]

A landmark in this controversy was reached in 1898 when Birch wrote a detailed memorandum on the subject of irrigation. According to him, irrigation was not only desirable but a matter of dire necessity in the Federation. As he saw it, the prime consideration was the population, for without it the *raison d'être* of British administration would be lost; without it, when the tin deposits were exhausted, revenues would decrease, towns would be depopulated, and railways would run at a loss. The population of the Federation consisted of migratory and settled groups with the former predominating and including Asian, and foreign Malay, immigrants who did not regard the Peninsula as their home. The authorities, ever since intervention, had tried very hard to attract and induce immigration and expended much money to bring aliens, supply them with funds to establish themselves, and give them buffaloes, rice, and padi seeds. Remissions of land rent were arranged to make it easier for the newcomers to eke out a hand-to-mouth existence. Much of these advances were written off as irrecoverable and the lands squatted on were, sooner or later, deserted. The worst consequence of this policy, however, was the growth of *lalang* wastes where forests had been destroyed and land rendered temporarily useless, due either to the inability of the people to secure regular harvests, or the inability of the Government to prepare irrigated tracts of land to receive immigrants. Both those who were already there, and those brought there, were forced to grow a crop or two of hill padi and then move on to other land.[166]

Such an eventuality, in a way, was understandable because, in the early years, the authorities did not possess surplus revenue to initiate a comprehensive system of irrigation. The bulk of the money had to be spent in opening up the country by roads and railways and in encouraging tin mining which was the mainstay of the economy. But by the end of the nineteenth century a stage was reached where the Government was urged to guarantee, for the population, a secure livelihood through the production of its staple commodity, and to prepare unalienated lands in such a manner as would induce the population of the future to remain. Some British administrators argued that it was wrong to cultivate a product that was unremunerative and that Malays grew rice out of habit rather than because it paid them to do so. Birch, however, insisted that the bulk of the rice fields had been worked by the Malays for generations and the land they occupied was, in most cases, unsuited to any other species of cultivation. Birch maintained that they should be encouraged to continue planting rice and the authorities could help by providing an adequate water supply. Irrigation schemes would have the added advantage not only of decreasing the dependence on imported rice but also of facilitating the growth of a settled population, introducing a reliable supply of good drinking water, and ensuring self-sufficiency in times of war.[167]

This impassioned plea resulted in the dispatch of Murray, the Colonial Engineer, to Perak with the object of reviewing the Krian Irrigation Scheme and reporting on its diverse aspects. The assessment was completed towards the end of 1898 and the recommendations, accepted by the Acting Governor, Sir James Swettenham,[168] were adopted by the Government of Perak which set aside $656,000 for the project.[169] The Colonial Office ratified the plans[170] and 100 Chinese labourers started work in Krian in April 1899. Initially, progress was extremely laborious but in January 1900 it increased in momentum, but by then the estimated cost had risen to $1,000,000.[171] The works were practically completed by the end of 1905 at a cost of $1,500,000 and the administration was confident that enormous benefits would accrue to the district.[172] It was recognized that success could only be ensured by, and depended entirely on, the very sympathetic and careful handling of the people. It was vital for the

Department of Agriculture to play a more positive role in the cultivation of padi, and the District Officer of Larut, Hale, urged the Government to make agricultural loans available to enable Malays to free themselves from debts due to usurers.[173]

The prosperity brought to the agriculturalists by the Krian Irrigation Scheme, with the 63,000 acres that thrived as a result of the project, did not, however, presage the launching of similar irrigation works elsewhere in the Federation. The authorities remained, as a rule, reluctant to embark on any heroic schemes and the common excuse proferred was that the number of potential rice cultivators was too small to justify further large-scale expenditure.[174] This malaise on the part of the administration provoked a sharp reaction from a Selangor Raja, Bot, in August 1902. Bot, the son of Raja Snay and the grandson of Sultan Muhammad, was taken in 1858 at the age of eleven by McPherson, the Resident in Malacca, and educated in an English school. Ten months later, on the departure of McPherson for Singapore, Bot was looked after by a Chinese merchant, Baba Chi Yamchwan, with whom he stayed for about a year. On his return to Lukut he became a close confidant of the Sultan of Selangor. Bot's views on padi planting, set out in a letter to Sultan Suleiman and the Resident-General, called for a large-scale revival of that economic activity and as a starting point he proposed a meeting between the Sultans, the Resident-General, and the Resident of Selangor with the idea of enacting new legislation that would specify methods of working and planting padi and compel 'planting by the imposition of rigorous punishment (gaol or fine) on the disobedient and lazy'. He was convinced that in the absence of strong legislation, enforced by a strong hand, padi cultivation could never prosper.[175] This powerful plea, however, had little effect on the authorities who regarded Bot as a busybody and sadly lacking in discretion.[176] The administration was, in any case, more interested in economic activities like rubber planting and tin mining and in the rapid expansion of the communications system. To be fair it should be mentioned that in the prevailing political and economic atmosphere there was a definite lack of incentive on the part of the Malays to produce more rice than was required for subsistence. The cash attraction of rubber was too tempting for the farmers to concentrate on padi.

The issue was allowed to languish for the next fifteen years and it was not until 1917 that the British authorities decided to act on the question of extending rice cultivation. In that year 'The Rice

Lands Enactment, 1917'[177] was passed with the purpose of reserving land for the express purpose of padi planting. The common view that there were not enough Malays interested in growing rice was, to some extent, dented by a statement by the Sultan of Selangor who announced that in Selangor alone 10,000 people were willing to grow the crop. He suggested that each cultivator be given three acres of land[178] and a certain amount of financial help. It also emerged that in Negri Sembilan many old padi fields had been destroyed by silt washed down from tin mines and rubber estates and needed extensive effort to render them suitable for padi again.[179]

The problems of Malay padi farmers were compounded by the fact that, prior to the construction of the Government Rice Mill in Krian in 1918, all milling and marketing facilities were controlled by Chinese entrepreneurs.[180] These buyers not only collected the padi from the *kampong* but also provided ready cash advances on the pledge of the next season's harvest. In return the Malays were forced to accept whatever prices were quoted by the buyers. The local Chinese provision shop too came into the picture by welcoming padi in return for goods taken on credit, or for cash loans.[181] As if these pressures were not serious enough, cash loans at high rates of interest were obtainable from Chettyar money-lenders for which padi land was pledged as security.[182]

In the final analysis, then, British rule, while establishing stable and peaceful conditions, did very little else for the average Malay. In spite of the occasional lofty pronouncements of prominent British officials over the years, the Malays remained confined to their own social and economic backwaters while all around them the Federation experienced an unprecedented boom and the British and other aliens benefited both economically and socially from the changed circumstances. The Government of the country was firmly in the control of British officials and it was widely acknowledged that the Malays neither had nor ought to have any vested interest in it.[183]

In education the principle underlying the organization of the Malay Vernacular Schools system was one of not wanting to over-educate the students so that, on leaving school, they would tend to follow the vocations of their parents and relations in the field of agriculture.[184] It was never the intention to educate the Malays so that they could significantly improve their lot in life. The one exception was the establishment of the élite-orientated Malay College in Kuala Kangsar which was geared to turn out prospective recruits for the lower rungs of the administrative service. The scale of the operation, however, was so small that in practice it represented only a spasmodic attempt by the authorities to create a class of Malays able to compete successfully with the Chinese and Indian immigrants who, till then, had dominated the subordinate ranks of the Civil Service.

In terms of employment little was accomplished in the attempt to infuse a significant Malay element into the government service. The only posts in which the Malays' monopoly was not threatened were the *penghulu*. In every other sector of the administrative service the Malays felt themselves discriminated against. British officials, in positions of power and responsibility, constantly ignored the directive which stated that Malays ought to be given preference over applicants of foreign origin.[185]

The Malay Agricultural Settlement established on the outskirts of Kuala Lumpur was an effort to engineer an urban Malay community able to take advantage of the better and more up-to-date facilities available in the larger towns of the Federation. The experiment, however, remained an isolated one and, even in that particular case, was not an outstanding success.

The Malay Reservations Enactment of 1913 was another irresolute attempt to safeguard the interests of the Malays. Besides the fact that the measure was introduced far too late, the administration did little, in the initial years of its application, to give effect to the spirit behind the legislation. In Negri Sembilan in 1916, for example, all that was done was to declare all important centres of Malay population as Malay Reservations. On the face of it this act was a creditable one but it did not take into account the fact that some of the valleys given up entirely to tin mining had, in the past, supported Malay settlements and, although these had been worked out and were not worth dredging, no steps were taken to return them to Malay possession.[186] The Bill was also riddled with loopholes which enabled Chinese and Indian capitalists to exploit gullible Malay peasants and acquire traditional Malay lands.

Extensive irrigation projects and the consequent encouragement of rice planting would have been one of the most practical methods of improving the economic position of the Malays. In the early years of the Federation the reluctance to commit large-scale expenditure, from not too large a revenue, confined British policy to the Krian Irrigation Scheme. But the persistence of these same attitudes, in years where the economic successes of rubber and tin ensured regular revenue surpluses, was incomprehensible. The Government remained totally uncommitted to helping the Malay agriculturalists and Krian was the only area where a large sum of money was expended in the period before 1920. Much land given out on *mukim* extracts soon became unsuitable for padi cultivation because the country had dried up to a large extent. The indiscriminate felling of jungle resulted in water running off rapidly making it impossible to grow padi. Areas around the Ipoh district that used to be under padi became too dry but in Pahang there were large tracts on which, if money was spent on irrigation schemes, padi could be grown.[187]

It took the First World War, the resultant shortage of rice, and the high prices charged for it, to convince the authorities that valuable opportunities had been lost over the years to put rice planting on a sound footing. The emergencies created by the war provoked the appointment of Food Control Committees in the Colony and the Federated Malay States, in December 1917, with F. S. James as Food Controller. Towards the end of 1918 the Government managed to purchase 60,000 tons of Thai rice in the market which proved invaluable in the subsequent years when rice became a very rare commodity indeed. Rampant speculation and the resulting price inflation created shortages throughout the country. At the request of the Food Controller a conference of the leading residents of Malaya was convened in Singapore on 15 May 1919 and it was decided that the Government should take over the entire control and distribution of rice. In May 1919 W. Peel was appointed Food Controller and a control scheme came into force on 1 July: the stocks of importers and wholesalers were taken over and no rice or padi could be imported into the country, except by the Controller. The movement of rice was also thenceforth dictated by the administration. The situation was so grave that a Food Production Department was set up to encourage the planting of foodstuffs such as *ragi* and hill padi. Thousands of acres were planted with these crops to assist the food situation.[188]

Another development that rankled with the Malays but attracted little concern from the Government was the increased presence of Chinese petty traders and itinerant vendors in Malay *kampong*. It was alleged that the Chinese tempted Malay women, when their husbands were away, to incur debts which they were later too ashamed to admit. The Chinese also advanced cash to Malays to collect jungle produce without licence and, in the event of the Malays being arrested, escaped punishment themselves, kept a double set of accounts, and produced the false set in civil suits; established piggeries to the annoyance of the Muslims; and were generally a source of great mischief in the Malay States.[189] The authorities, however, were unable to look at the problem from the Malay point of view and concerned themselves with the theory that all trade and commercial activity, however nefarious, should be left unrestricted.

In conclusion it may be said that British policies did not affect the rate of socio-economic change at the village level or the organization of Malay rural life. According to Roff the Malays were isolated from the economic and social stimuli that might have enabled them to create social structures and patterns of life more in harmony with twentieth-century conditions.[190] In its essence the situation represented yet another contradiction that British administration was a form of indirect rule designed primarily to benefit the indigenous population.

1. T. J. Newbold, *Political and Statistical Account of the British Settlements in the Straits of Malacca*, London, 1839; reprinted, Kuala Lumpur, 1971, Vol. 1, p. 418.

2. H. Marriott, 'Population of the Straits Settlements and Malay Peninsula during the last century', *JSBRAS*, No. 62, 1912, p. 31.

3. On his retirement Sir Orfeur Cavenagh wrote *Reminiscences of an Indian Official*, London, 1884.

4. Sadka, *The Protected Malay States*, p. 3.

5. J. F. A. McNair, *Perak and the Malays*, London, 1878, p. 156. The author was Colonial Engineer and Surveyor-General, Straits Settlements.

6. See Sadka, *The Protected Malay States*, p. 3, but Gullick, *Indigenous Political Systems*, p. 23, quoting the *Perak Annual Report*, 1888, put the total at 31,553.

7. J. Anderson, *Political and Commercial Considerations relative to the Malayan Peninsula and the British Settlements in the Straits of Malacca*, Prince of Wales Island, 1824; facsimile reprint *JMBRAS*, Vol. XXXV, No. 4, 1962, introduced by J. S. Bastin, pp. 190–202.

8. Sadka, *The Protected Malay States*, p. 3.

9. Gullick, *Indigenous Political Systems*, p. 23.

10. In Selangor in 1871–3 large numbers of settlers from the Selangor River fled to the Bernam valley in the north. See Sadka, *The Protected Malay States*, p. 4.

11. Ibid., pp. 4–6.

12. *Census of the State of Perak, 1891*, Taiping, 1892; Merewether, *Report on Census of April 1891*.

13. The population of the FMS in 1891 was 418,509. See A. M. Pountney, *The Census of the F.M.S., 1911*, London, 1911, p. 18.

14. The total population in 1901 was 678,595; in 1911 it had increased to 1,036,999; and in 1921 it reached 1,324,890. See Pountney, *Census of FMS, 1911*, p. 17; and Nathan, *Census of 1921*, p. 18.

15. The Chinese urban population in the same period changed from 67.2 per cent to 66.2 per cent in Perak, 67.4 per cent to 63.1 per cent in Selangor, 64.1 per cent to 68.5 per cent in Negri Sembilan, and 57.3 per cent to 66.1 per cent in Pahang. The Indian proportion moved from 19.1 per cent to 21.4 per cent, 18.1 per cent to 24.2 per cent, 16.4 per cent to 18.0 per cent, and 15.9 per cent to 15.0 per cent respectively. Ibid., pp. 27 and 42.

16. Pountney, *Census of FMS, 1911*, p. 27.

17. F. A. Swettenham, 'British Rule in Malaya', *Royal Colonial Institute*, Vol. XXVII, 1895–6, p. 276.

18. Swettenham, *Royal Colonial Institute*, Vol. XXVII, p. 276.

19. Clifford, *North American Review*, Vol. 177, 1903, pp. 399–409.

20. FMS Annual Report, 1900, Cmd. 815, *Parliamentary Papers*, Vol. LXVI, 1902. This was in accordance with Clifford's belief that the Malays should be guided rather than forced. The so-called natural indolence of the Malays was regretted but officials were reluctant to compel them to labour against their will. See Clifford, *North American Review*, Vol. 177, 1903, pp. 399–409.

21. These savings and remittances to India were, however, made at the cost of a frugal and stingy existence at a level barely bordering on subsistence. This contributed to the high incidence of ill-health among South Indian labourers. See Arasaratnam, *Indians in Malaysia and Singapore*, pp. 62–3.

22. For details see Jackson, *Planters and Speculators*; Jackson, *Immigrant Labour and the Development of Malaya*.

23. FMS Annual Report, 1902, Cmd. 1819, *Parliamentary Papers*, Vol. LX, 1904.

24. Editorial, *The Malay Mail*, 6 September 1898.

25. Ibid., 6 December 1897, 8 December 1897, and 6 September 1898.

26. R. J. Wilkinson, *Malay Beliefs*, Singapore, 1960, p. 81.

27. Ibid.

28. Quoted in Editorial, *The Malay Mail*, 21 February 1899.

29. It was claimed that before Federation, Malay headmen knew their few British officials and the few British officials knew them. Federation, instead of simplifying administration, had merely amplified it with little or no corresponding advantages to the Malays. Editorial, *The Malay Mail*, 11 April 1908.

30. Ibid., 6 December 1897, 8 December 1897, and 6 September 1898.

31. Ibid., 31 December 1897.

32. R. J. Wilkinson (ed.), *Papers on Malay Subjects*, introduced by P. L. Burns, Kuala Lumpur, 1971, p. 5.

33. *Proceedings of the Conference of Residents*, 3 to 7 December 1906.

34. Wilkinson, *Papers on Malay Subjects*, pp. 5–6.

35. R. O. Winstedt, born in August 1878, arrived in Perak in December 1902. He was appointed Inspector of Schools, Perak, and was later Assistant District Officer, Tapah, and Matang. In 1916 he was appointed Assistant Director of Education, SS and FMS. For more details see J. S. Bastin and R. Roolvink (eds.), *Malayan and Indonesian Studies*, Oxford, 1964, pp. 1–24.

36. A useful guide to the early editions of the Papers is C. A. Gibson-Hill, 'Notes on the Series "Papers on Malay Subjects" ', *JMBRAS*, Vol. XXV, Part 1,

1952, pp. 194–9. Also see R. O. Winstedt, 'Richard James Wilkinson (1867–5 December 1941)', *JMBRAS*, Vol. XX, Part 1, 1947, pp. 143–4.

37. Editorial, *The Malay Mail*, 15 January 1903.

38. *The Malay Mail*, 15 January 1903.

39. Unrestricted immigration policies and the subsequent construction of railways, for example, had led to the abandonment of the upkeep of cart roads along routes used frequently by bullock carts driven by Malays. This was especially true of routes between Klang and Kuala Lumpur. Editorial, *The Malay Mail*, 26 November 1909.

40. The Malays considered immigrants as greedy, less polite, and better accustomed to taking other people's property by guile. They asked the British to give the Malays a chance by quoting from a local saying which went, 'Don't starve the boatman because the greedy drought has dried up the river.' 'What the Malays Think', translated from *Utusan Melayu* and reprinted in *The Malay Mail*, 30 April 1908.

41. Editorial, *The Malay Mail*, 11 April 1908.

42. H. R. Cheeseman, 'Education in Malaya, 1900–1941', *The Malayan Historical Journal*, Vol. 2, No. 1, July 1955, p. 31.

43. FMS Annual Report, 1901, Cmd. 1297, *Parliamentary Papers*, Vol. LXVI, 1902.

44. The British were urged to maintain and revive the Malays' interest in the best of their traditions rather than encourage them to assume habits of life not really suited to their character, constitution, climate or the circumstances in which they lived. See Swettenham, *Royal Colonial Institute*, Vol. XXVII, 1896, pp. 288–90.

45. FMS Annual Report, 1920, *FMS Government Gazette*, 1921; also see G. Maxwell, 'Some Problems of Education and Public Health in Malaya', *United Empire*, Vol. XVIII, 1927, pp. 209–19.

46. Perak Annual Report, 1896, Cmd. 8661, *Parliamentary Papers*, Vol. LXI, 1898.

47. The 1891 Census of Perak put the Malay population of the State at 96,719.

48. Editorial, *The Malay Mail*, 6 December 1897.

49. Roff, *The Origins of Malay Nationalism*, p. 76.

50. Governor to CO, Confidential Desp., 18 August 1896, CO 273/1896.

51. The alternative was Malacca, but Swettenham wanted the school to be in Perak because more Malays would be attracted if the institution were to be sited in a Malay State. RG to HC, 21 February 1899, on Governor to CO, Desp. No. 49, 3 March 1899, CO 273/1899.

52. Perak Annual Report 1898, in Reports on the FMS for 1898 [Cmd. 9524], *Parliamentary Papers*, Vol. LXI, 1899.

53. Roff, *Origins of Malay Nationalism*, p. 132.

54. Ibid., p. 133.

55. Report on the Educational System of the FMS, January 1902, in Special Reports on Educational Subjects, Vol. 14, Part III [Cmd. 2379], *Parliamentary Papers*, Vol. XXVI, 1905, p. 385.

56. FMS Annual Report, 1909, Cmd. 5373, *Parliamentary Papers*, Vol. LXVI, 1910.

57. Roff, *Origins of Malay Nationalism*, p. 135.

58. FMS Annual Report, 1913, Cmd. 7709, *Parliamentary Papers*, Vol. XLVI, 1914–16.

59. FMS Annual Report, 1914, Cmd. 8155, *Parliamentary Papers*, Vol. XLVI, 1914–16.

60. *Federal Council Proceedings*, 1915.

61. HC to CO, Desp. No. 456, 2 December 1915, CO 273/1915.

62. Report by R. O. Winstedt, Assistant Director of Education, SS and FMS, On Vernacular and Industrial Education in the Netherlands East Indies and the Philippines, *SS Legislative Council Proceedings*, Council Paper No. 22, 1917.

63. This contrasted radically with the earlier views of Mitchell who was too obsessed with the necessity of imparting a literary type of education to Malay youth and was averse to any form of technical instruction for Malay school-teachers. Mitchell fervently believed that technical instruction had no place in fitting Malays for the profession of a schoolmaster. The Colonial Office, how-ever, did not agree and felt that the creation of a Malay 'Babu' on the Bengal plan was to be avoided with all possible care. Fiddian to Lucas, 3 May 1899, on Governor to CO, Desp. No. 49, 3 March 1899, CO 273/1899.

64. Report by Winstedt, *SS Legislative Council Proceedings*, 1917. For a critical examination of the Report and its repercussions, see Roff, *The Origins of Malay Nationalism*, pp. 136–42.

65. FMS Annual Report, 1916, *FMS Government Gazette*, 1917.

66. Roff, *The Origins of Malay Nationalism*, p. 135.

67. FMS Annual Report, 1898, Cmd. 9524, *Parliamentary Papers*, Vol. LXI, 1899.

68. FMS Annual Report, 1901, Cmd. 1297, *Parliamentary Papers*, Vol. LXVI, 1902.

69. FMS Annual Report, 1903, Cmd. 2243, *Parliamentary Papers*, Vol. LIV, 1905.

70. Wilkinson to RG, 24 February 1904, in *Minutes of the Conference of Residents*, March 1904.

71. Ibid.

72. Wilkinson to RG, in *Minutes of the Conference of Residents*, March 1904.

73. The Art School was established in Kuala Kangsar at the end of 1902 and provided practical teaching of weaving and embroidery; wood-carving and silversmiths' work; plaiting mats and making hats; and modelling artistic pottery. The teachers were all local Malays from different parts of Perak and were induced to settle in Kuala Kangsar by the Sultan and the Raja Muda, both of whom were keenly interested in the project. See Perak Annual Report, 1902, Cmd. 1819, *Parliamentary Papers*, Vol. LX, 1904.

74. Wilkinson to RG, in *Minutes of the Conference of Residents*, March 1904.

75. Rodger cited the existence of similar institutions in British India and the Dutch East Indies. His suggestion aimed at the possibility of appointing 'native gentlemen' to a Lower Division of the Civil Service distinct from, and superior to, the clerical service. Resident, Perak, to RG, 6 August 1903, on HC to CO, Desp. No. 480, 17 September 1904, CO 273/1904.

76. RG to HC, 2 September 1903, in ibid. For an account of the Raffles Institution, see E. Wijeysingha, *A History of the Raffles Institution*, Singapore, 1963. An interesting account of the Victoria Institution can be found in R. J. H. Sidney, *In British Malaya Today*, London, n.d.

77. Swettenham proposed the grant of ten scholarships annually, paying for board and education for a period of three to four years. These scholarships would be awarded on condition that they could be withdrawn or suspended if the holders failed to make satisfactory progress or if their conduct was unsatisfactory. HC to RG, 16 September 1903, in HC to CO, 17 September 1904, CO 273/1904.

78. RG to Acting HC, 12 March 1904, on ibid.

79. RG to Acting HC, 12 March 1904, on HC to CO, 17 September 1904, CO 273/1904.

80. Taylor also referred to the situation in Ceylon where the sons of chiefs and headmen got their education, not in any special institution, but in schools such as the Royal College, St. Thomas' College, and Trinity College, Kandy. After their education they entered government service in subordinate posts such as Native Writers, and rose to be Mudaliyars, Ratemahatmays, and Presidents of Village Tribunals, with salaries of between Rs. 1,200 and Rs. 1,800 a year. OAG to RG, 28 March 1904, in HC to CO, 17 September 1904, CO 273/1904.

81. For general accounts of English education in the Federation and the Straits Settlements see J. S. Nagle, *Educational Needs of the Straits Settlements and Federated Malay States*, Baltimore, 1928; J. S. Furnivall, *Educational Progress in Southeast Asia*, New York, 1944; D. D. Chelliah, *A Short History of the Educational Policy of the Straits Settlements, 1800–1925*, Kuala Lumpur, 1947; R. O. Winstedt, 'Education in Malaya, British Empire Exhibition', *Malayan Series Pamphlets*, No. XIV, London, 1924; H. R. Cheeseman, *The Malayan Historical Journal*, Vol. 2, No. 1, July 1955, pp. 30–47; H. R. Cheeseman, 'Education in Malaya', *Overseas Education*, Vol. XVII, No. 4, July 1946, pp. 346–54; and Vol. XVIII, No. 1, October 1946, pp. 391–400; J. B. Elcum, 'Education', *Twentieth Century Impressions of British Malaya*, pp. 267–80; H. C. Banner, 'The Growth of Education in Malaya', *The Asiatic Review*, Vol. XXVIII, No. 93, January, 1932, pp. 103–7.

82. The intelligent boys who won certificates and Queen's Scholarships were valuable advertisements to their teachers and were humoured rather than controlled. As a result the students became vain and made unreliable officials. Wilkinson knew every Queen's Scholar from 1896 to 1903 but only in one case was he confident in the ability of the boy to give advice which implied trust in his diligence and economy. Wilkinson had also seen most of the students at work in Cambridge and conversed with some of their tutors but did not think their successes had been commensurate with their abilities. The only exception was Dr. Guoh Lean Tuck who later joined the Institute of Medical Research, Kuala Lumpur. The Inspector of Schools concluded that, without attempting to deprecate what they had done, the existing schools were bad training grounds for character. Wilkinson to RG, 12 December 1903, in HC to CO, 17 September 1904, CO 273/1904.

83. Ibid.

84. RG to HC, 30 July 1904, in HC to CO, 17 September 1904, CO 273/1904.

85. For details see H. Drennan, 'A Short History of the Malay College', *Malay College Magazine*, Vol. 2, No. 5, 1955, pp. 8–15.

86. See Roff, *Origins of Malay Nationalism*, pp. 102–3; Raja Haji Kamarulzaman, 'Some Early Impressions at College, 1905–1908', *Malay College Magazine*, Vol. 2, No. 1, 1950, p. 60.

87. Roff, *Origins of Malay Nationalism*, p. 105.

88. *FMS Education Report, 1904*, Kuala Lumpur, 1905.

89. *FMS Education Report*, 1904.

90. Salaries offered to Malays were sometimes below those offered to other Asians in the Federation. The official rate of wages for Chinese coolies was higher than that for Malays. Malay assistant teachers were paid lower salaries than Tamil peons. For some time Malay policemen were paid less than their Sikh counterparts. In addition, Jaffna Tamil clerks were granted half-pay leave to return to their homes, while Malay clerks who wished to visit their parents on leave did so on no-pay leave. See B. O. Stoney, 'The Malays of British Malaya', Wright and Cartwright (eds.), *Twentieth Century Impressions of British Malaya*, p. 228.

91. *FMS Education Reports*, 1904.

92. R. J. Wilkinson, 'Malay Literature', *Papers on Malay Subjects*, Series 1, Part 1, Kuala Lumpur, 1907, p. 61.

93. For details see R. O. Winstedt, 'A History of Malay Literature', *JMBRAS*, Vol. XVII, 1939, pp. 1–243; reprinted Kuala Lumpur, 1969.

94. The question posed was whether such a system could be considered national and was it the end envisaged by its founders? The answer, it was believed, could only be obtained by a study of the people concerned. See R. J. Wilkinson, 'The Education of Asiatics', July 1901, in 'Special Reports on Educational Subjects', Vol. 8 [Cmd. 835], *Parliamentary Papers*, Vol. XXVI, 1902, p. 335.

95. Wilkinson to RG, in *Minutes of the Conference of Residents*, March 1904.

96. For more details see Sadka, *The Protected Malay States*, pp. 286–9.

97. Editorial, *The Malay Mail*, 8 March 1901.

98. See Sadka, *The Protected Malay States*, p. 114.

99. Perak Annual Report, 1900, Cmd. 815, *Parliamentary Papers*, Vol. LXVI, 1902.

100. Treacher did not subscribe to this argument and felt that it was a mistake to use such logic in a situation where the Government preferred its European officers to possess a fair knowledge of Malay or at least to be able to read and write it when it was written or printed in Roman characters, see W. H. Treacher, *Notes of Visits to Districts in Selangor, 1894*, Kuala Lumpur, n.d., p. 19.

101. E. W. Birch, 'The Malay Race in the FMS', 28 May 1906, Birch Papers. Quoted in Burns, Ph.D. Dissertation, University of London, 1966, pp. 295–6.

102. Editorial, *The Malay Mail*, 8 March 1901.

103. Editorial, *The Malay Mail*, 6 December 1897.

104. It was proposed that Government officers should not be allowed to engage Indians or hybrid Penang men as peons when there were plenty of Malays ready to fill the appointments. Also if the Thai and the Javanese railways could be entirely worked by the people of those countries, surely a few Malays could be employed in the FMS Railways as guards and ticket collectors. Editorial, *The Malay Mail*, 7 September 1897.

105. FMS Annual Report, 1902, Cmd. 1819, *Parliamentary Papers*, Vol. LX, 1904.

106. Resident, Perak, to RG, 6 August 1903, in HC to CO, Desp. No. 480, 17 September 1904, CO 273/1904.

107. HC to RG 16 September 1903, in HC to CO, Desp. No. 480, 17 September 1904, CO 273/1904.

108. The Memorial was signed by Mahomed Abas Inche Teh, and Mahomed

Cassim. Memorial to Acting State Engineer, Taiping, 6 June 1903, in HC to CO, 17 September 1904, CO 273/1904.

109. RG to Acting HC, 12 March 1904, in ibid.

110. Minutes of the Second Conference of Chiefs, 20 to 23 July 1903.

111. Rodger said that it was unfair to expect Malays to pass the same examinations that cadets sat for. He found it difficult, however, to over-estimate the value of responsibility in forming the character of young Malays and recommended that they be trained, in government departments, and be eventually fitted to fill important appointments in the administration of their own states. Ibid.

112. The Proclamation read: 'It is hereby proclaimed that in the opinion of the British Resident there will shortly be plenty of work to be had in the rubber plantations in Perak. This is the kind of employment familiar to Malays and they would exhibit both intelligence and industry in it. One man should be capable of tending 50 to 70 rubber trees. There can be no possible doubt that this kind of work is suited to Malays. It is easy work and moreover it is conducted in the shade and not in the heat of the sun. The European gentlemen who own these rubber plantations might find employment for two or three thousand Malays if they applied for it. We trust that when European gentlemen offer employment in the rubber plantations to persons of Malay race they will accept it and earn wages.' Quoted in Editorial, *The Malay Mail*, 20 July 1906.

113. Pountney, *Census of the FMS, 1911*.

114. In 1909 some indications were beginning to emerge that the administration was thinking along the same lines. As an instance, the Perak Government Gazette of November 1909 announced twenty vacancies for the entrance of probationers for the Survey Department into the Technical School in Kuala Lumpur, and stated that an endeavour would be made to give preference to Malays. In addition the Resident of Perak in his Annual Report drew attention to opportunities for Malays on rubber plantations not only in the area of tapping rubber but also in estate stores using machinery. The Report, however, acknowledged that so long as the price of rubber was high there was little inducement for *kampong* Malays, provided they had the foresight to catch the boom, to tap any other rubber but their own. Editorial, *The Malay Mail*, 26 November 1909.

115. Memorandum on the principal differences between the 1910 and 1917 schemes, in HC to CO, Desp. No. 182, 18 June 1917, CO 273/1917.

116. J. M. Gullick, 'The Malay Administrator', *The New Malayan*, Vol. 1, 1957, p. 78.

117. In 1895 there were 4; in 1905, 5; in 1915, 25; and in 1925, 28. These figures, even at their best, did not even amount to 25 per cent of the European MCS total. See Allen, *Comparative Studies in Society and History*, Vol. 12, No. 2, p. 177.

118. Memorandum on the differences between the 1910 and 1917 schemes, CO 273/1917.

119. *Scheme for Malay Officers*, 1 July 1917, Kuala Lumpur, 1917.

120. HC to CO, Desp. No. 108, 5 April 1917, CO 273/1917.

121. Raja Said Tauphy, born in 1878, was ex-Sultan Abdullah's fourth son. He was appointed settlement officer in 1900 and passed the cadets' examination in law in 1911. During the war he acted as Assistant District Officer and before his promotion to the MCS was a Malay Magistrate in Perak. HC to CO, Desp. No. 108, 5 April 1917, CO 273/1917.

122. HC to CO, Desp. No. 268, 4 September 1917, CO 273/1917.

123. HC to CO, Desp. No. 316, 25 October 1917, CO 273/1917.

124. Report of the Committee to Enquire into Salaries paid to the Office of the General Clerical Service, Council Paper No. 18, 1919, *Federal Council Proceedings*, 1919.

125. Interim Reports of the Retrenchment Committee, Council Paper No. 15, 1923, *Federal Council Proceedings*, 1923. The forty-first Interim Report was on the Employment of Malays in government service, and was compiled by a committee consisting of Y. S. Adams, Hamzah bin Abdullah, Mohammed Eusoff, and Raja Aznam Shah.

126. Allen, *Comparative Studies in Society and History*, Vol. 12, No. 2, p. 177.

127. Perak's first-ever non-MCS Mentri Besar was the Dato Panglima Bukit Gantang who had earlier been refused entry to the MCS and had turned down the MAS. This tendency strengthened the federal structure and accounted for the Malay dominance of the nationalist movement. Ibid., p. 177.

128. Selangor Annual Report, 1899, Cmd. 382, *Parliamentary Papers*, Vol. LV, 1900.

129. The area lay on what was then the north-eastern edge of Kuala Lumpur. The name of the settlement was later changed to 'Kampong Bahru' and remains so to this day.

130. The scheme was launched largely on the initiative of Douglas Campbell, the District Officer, Kuala Lumpur, and the Raja Muda of Selangor. The first meeting of the Board of Management took place on 11 March 1900 and was attended by the Raja Muda, Campbell, Robson, and Hale, Tamby Abdullah being absent. As the years went by the Board was enlarged. For details see J. Hands, 'Malay Agricultural Settlement, Kuala Lumpur', *The Malayan Historical Journal*, Vol. 2, No. 2, December 1955, pp. 146–62. Hands was an engineer who owned a rubber factory in Kajang and was a member of the Board from 1933 and Secretary from 1939 to 1941. He is best remembered for assisting the unemployed and distressed during the slump of the early 1930s and was the only non-Asian to be awarded the Malayan Certificate of Honour.

131. It was suggested that the Board should also insist on decent hedges being grown and supply the settlers with fruit-tree seedlings from one of the many Government experimental plantations. Editorial, *The Malay Mail*, 15 October 1907.

132. Selangor Annual Report, 1900, Cmd. 815, *Parliamentary Papers*, Vol. LXVI, 1902.

133. It was hoped that the improved access would attract more settlers. Selangor Annual Report, 1901, Cmd. 1297, *Parliamentary Papers*, Vol. LXVI, 1902.

134. Selangor Annual Report, 1902, Cmd. 1819, *Parliamentary Papers*, Vol. LX, 1904.

135. The Raja Muda became Chairman of the Board in May 1902 and the other members were E. Pratt (Secretary), Jelf, McCrakett, Shaw, Raja Mahmud, Raja Ali, and Penghulu Khatib Koyan. See Hands, *The Malayan Historical Journal*, Vol. 2, No. 2, p. 149.

136. Ibid., p. 149.

137. *The Malaysia Message*, February 1904.

138. Hands, *The Malayan Historical Journal*, Vol. 2, No. 2, p. 149.

139. Ibid., pp. 151–2.

140. Selangor Annual Report, 1908. Cmd. 4722, *Parliamentary Papers*, Vol. LXI, 1909.

141. Hands, *The Malayan Historical Journal*, Vol. 2, No. 2, p. 153.

142. A similar settlement was projected for Kinta Malays who had been ousted from their old homes by mining operations. It was to be situated about a mile out of Kampar. Editorial, *The Malay Mail*, 15 October 1907.

143. Selangor Annual Report, 1905, Cmd. 3186, *Parliamentary Papers*, Vol. LXXVIII, 1906.

144. Selangor Annual Report, 1906, Cmd. 3741, *Parliamentary Papers*, Vol. LXXIII, 1908.

145. It is interesting to note that between 1906 and 1913 rubber lands in Malaya increased from less than 100,000 acres to about 685,000 acres and were mainly European-owned. In the FMS in 1913, 408,000 acres were under rubber and a further 400,000 acres had been alienated for rubber and coconut plantations. See C. R. Akers, *The Rubber Industry in Brazil and the Orient*, London, 1914, pp. 171–3.

146. Speech by the Chief Secretary, *Federal Council Proceedings*, 9 July 1913.

147. *Minutes of the Conference of Residents*, 20 October 1908.

148. Speech by Sultan of Perak, *Federal Council Proceedings*, 9 July 1913.

149. Speech by J. O. Anthonisz, Acting Resident, Selangor, *Federal Council Proceedings*, 8 May 1911.

150. Editorial, *The Malay Mail*, 25 April 1910.

151. Perak Annual Report, 1911, Cmd. 5902, *Parliamentary Papers*, Vol. LX, 1912–13.

152. Perak Annual Report, 1912, Cmd. 7208, *Parliamentary Papers*, Vol. LX, 1914.

153. Perak Annual Report, 1913, Cmd. 7709, *Parliamentary Papers*, Vol. XLVI, 1914–16.

154. Speech by Legal Adviser, FMS, *Federal Council Proceedings*, 9 July 1913.

155. The danger had been foreseen by the Dutch in the Netherlands East Indies where the Government had decreed that no native of Java or the other islands in the archipelago could dispose of his land to a foreigner. The most he could do was to lease his holding for a term of years. Speech by Chief Secretary, *Federal Council Proceedings*, 9 July 1913.

156. For details of the Enactment, see A. B. Voules (ed.), *The Laws of the Federated Malay States, 1877–1920*, London, 1921, Vol. 2, pp. 505–8.

157. Although for the sake of convenience any alienated or State land could be included in a Malay Reservation, the restrictive effect of the Enactment was expected, in the case of alienated land, to operate only on the rights of people who were 'Malays' within the meaning of the Bill. See Report for the Secretary of State on FMS Enactment No. 15 of 1913, by the Legal Adviser, FMS, 24 February 1914, in HC to CO, Desp. No. 108, 3 March 1914, CO 273/1914.

158. Arasaratnam, *Indians in Malaysia and Singapore*, pp. 93–5.

159. Perak Annual Report, 1895, Cmd. 8257, *Parliamentary Papers*, Vol. LVIII, 1896.

160. The retail price in 1833 was 3 cents per *chapah* and this rose to 5 cents in January 1893. The field wages of Chinese labourers in 1833 were $4.36 per month, Indians and Malays being paid $2.90 per month; these rose in 1893 to

$7.12 and $4.75 per month respectively. In terms of percentages the price of rice rose by 66 per cent whilst wages rose between 63 per cent and 64 per cent. Minute by CS on Encouragement of Rice Cultivation in the Malay Peninsula, 28 January 1893, in Reports on the best means of encouraging the cultivation of rice in the Malay Peninsula, SGR, 1893.

161. Governor to CO, Desp. No. 187, 14 December 1897, CO 273/1897.

162. Governor to CO, 14 December 1897, CO 273/1897.

163. Ibid.

164. Cameron to Lucas, 17 February 1898, and Lucas to Selborne, 23 February 1898, on Governor to CO, 14 December 1897, CO 273/1897.

165. Swettenham to CO, 16 March 1898, CO 273/1898.

166. E. W. Birch, A Memorandum on the Subject of Irrigation for the Resident-General, Selangor Printing Office, 1898, enclosed in OAG to CO, Desp. No. 193, 17 May 1900, CO 273/1900.

167. The Perak, Pahang, Muar, Bernam, Selangor, Krian, and Linggi Rivers together with the countless streams of major and minor importance, and the innumerable valleys varying in size but alike in fertility, gave the Malay States an immense advantage in the formulation of irrigation schemes. Silt from the mines had caused a certain amount of damage to the padi fields but since mining arrangements were under Government control it was possible to work out some way whereby the padi farmer and the miner could co-exist. See Birch, Memorandum on Irrigation, CO 273/1900.

168. J. A. Swettenham was the elder brother of F. A. Swettenham. He was appointed writer in the Ceylon Civil Service in 1868 and served there till 1883 when he was transferred to Cyprus. In 1895 he was appointed Colonial Secretary, Straits Settlements. In 1901 he went to British Guiana as Governor and from 1904 to 1907 was Governor of Jamaica.

169. Acting Governor to CO, Desp. No. 188, 1 December 1898, CO 273/1898.

170. CO to OAG, Desp. No. 207, 16 July 1900, CO 273/1900.

171. The engineer-in-charge was Anderson who had some experience of irrigation in Australia. He soon discovered that O'Shaughnessy's estimates were founded on unreliable surveys and levels and were therefore useless. In May 1901, 2,000 labourers were employed and 12 miles of narrow gauge railway, 3 locomotives, and 180 wagons were in use. OAG to CO, Desp. No. 197, 25 May 1901, CO 273/1901.

172. It was expected that in the future Krian would have a settled population, in permanent houses, that could look forward to a sure grain crop every year. Bagan Serai became an important town overnight and showed signs of growing prosperity. Perak Annual Report, 1905, Cmd. 3186, *Parliamentary Papers*, Vol. LXXVIII, 1906.

173. Hale went on to say: 'It may be a matter for congratulation that the scheme will be a very profitable source of revenue, perhaps thinking men will also consider that the greater success will be achieved if a contented population is kept on the land, and two blades of padi are made to grow where only one grew before.' He also believed that padi deserved at least as much attention as rubber. Perak Annual Report, 1908, Cmd. 4722, *Parliamentary Papers*, Vol. LXI, 1909.

174. FMS Annual Report, 1900, Cmd. 815, *Parliamentary Papers*, Vol. LXVI, 1902.

175. Bot recalled the reign of Sultan Muhammad when on the Selangor River

from Telok Penyamun, on the right and left banks, as far as Kampong Kedah in the interior, nothing but padi fields predominated. Also on the Langat River, from Pendamaran to the Rambay River, many Malays worked on their dry rice fields or *ladang*. During Abdul Samad's reign rinderpest broke out and the bulk of the buffaloes in Selangor died; the majority of the Malays abandoned their rice fields having lost the principal implement of their trade. Raja Bot was critical of Abdul Samad for not being tough enough to insist on the activity being continued. The Selangor Civil War, in the late 1860s and early 1870s, caused further problems to the peasants and many Malays fled to places like Muar, Malacca, Perak, and Penang. See Letter from Raja Bot, giving his view on the subject of extending the area of rice cultivation, to Sultan Suleiman Aladdin Shah of Selangor and to the Resident-General, W. H. Treacher, 22 August 1902, in Governor to CO, Desp. No. 498, 11 December 1902, CO 273/1902. Also published in *The Malay Mail*, 14 November 1902.

176.   Governor to CO, Desp. No. 498, 11 December 1902, CO 273/1902.

177.   For details of the Enactment, see Voules, *Laws of the Federated Malay States*, pp. 125–7. Other sources relating to the need to maintain rice cultivation are A. S. Haynes, 'Memorandum on Extension of Rice Cultivation in the Federated Malay States: Need for a Definite Policy', Council Paper no. 28 of 1933, *Federal Council Proceedings*, 1933; E. J. Butler, 'Report on the Agricultural Department', Council Paper No. 19 of 1919, *Federal Council Proceedings*, 1919; Ding Eing Tan Soo Hai, *The Rice Industry in Malaya, 1920–1940*, Singapore, 1963.

178.   Although much land had been alienated for other forms of planting and belonged to private individuals and rubber companies there were still many forest reserves suitable for rice cultivation. Speech by Sultan of Selangor, *Federal Council Proceedings*, 17 November 1917.

179.   The damage caused by railway and road embankments was also considerable. The Resident, A. H. Lemon (1912–20), believed that so long as the Malay population produced all the padi it required for its own use they were unlikely to carry out irrigation works of any magnitude in new localities, and it was therefore necessary that these should be undertaken by the Government. It was also unfortunate that the Irrigation Department had not been able to devote much time to working out schemes of this kind. In this respect it was better to irrigate small areas with settled populations accustomed to padi planting rather than undertake grandiose schemes in areas that had no such populations. Negri Sembilan Annual Report, 1917, Cmd. 26, *Parliamentary Papers*, Vol. XXXVI, 1919.

180.   *Report of the Rice Cultivation Committee, 1931*, Vol. 1, para. 126.

181.   FMS Annual Report, 1922, *FMS Government Gazette*, 1923.

182.   Arasaratnam, *Indians in Malaysia and Singapore*, p. 93.

183.   Editorial, *The Malay Mail*, 11 April 1908.

184.   In one particular year, of the 2,900 boys who left school almost all went into agricultural pursuits. See E. W. Birch, 'The Federated Malay States', *United Empire*, New Series, Vol. III, 1912, p. 444.

185.   Interim Reports of the Retrenchment Committee, Paper No. 15 of 1923, *Federal Council Proceedings*, 1923.

186.   Negri Sembilan Annual Report, 1916, *Negri Sembilan Government Gazette*, 1917.

187.   Speech by A. W. Kenion, *Federal Council Proceedings*, 24 July 1917.

188. 'Memorandum on Food Control in Malaya' by W. Peel, 20 October 1919, in OAG to CO, Confidential Desp., 24 November 1919, CO 273/1919.

189. When Birch was Acting Resident in Negri Sembilan in 1897 he maintained strong views on these subjects and believed that the allegations mentioned were the inciting cause of several murders of Chinese. In such cases the clanship among the Malays baffled all efforts by the police to discover the culprits. Negri Sembilan Annual Report, 1897, Cmd. 9108, *Parliamentary Papers*, Vol. LXI, 1899.

190. Roff, *The Origins of Malay Nationalism*, p. 124.

RETROSPECT

THE signposts of change for the period under review are clear enough. The first was the constitutional measure which brought about the Federated Malay States and which represented the hopes and aspirations of the more prominent and ambitious British personalities in Malaya and London. Two decades of the Residential System had served to expose all the weaknesses inherent in an arrangement that did not place sufficient emphasis on uniformity of action and identity of purpose. The Treaty of Federation was a conscious effort to streamline the administration of the four Protected States and thus create a more suitable climate for the economic exploitation of the territory. In essence Federation was a British solution to the problems of the Malay States and was designed to further the interests of the colonial power. The principal responsibility for the future of the States was vested in the person of the Resident-General who, because of the vagueness of the Treaty, could act very much on his own initiative. During the first few years the ideas of Swettenham, and his strength of character and vast knowledge of the country, resulted in the introduction of proposals that strengthened the cohesiveness of the Federation. The succeeding Residents-General, Treacher and Taylor, lacked this dynamism and were unable to maintain either the momentum or the degree of harmony that had existed previously. Cracks emerged in the fabric of British administration. Residents became restive and dissatisfied, and some suggested changes were openly challenged.

The Federal Council Agreement of 1909, the next constitutional landmark, was an attempt to iron out the problems arising out of Federation. Anderson, the moving force behind the Agreement, was apprehensive of the growing importance of the Resident-General and sought to impose the personality of the High Commissioner on Malay States affairs. To justify this step he interpreted the uneasiness of Residents as being symptomatic of the failure of Residents-General to maintain an adequate balance between the central government and state administrations. Anderson argued that the direct participation of the High Commissioner in the details of Federal

Government would allay the fears of the Residents and the State governments. Subsequent events proved otherwise and the tendencies towards greater concentration of power and centralization of government continued unabated. The composition and the working of the Federal Council itself reflected Anderson's true motives. In this institution the official element was dominant, the Sultans were individual members and were equal in number with unofficials representing planting and mining interests. The presence of the unofficials was an added recognition of the importance of commercial and business enterprises in the development of the country.

Within the framework of these two sets of constitutional reforms economic considerations were foremost in the minds of the authorities and stringent efforts were made to encourage planters and miners to invest in enterprises within the Federation. Thus, government land policies treated European and Chinese land seekers with the utmost generosity and consideration. Realizing that an adequate labour force was a prerequisite to successful economic exploitation, the administration went to great lengths, and spent large sums of money, to devise ways and means of attracting an increasing number of immigrants from China and India for work on tin mines, agricultural plantations, and public works. In the beginning these efforts met with only moderate success but by 1920 the Federation had most of its labour requirements. But the officials and the private employers involved in this immigrant traffic were so preoccupied with the economic advantages that they failed to recognize the social and political problems this would create. As it happened, a plural society emerged where Malays, Chinese, and Indians formed separate and distinct entities each with its own religion, culture and language, and way of life. No attempts were made to integrate the three communities and although, as individuals, they did come into contact with one another these meetings were superficial and confined largely to the market place in the course of buying and selling.

Even the construction of roads and railways was undertaken not because of their social usefulness but with an eye to the exploitation of the economic potential of the country. The primary intention was to open up the remote areas and link the centres of business and commercial enterprise with the ports of the Federation. The railway system, in particular, was planned to meet the specific requirements of foreign entrepreneurs and to serve the urban, largely non-Malay, communities that had become the hubs of all financial transactions.

So far as the practical organization of day-to-day administration was concerned the most significant developments involved fundamental changes in the character of the civil service. It was converted from a narrow state-based service, recruited on an informal basis, into a unified institution serving the needs of the Federated Malay States and the Straits Settlements chosen as the result of a competitive examination held in London. These Civil Servants as a group were the undisputed leaders of the European community in Malaya because they had preceded the arrival of the handful of merchants, missionaries, and other categories with important financial influences. This factor, together with the positions they occupied in government, enabled the Civil Service to maintain its pre-eminence and ensured that its opinions on all issues were given sufficient consideration. According to Allen, the Civil Servants' dominance was strengthened by the fact that, by English standards, they belonged to a higher social stratum than those in other Government departments and had more 'gentlemen' than the planting community which was decidedly middle class.[1] The creation and growth of federal departments and specialized government agencies further contributed to the uniformity of practice and injected an air of purpose into subjects like education, legislation, land tenure, and financial management. Essentially, the role of the Civil Service was twofold. Firstly, it fulfilled its obligations as the organ which implemented policies worked out in Whitehall, Singapore, and Kuala Lumpur, and kept itself detached from the rest of the European community. Secondly, as a privileged group in Malaya, it represented the highest stratum of society in the country, zealously tried to maintain the *status quo*, and, in doing so, ensured its own comfortable position. Members of the service were unaware of any dichotomy in these two functions, and, throughout the period under review, succeeded in reconciling the two seemingly contrasting roles and avoiding any obvious dilemmas.[2]

This superstructure erected by the British authorities in the Federated Malay States achieved all the goals for which it was designed. Government administrative procedures were smooth and efficient, a favourable economic climate was created, and Federal finances looked remarkably healthy. But the repercussions these measures had on the traditional ruling élite and on the Malay peasantry were not wholly satisfactory. A characteristic of British policy towards the Malay aristocracy was that it was based on an alliance of convenience. The Sultans were provided with generous monetary allowances, allowed to enjoy the superficial trappings of pomp and ceremony, and freed from the uncertainties that could be created by rebellious subjects and court intrigues. In return for this security of tenure the Rulers were required to surrender most of their real powers and authority. In the beginning these arrangements were welcomed by the sovereigns who were tired of having to cope with uprisings, civil wars, and petty disturbances which had plagued the Malay States in the period preceding British intervention. The shift in the balance of power was, generally, made all the more palatable by the tact and diplomacy used by the British officials. The incident involving Sultan Abdullah of Perak and the Resident, J. W. W. Birch, was an exception but, even in this case, the situation was speedily rectified and cordial relations were established. Stringent efforts were made to create the impression that what was happening in the Protected Malay States was a form of indirect rule with the Sultans governing on the advice of Residents who were, in some sense, their servants. After Federation, however, the fiction of indirect rule was largely ignored and relations between the Sultans and the British authorities underwent significant changes. The honeymoon was over and some of the Rulers, comparing their positions with those of their counterparts in States not formally under British protection, realized that they had been stripped of all effective power. Efforts to turn the clock back were made by the Sultans of Perak and Pahang, and the Yamtuan Besar of Negri Sembilan, but their protestations were quickly dismissed by Swettenham and Anderson. Such arbitrary treatment was resented by the Rulers, and Sultan Idris of Perak even threatened to write to the King in England but there was nothing they could really do in the way of retaliation. They realized too late that they had become prisoners of their own devices and had only themselves to blame for the predicament they were in. The establishment of the Federal Council did nothing to improve matters and the sovereigns were forced to reconcile themselves with their reduced status and to make the best of the circumstances.

The loss in political power encompassed Malay princes and chiefs as well. British administration deprived them of their governmental functions, rights to levy and collect taxes, and privileges of exercising territorial independence. But they too were compensated in some ways by the authorities. By being appointed to State Councils they were given deliberative, albeit limited, roles in State government. In addition some of them, in their capacities as district chiefs, continued to exert a certain degree of responsibility in Malay customary life, were granted State pensions and allowances, and given preference in their applications for land mining rights, and so on. Early in the twentieth century the younger generation of Malay aristocrats were given an unexpected bonus in the shape of privileged educational facilities at the Malay College, Kuala Kangsar. Hopes were entertained that this élite institution would somehow improve the general position of the Malays and prepare them for life in the twentieth century. A scheme was formulated whereby the graduates from the College would be entitled to join a specially created Malay Administrative Service which, although distinctly inferior to the Malayan Civil Service, was sufficiently exclusive to set its members apart from the ordinary Malays. Perhaps what made the service even more prestigious was that non-Malays, although generally better off economically, were barred from the administrative ranks of the public service. Unfortunately, in the period up to 1920, the number of Malay boys who joined the Administrative Service did not reach sizeable proportions and even those who were recruited were often dissatisfied with the lack of promotion prospects.

The Raja Chulan case, and the unpleasantness this created between a prominent Perak Malay royal family and the authorities, was unique but clearly demonstrated some of the contradictions that could arise in the theory and practice of British policy. This episode, more than any other, highlighted one of the few flaws in the administrative system and, because of the obvious injustice to which the family of ex-Sultan Abdullah was subjected, remained a constant source of embarrassment to the Colonial power.

In contrast to the frequent, if superficial, contact between the traditional Malay ruling classes and the British administration, relations between the authorities and the Malay peasantry were kept to the bare minimum. The Government was particularly anxious not to introduce any measures which would disrupt or disorganize Malay village life for fear that these could cause economic discontent and social unrest. The idea was to keep the Malays in their traditional environment and encourage them to stick to their customary occupations. Thus in the alienation of land to European and Chinese agricultural and mining enterprises care was taken not to encroach, to any large extent, on Malay-held areas. The existence of large tracts of unoccupied land facilitated this operation and prevented the clash between modern techniques and traditional methods. Such a compartmentalization, however, broke down towards the end of the first decade of the twentieth century when shrewd and unscrupulous Chinese and Indian land speculators began to acquire more and more land belonging to Malays. Even so the administration was very reluctant to intervene and it was not until 1913 that the Malay Reservations Enactment was passed. Ostensibly the Act was designed to protect and maintain Malay land rights and thus ensure the continuance of a stable landed Malay peasantry, but the passage of the law was not accompanied by concerted attempts to implement the sentiments expressed. The result was that Malays continued to lose control of their hereditary holdings and were thus put at a greater disadvantage *vis-à-vis* the immigrant communities.

In the matter of education the British believed that Malay vernacular schools most suited the needs of the indigenous population. The aim was not so much to produce a core of educated Malays trained to take their rightful place in the new society that was emerging in Malaya, but to create a vigorous and self-respecting agricultural community. The emphasis was on the 3 R's and so long as this was achieved the authorities were satisfied. Accordingly Malay vernacular education failed to progress and was plagued by inefficient administration, unqualified teachers, and a high degree of pupil absenteeism.

The education policy might have made sense if constructive efforts to promote Malay agricultural enterprise had accompanied it. But between 1896 and 1920 the only tangible project undertaken by the Government was the Krian Irrigation Scheme which opened up a substantial area for padi cultivation. Since rice growing was dominated by Malay peasants it would have been the logical activity for the administration to have supported but, despite the success of the Krian padi farmers, the authorities preferred to leave future irrigation works to the initiative of private individuals. The bona fides of the British thus remained unproven, the output of rice continued to decrease, and the Malay masses became more and more impoverished. The lack of suitable alternative employment made matters worse and although there were no violent demonstrations, or even peaceful protests, it was clear that the Malays were getting a raw deal. The policies implemented by the Government, taken as a whole, only served to underline the fact that, in the period under review, socio-economic changes among the indigenous population were kept at a minimum.

It must, however, be pointed out that not everything done by the British was bad or harmful to the Malays. There is no doubt that the general conditions of life were improved, the bulk of the population was freed from the scourges of disease, and many of the superstitious beliefs that had formerly guided most actions were dissipated. The constant threat of local warfare was removed and the people could reap their rice, tap rubber, and engage in other private enterprises relatively unmolested. The Malays were also no longer subjected to unfair levies of taxation and could look forward to being treated impartially by the law.

By 1920, therefore, the situation within the Federated Malay States was clear. In the administration of the country the British authorities were all-powerful and made the important decisions. The Sultans, although leading comfortable lives, were reduced to positions of political nonentities with ceremonial functions only. Opportunities for the rest of the Malay aristocracy were severely limited and prospects for the emergence of a highly qualified and progressive indigenous élite were dim. The Malay peasantry, however, was in dire straits and was in danger of being completely submerged by the hardworking and materialistic Chinese and Indian immigrants. In the circumstances, if the interests of the indigenous inhabitants of the country were at all of concern to the British authorities a radical change of outlook was called for. The arrival, in 1920, of a new High Commissioner and the appointment of W. G. Maxwell as Chief Secretary to the Government held out distinct possibilities, but the events of succeeding years are beyond the scope of this dissertation.

1. J. de V. Allen, 'The Malayan Civil Service, 1874–1941: Colonial Bureaucracy/Malayan Elite', *Comparative Studies in Society and History*, Vol. 12, No. 2, April 1970, p. 171.

2. For details see Allen, *Comparative Studies in Society and History*, Vol. 12, No. 2, pp. 149–50.

APPENDICES

1. TREATY OF FEDERATION, 1895

AGREEMENT between the Governor of the Straits Settlements, acting on behalf of the Government of Her Majesty the Queen, Empress of India, and the Rulers of the following Malay States:– that is to say, Perak, Selangor, Pahang and the Negri Sembilan.

1. In confirmation of various previous Agreements, the Sultan of Perak, the Sultan of Selangor, the Sultan of Pahang, and the Chiefs of the States which form the territory known as the Negri Sembilan, hereby severally place themselves and their States under the protection of the British Government.

2. The above-named Rulers and Chiefs of the respective States hereby agree to constitute their countries a Federation, to be known as the Protected Malay States, to be administered under the advice of the British Government.

3. It is to be understood that the arrangement hereby agreed upon does not imply that any one Ruler or Chief shall exercise any power or authority in respect of any State other than that which he now possesses in the State of which he is the recognised Ruler or Chief.

4. The above-named Rulers agree to accept a British Officer, to be styled the Resident-General, as the agent and representative of the British Government under the Governor of the Straits Settlements. They undertake to provide him with suitable accommodation, with such salary as is determined by Her Majesty's Government, and to follow his advice in all matters of administration other than those touching the Muhammadan religion. The appointment of the Resident-General will not affect the obligations of the Malay Rulers towards the British Residents now existing or to be hereafter appointed to offices in the above-mentioned Protected States.

5. The above-named Rulers also agree to give to those States in the Federation which require it such assistance in men, money, or other respects as the British Government, through its duly appointed officers may advise; and they further undertake, should war break out between Her Majesty's Government and that of any other Power,

to send, on the requisition of the Governor, a body of armed and equipped Indian troops for service in the Straits Settlements.

Nothing in this Agreement is intended to curtail any of the powers or authority now held by any of the above-named Rulers in their respective States, nor does it alter the relations now existing between any of the States named and the British Empire.

The above Agreement was signed and sealed by the undermentioned Rulers and Chiefs of the various States in July, 1895.

His Highness the Sultan of Perak
His Highness the Sultan of Selangor
His Highness the Sultan of Pahang
His Highness the Yam Tuan Besar of Sri Menanti
The Dato' Bandar of Sungei Ujong
The Dato' of Johol
The Dato' of Jelebu
The Dato' of Rembau
The Tungku Dewa of Tampin

2. AGREEMENT FOR THE CONSTITUTION OF A FEDERAL COUNCIL, 1909

AGREEMENT between the High Commissioner of the Federated Malay States acting on behalf of the Government of His Majesty the King, Emperor of India, and the Rulers of the Federated Malay States of Perak, Selangor, Pahang and Negri Sembilan.

Whereas by the Treaty entered into in July, 1895, known as the Treaty of Federation the above-named Rulers agreed to constitute their countries a Federation to be known as the Protected Malay States to be administered under the advice of the British Government, and whereas the above-named Federation was duly constituted as provided in above-named Treaty, and whereas the above-named Rulers further desire that means should be provided for the joint arrangement of all matters of common interest to the Federation or affecting more than one State and for the proper enactment of all laws intended to have force throughout the Federation or in more than one State, it is hereby agreed:

1. That on and after a date to be fixed by His Majesty a Council shall be established to be known as the Federal Council of the Federated Malay States.

2. In the first instance the following shall be members of the Council:

The High Commissioner
The Resident-General
The Sultan of Perak
The Sultan of Selangor
The Sultan of Pahang
The Yam Tuan of Negri Sembilan as representing the Undang of the Negri Sembilan
The Resident of Perak
The Resident of Selangor
The Resident of Pahang
The Resident of Negri Sembilan
Four unofficial members to be nominated by the High Com-

missioner with the approval of His Majesty. The absence of any member shall not invalidate any proceedings of the Council at which he has not been present.

3. If hereafter it should in the opinion of the High Commissioner be desirable to add to the Council one or more of the heads of the various public departments, he may do so subject to the approval of His Majesty, and may in such case and subject to the like consent also nominate not more than one additional unofficial member for every official member so added to the Council.

4. A head of a department who is nominated to the Council shall hold office so long as the High Commissioner thinks fit. Unofficial members shall hold office for three years.

5. The High Commissioner shall be President of the Council and in his absence the Resident-General shall be President.

5A. The Legal Adviser of the Government may attend any sitting of the Council and assist in the discussion of any legal questions which may arise in the course of its proceedings but shall not be entitled to a vote; and any head of a public department may similarly attend and assist in the discussion of any matter affecting his department but shall not be entitled to a vote.

6. If any of the Rulers above-named is unable to be present he may nominate one of the members of his State Council to represent him. In the case of Negri Sembilan, the nomination shall be by the Undang.

7. The Council shall meet at least once in every year at a place to be appointed from time to time by the High Commissioner.

8. Unless the President of the Council shall certify in writing that it is a matter of urgency every law proposed to be enacted by the Council shall be published in the Government *Gazette* at least one month before being submitted to the Council.

9. Laws passed or which may hereafter be passed by the State Councils shall continue to have full force and effect in the State except in so far as they may be repugnant to the provisions of any law passed by the Federal Council, and questions connected with the Mohammedan Religion, Mosques, Political Pensions, Native Chiefs and Penghulus and any other questions which in the opinion of the High Commissioner affect the rights and prerogatives of any of the above-named Rulers or which for other reasons he considers should properly be dealt with only by the State Councils shall be exclusively reserved to the State Councils.

10. The Draft Estimates of Revenue and Expenditure of each State

shall be considered by the Federal Council, but shall immediately on publication be communicated to the State Councils.

11. Nothing in this Agreement is intended to curtail any of the powers or authority now held by any of the above-named Rulers in their respective States, nor does it alter the relations now existing between any of the States named and the British Empire as established by previous Treaties.

The above Agreement was signed and sealed by His Excellency Sir John Anderson, G.C.M.G., High Commissioner for the Federated Malay States, on the twentieth day of October, 1909, having been signed and sealed before that date by the undermentioned Rulers and Chiefs of the Federated Malay States:

His Highness the Sultan of Perak
His Highness the Sultan of Selangor
His Highness the Regent of Pahang
His Highness the Yang-di-Pertuan Besar of Negri Sembilan
The Dato' Klana Petra of Sungei Ujong
The Dato' of Johol
The Dato' of Jelebu
The Dato' of Rembau
The Tungku Dewa of Tampin

3. FMS ENACTMENT NO. I OF 1911

An Enactment to Incorporate the Chief Secretary to Government

John Anderson,
President of the Federal Council
(19 January, 1911)

Whereas by an Agreement signed and sealed in the month of July, 1895, the Rulers and Chiefs of Perak, Selangor, Pahang and Negri Sembilan agreed to constitute their countries a Federation to be administered under the advice of the British Government and agreed further to accept a British Officer, to be styled the Resident-General, as the agent and representative of the British Government under the Governor of the Straits Settlements and undertook amongst other things to follow his advice in all matters of administration other than those touching the Muhammadan religion, but so that the appointment of the Resident-General should not affect the obligations of the said Rulers towards the British Residents then existing or to be thereafter appointed to offices in the above mentioned States: And whereas by certain Enactments passed by their Highnesses the Sultans of Perak, Selangor, and Pahang and by His Highness the Yang di Pertuan and Chiefs of Negri Sembilan in Council in and for their respective States it is among other things enacted that the British Officer appointed in pursuance of the above-named agreement to be the Resident-General and his successors shall be a body corporate, and for the purposes of the said Enactments have the name of 'The Resident-General' and shall and may have and use a corporate seal, and the said seal may from time to time break, change, alter and make anew as to the said Corporation may seem fit; and the said Corporation is by the said Enactments empowered to sue, and be sued, to enter into contracts, to acquire, purchase, take, hold and enjoy movable and immovable property of every description, and to sell, convey, assign, surrender and yield up, mortgage, demise, reassign, transfer or otherwise dispose of any movable and immovable property vested in the said Corporation upon such terms as to the said Corporation may seem fit.

And whereas the Rulers of the States hereinbefore named, with the consent of the British Government, are minded that the British Officer appointed or hereinafter to be appointed in pursuance of the agreement above referred to shall hereafter be styled 'the Chief Secretary to Government' and not as heretofore 'the Resident-General' but shall nevertheless possess and enjoy all and every one of the rights, privileges and powers conferred, and exercise all and every one of the duties imposed upon the Resident-General by the agreement and Enactments hereinbefore referred to and by any law heretofore enacted by the Ruler or the Ruler and Chiefs of any of the above mentioned States in Council or by the Rulers of the Federated Malay States in Council except in so far as such law shall have been or may hereafter be repealed by the Rulers of the Federated Malay States in Council or by the Ruler or Ruler and Chiefs in Council of the State in and for which it was enacted.

Now therefore it is hereby enacted by the Rulers of the Federated Malay States in Council as follows:

Short title and Commencement	1. This Enactment may be cited as 'The Chief Secretary (Incorporation) Enactment, 1911' and shall come into force upon the 1st day of February, 1911.
Repeal	2. On the coming into force of this Enactment the Enactments specified in the schedule hereto shall be repealed in so far as the continued operation of the said Enactments is or might be inconsistent with the provisions of this Enactment or the operation thereof.
The Incorporation of Chief Secretary to Government	3. Sir Arthur Henderson Young, Knight Commander of the Most Distinguished Order of St. Michael and St. George, and his successors in the office of Chief Secretary to Government shall be a body corporate, and shall for the purposes of this Enactment have the name of 'Chief Secretary to Government' and by that name have perpetual succession and shall and may have and use a corporate seal, and the said seal may from time to time break, change, alter and make anew as to the said Corporation may seem fit; and the said Corporation is hereby empowered to sue and be sued, to enter into contracts, to acquire, purchase, take, hold and enjoy movable and im-

movable property of every description and to sell, convey, assign, surrender and yield up, mortgage, demise, reassign, transfer or otherwise dispose of any movable or immovable property vested in the said Corporation upon such terms as to the said Corporation may seem fit.

Model of sealing deeds

4. All deeds, documents and other instruments requiring the seal of the said Corporation shall be sealed with the seal of the said Corporation in the presence of the said Sir Arthur Henderson Young or in the presence of his successor for the time being in the office of Chief Secretary to Government, and shall also be signed by the said Sir Arthur Henderson Young or by his said successor, and such signing shall be, and shall be taken as, sufficient evidence of the due sealing of such deeds, documents or other instruments.

Property to vest

5. All property, movable and immovable, of whatever description which immediately before the commencement of this Enactment was vested in the Resident-General shall on such commencement vest in the Chief Secretary to Government, and all rights, powers and authority belonging to or attaching immediately before such commencement to the Resident-General or which would have thereafter accrued to the Resident-General by virtue of anything done before such commencement and all duties imposed upon the Resident-General shall belong, attach, accrue or be deemed imposed upon the Chief Secretary to Government.

Written laws or documents

6. Wherever in any written law or document passed or made before the commencement of this Enactment the words 'Resident-General' occur such written law or document shall be read as if the words 'Chief Secretary to Government' were from the commencement of this Enactment substituted for the words 'Resident-General'.

Actions pending

7. All actions and proceedings commenced by or in the name of the Resident-General before the commencement of this Enactment may be con-

tinued, carried on and completed after such commencement by or in the name of the Chief Secretary to Government.

Seal of Resident-General may be continued in use

8. Until a new seal has been made for the use of the Chief Secretary to Government the seal in use at the commencement of this Enactment as the seal of Resident-General may be used and shall if and so long as it is used after the commencement of this Enactment be deemed to be the seal of the Chief Secretary to Government.

Appointment of successors and of acting officers

9. If at any time after the commencement of this Enactment the Chief Secretary to Government for the time being shall be absent from the Federated Malay States or shall otherwise be incapable of performing all or any of the duties or exercising any of the rights, powers or authority belonging to or attaching to the office of Chief Secretary to Government or shall have resigned or been removed from such office it shall be lawful for the High Commissioner with the approval of the British Government to appoint some other person to be his successor in the office of Chief Secretary to Government or to act temporarily for him in the said office, as the case may be, and a notification in the Gazette of such appointment shall be conclusive evidence for all purposes that such person was duly so appointed and it shall be lawful for any person so appointed to act in the office of Chief Secretary to Government to do and perform the continuance of such appointment all or any of the things which may lawfully be done or performed by the Chief Secretary to Government and anything so done or performed shall be deemed to have been done or performed by the Chief Secretary to Government.

SCHEDULE

State	No. and Year	Short title
Perak	18 of 1898	Resident-General's (Incorporation) Enactment, 1898
Selangor	19 of 1898	do.
N. Sembilan	15 of 1898	do.
Pahang	4 of 1899	Resident-General's (Incorporation) Enactment, 1899

Passed this 19th day of January, 1911

Claud Severn,
Clerk of Council

BIBLIOGRAPHY

I PRIMARY SOURCES

(a) *Official: Unpublished*

The principal sources for the period are the series of Colonial Office papers

CO 273 Straits Settlements and Malay States original correspondence 1838–1919

CO 717 Malay States original correspondence from 1920 onwards

CO 537 Additional Despatches, 1873–1898

which should be used in conjunction with

CO 426 Straits Settlements Register of Correspondence 1867–1919

All the above can be found at the Public Record Office, London. Further manuscript collections of records located at the Arkib Negara Malaysia, Kuala Lumpur, include

Selangor Government Records 1874–1920

Selangor State Council Proceedings, 1877–1941.

(b) *Official: Published*

(i) PARLIAMENTARY PAPERS (GREAT BRITAIN)

Protected Malay States and Federated Malay States Annual Reports can be found in:

1874: Vol. XLV, Cmd. 1111, pp. 611 et seq.

1875: Vol. LIII, Cmd. 1320, pp. 55 et seq.

1876: Vol. LIV, Cmd. 1505, pp. 287 et seq.; Cmd. 1512, pp. 669 et seq.

1877: Vol. LXI, Cmd. 1709, pp. 395 et seq.

1879: Vol. LI, Cmd. 2410, pp. 409 et seq.

1882: Vol. XLVI, Cmd. 3285, pp. 661 et seq.; Cmd. 3428, pp. 705 et seq.; Cmd. 3429, pp. 683 et seq.

1884: Vol. LV, Cmd. 4192, pp. 419 et seq.

1886: Vol. XLVI, Cmd. 4627, pp. 603 et seq.

1887: Vol. LVIII, Cmd. 4958, pp. 357 et seq.

1888: Vol. LXXII, Cmd. 5352, pp. 813 et seq.; Cmd. 5566, pp. 669 et seq.

1889:   Vol. LVI, Cmd. 5884, pp. 629 et seq.
1890–1:   Vol. LVII, Cmd. 378, pp. 513 et seq.; Cmd. 6222, pp. 351 et seq.; Cmd. 6290, pp. 445 et seq.
1892:   Vol. LVI, Cmd. 6576, pp. 333 et seq.
1893–4:   Vol. LXI, Cmd. 6858, pp. 255 et seq.; Cmd. 7228, pp. 357 et seq.
1894:   Vol. LVII, Cmd. 7546, pp. 431 et seq.
1895:   Vol. LXX, Cmd. 7784, pp. 773 et seq.; Cmd. 7877, pp. 695 et seq.
1896:   Vol. LVIII, Cmd. 8257, pp. 303 et seq.
1898:   Vol. LIX, Cmd. 8661, pp. 20 et seq.
1899:   Vol. LXI, Cmd. 9108, pp. 1 et seq.; Cmd. 9524, pp. 79 et seq.
1900:   Vol. LV, Cmd. 382, pp. 459 et seq.
1902:   Vol. LXVI, Cmd. 815, pp. 863 et seq.; Cmd. 1297, pp. 957 et seq.
1904:   Vol. LX, Cmd 1819, pp. 307 et seq.
1905:   Vol. LIV, Cmd. 2243, pp. 527 et seq.
1906:   Vol. LXXVIII, Cmd. 2777, pp. 355 et seq.; Cmd. 3186, pp. 455 et seq.
1908:   Vol. LXXIII, Cmd. 3741, pp. 597 et seq.
1909:   Vol. LXI, Cmd. 4471, pp. 1 et seq.; Cmd. 4722, pp. 33 et seq.
1910:   Vol. LXVI, Cmd. 5373, pp. 779 et seq.
1911:   Vol. LIII, Cmd. 5902, pp. 209 et seq.
1912–13: Vol. LX, Cmd. 6562, pp. 145 et seq.
1914:   Vol. LX, Cmd. 7208, pp. 331 et seq.
1914–16: Vol. XLVI, Cmd. 7709, pp. 299 et seq.; Cmd. 8155, pp. 343 et seq.
1916:   Vol. XXXVI, Cmd. 26, pp. 299 et seq.
1920:   Vol. XXXIII, Cmd. 1094, pp. 577 et seq.

In addition to the Annual Reports the above papers also deal with appointments of British Residents to the Malay States as well as subjects like land ownership and the case of ex-Sultan Abdullah of Perak.

Parliamentary Papers dealing with special subjects include

'The Education of Asiatics', by R. J. Wilkinson in *Special Reports on Educational Subjects*, Vol. 8, Cmd. 835 of 1902, pp. 335 et seq.

'The System of Education in the FMS' and 'The System of Education in the SS', in *Special Reports on Educational Subjects*, Vol. 14, Cmd. 2379 of 1905, pp. 385 et seq.

'*Report by the Rt. Hon. W. G. A. Ormsby-Gore on his visit to Malaya, Ceylon and Java in 1928*', Cmd. 3235 of 1928–9, pp. 791 et seq.

'*Report by Sir Samuel Wilson on his visit to Malaya*', Cmd. 4276 of 1932–3, pp. 501 et seq.

(ii) COUNCIL PAPERS (FEDERAL COUNCIL, FMS)
Papers printed with the Federal Council Proceedings
'Report of the Committee on General Clerical Service Salaries', No. 18 of 1919.
'Interim Reports of the Retrenchment Commission' including 'Report of a Committee on Employment of Malays in the Government Service', No. 15 of 1923.
Papers printed separately
Final Report of the Retrenchment Commission, Kuala Lumpur, 1923, No. 16 of 1923.
Report of the Rice Cultivation Committee, Kuala Lumpur, 1931, No. 24 of 1931, 2 vols.

(iii) COUNCIL PAPERS (LEGISLATIVE COUNCIL, SS)
Papers printed with the Legislative Council Proceedings
'Report by Mr. R. O. Winstedt, Assistant Director of Education, SS and FMS, on Vernacular and Industrial Education in the Netherlands East Indies and the Philippines', No. 22 of 1917.

(iv) COUNCIL PROCEEDINGS
Proceedings of the Federal Council of the FMS, 1909–20.
Proceedings of the Legislative Council of the SS, 1895–1920.

(v) COLLECTIONS OF LAWS

Federal
FORRER, H. A. (comp.), *Chronological Lists of State and Federal Laws 1877–1932 with Rules*, Kuala Lumpur, 1933.
GIBSON, W. S. (comp.), *The Laws of the FMS and each of them in force on the 31 day of December, 1934*, London, 1935, 4 vols.
VOULES, A. B. (comp.), *The Laws of the FMS 1877–1920*, London, 1921, 3 vols.

Pahang
Pahang Laws passed by the State Council between the 31 December 1889 and 8 January 1896, Kuala Lumpur, 1897.

Perak

MAXWELL, W. G. (comp.), *The Perak Laws 1877–1903*, Kuala Lumpur, 1905, 2 vols.

TREACHER, W. H. (comp.), *The Orders of His Highness the Sultan of Perak in Council from 11 September 1897 to 29 February 1888*, Taiping, 1892.

VOULES, A. B. (comp.), *The Laws of Perak, Orders in Council and Enactments passed by the State Council, 1877–1896*, Taiping, 1899.

Negri Sembilan

BIRCH, E. W. (comp.), *The Laws of Negri Sembilan, 1887–1896*, Kuala Lumpur, 1900.

DESBOROUGH, C. E. M. (comp.), *Negri Sembilan Laws*, Kuala Lumpur, 1896.

DINSMORE, W. H. (comp.), *Negri Sembilan Laws, 1883–1902*, Singapore, 1900.

Selangor

KEMP, C. (comp.), *Regulations and Rules and Orders from 18 April 1877 to 31 December 1889*, Kuala Lumpur, 1892.

ROBSON, J. H. M. (comp.), *The Laws of Selangor, 1877–1895*, Kuala Lumpur, 1896.

VOULES, A. B. (comp.), *The Laws of Selangor, 1877–1899*, Kuala Lumpur, 1901.

Executive Orders

    Circulars and Schemes Issued by the Resident-General's Office 1896–1902, revised and amended to 6 March 1903, Kuala Lumpur, 1903.

    General Orders of the FMS, Taiping, 1900.

    General Orders of the FMS, revised up to November 1903, Taiping, n.d.

    General Orders of the FMS, revised up to December 1913, Kuala Lumpur, 1914.

ROBSON, J. H. M. and BERRINGTON, A. T. D. (comps.), *Selangor Orders and Notifications*, Kuala Lumpur, 1895.

Census Reports

    Census of the State of Perak, 1891, London, 1892.

DEL TUFO, M. V. (comp.), *Malaya: A Report on the 1947 Census of Population*, London, 1949.

MEREWETHER, E. M. (comp.), *Report of the Census of the Straits Settlements taken on 5th April, 1891*, Singapore, 1892.

NATHAN, J. E. (comp.), *The Census of British Malaya, 1921*, London, 1922.

POUNTNEY, A. M. (comp.), *The Census of the FMS, 1911*, London, 1911.

Report on the Census of the FMS, 1901, Kuala Lumpur, 1901.

VLIELAND, C. A. (comp.), *British Malaya: A Report on the 1931 Census*, London, 1932.

Miscellaneous Items

Abstract of Proceedings, Conference of Residents, 1905, 1907–9, 1911, and 1922–31, Kuala Lumpur, 1931.

Colonial Office Eastern Pamphlet No. 24A.

Colonial Office Lists, various years.

Correspondence Respecting the Federation of the Protected Malay States, May 1893–December 1895, Taiping, 1896.

FMS Civil Service Lists, 1904, 1920, and 1938, Kuala Lumpur, 1904, 1920, 1938.

HARVEY, J. A. (comp.), *Index of Decisions of Residents' Conferences, 1897–1928*, Kuala Lumpur, 1928.

Scheme for Salaries of Teachers in Government Schools, Kuala Lumpur, 1902.

Scheme for Malay Officers, 1 July 1917, Kuala Lumpur, 1917.

Scheme for Malay Inspectors of Police, Kuala Lumpur, 1917.

Scheme for Malay Officers in the Agricultural Department of the FMS, 1 June 1918, Kuala Lumpur, 1918.

(c) *Unofficial: Published*

NEWSPAPERS
The Malay Mail
The Singapore Free Press
The Straits Budget
The Straits Times

MONTHLY PERIODICAL
The Malaysia Message, Singapore. Issued by the Methodist Episcopal Mission, Singapore.

II SECONDARY SOURCES

(i) *Books*

ABDUL MAJID BIN ZAINUDDIN, *The Malays of Malaya, By One of Them*, Singapore, 1928.

AKERS, C. R., *The Rubber Industry in Brazil and the Orient*, London, 1914.

ALLEN, C. C. and DONNITHORNE, A. G., *Western Enterprise in Indonesia and Malaya*, London, 1957.

ANDERSON, J., *Political and Commercial Considerations relative to the Malayan Peninsula and the British Settlements in the Straits of Malacca*, Prince of Wales Island, 1824.

ANSON, A. E., *About Myself and Others*, London, 1920.

ARASARATNAM, S., *Indians in Malaysia and Singapore*, Kuala Lumpur, 1970.

BASTIN, J. S., *The Study of Modern Southeast Asian History*, An Inaugural Lecture delivered on 14 December 1959 at the University of Malaya, Kuala Lumpur, 1959.

BASTIN, J. S. and ROOLVINK, R. (eds.), *Malayan and Indonesian Studies*, Oxford, 1964.

BAUER, P. T., *The Rubber Industry*, London, 1948.

BEGBIE, P. J., *The Malayan Peninsula*, Madras, 1834; reprinted Kuala Lumpur, 1967.

BERTRAM, A., *The Colonial Service*, Cambridge, 1930.

BIRD, I. L., *The Golden Chersonese and the Way Thither*, London, 1883; reprinted Kuala Lumpur, 1967.

BLYTHE, W. L., *The Impact of Chinese Secret Societies in Malaya*, London, 1969.

BODELSEN, C. A., *Studies in Mid-Victorian Imperialism*, London, 1960.

BRADDELL, R., *The Law of the Straits Settlements*, Singapore, 1931. —— *The Legal Status of the Malay States*, Singapore, 1931.

CAMERON, J., *Our Tropical Possessions in Malayan India*, London, 1865.

CAMPBELL, P. C., *Chinese Coolie Emigration to Countries Within the British Empire*, London, 1971.

CAVENAGH, O., *Reminiscences of an Indian Official*, London, 1884.

CHAI HON CHAN, *The Development of British Malaya, 1896–1909*, Kuala Lumpur, 1964; reprinted Kuala Lumpur, 1967.

CHEESEMAN, H. R., *Bibliography of Malaya*, London, 1959.

CHELLIAH, D. D., *A Short History of the Educational Policy of the Straits Settlements*, Kuala Lumpur, 1947.

CLARKE, A., *India, Ceylon, and the Straits Settlements*, London, 1906.

CLIFFORD, H., *Expedition to Trengganu and Kelantan*, Kuala Lumpur, 1895.

—— *In Court and Kampong*, London, 1897.

—— *The Further Side of Silence*, New York, 1922.

—— *Bushwhacking and Other Asiatic Tales and Memories*, London, 1929.

CLODD, H. P., *Malaya's First British Pioneer: The Life of Francis Light*, London, 1948.

COMBER, L. F., *Chinese Secret Societies in Malaya, a Survey of the Triad Society from 1800 to 1900*, New York, 1959.

COURTENAY, P. P., *A Geography of Trade and Development in Malaya*, London, 1972.

COWAN, C. D., *Nineteenth Century Malaya, the Origins of British Political Control*, London, 1961.

—— (ed.), *The Economic Development of Southeast Asia*, London, 1964.

CRAWFURD, J., *Journal of an Embassy from the Governor General of India to the Courts of Siam and Indo-China . . .*, London, 1828; reprinted Kuala Lumpur, 1967.

DING EING TAN SOO HAI, *The Rice Industry in Malaya, 1920–1940*, Singapore, 1963.

DISSETT, J. W. (ed.), *Who's Who in Malaya*, Singapore, 1918.

EMERSON, R., *Malaysia: A Study in Direct and Indirect Rule*, New York, 1937; reprinted Kuala Lumpur, 1964.

Fifty Years of Railways in Malaya, 1885–1935, Kuala Lumpur, 1935.

FIRTH, RAYMOND, *Malay Fishermen: Their Peasant Economy*, London, 1946.

FIRTH, ROSEMARY, *Housekeeping Among Malay Peasants*, London, 1966.

FURNIVALL, J. S., *Netherlands India, a Study in Plural Economy*, Cambridge, 1944.

—— *Educational Progress in Southeast Asia*, New York, 1944.

—— *Colonial Policy and Practice, A Comparative Study of Burma and Netherlands India*, London, 1948.

GARVIN, J. L., *The Life of Joseph Chamberlain, Vol. III: 1895–1900*, London, 1934.

GINSBURG, N. and ROBERTS, P. E., *Malaya*, Singapore, 1958.

14

GRIST, D. H. (comp.), *An Outline of Malayan Agriculture*, Kuala Lumpur, 1936.

GUILLEMARD, L., *Trivial Fond Records*, London, 1937.

GULLICK, J. M., *Indigenous Political Systems of Western Malaya*, London, 1958.

—— *A History of Selangor, 1742–1957*, Singapore, 1960.

INNES, E., *The Chersonese With the Gilding Off*, London, 1885; reprinted Kuala Lumpur, 1966, 2 vols.

JACKSON, J. C., *Planters and Speculators*, Kuala Lumpur, 1968.

JACKSON, R. N., *Immigrant Labour and the Development of Malaya*, Kuala Lumpur, 1961.

JENKYNS, H., *British Rule and Jurisdiction beyond the Seas*, London, 1902.

JENNINGS, I. and YOUNG, S. M., *Constitutional Laws of the Commonwealth*, London, 1952.

JONES, S. W., *Public Administration in Malaya*, London, 1953.

JONG, P. E. DE J. DE, *Minangkabau and Negri Sembilan Socio-political Structure in Indonesia*, London, 1951.

KENDLE, J. E., *The Colonial and Imperial Conferences, 1887–1911*, London, 1967.

KHOO KAY KIM, *The Western Malay States, 1850–1873*, Kuala Lumpur, 1972.

KOEBNER, R. AND SCHMIDT, H. D., *Imperialism*, Cambridge, 1964.

Labour Research Department, *British Imperialism in Malaya*, London, 1926.

LANGER, W. L., *The Diplomacy of Imperialism*, New York, 1956, (2nd ed.).

LEGGE, J. D., *Britain in Fiji, 1858–1880*, London, 1958.

LIVINGSTON, W. S., *Federalism and Constitutional Change*, Oxford, 1956.

—— *Federalism in the Commonwealth*, London, 1965.

LOVAT, A., *The Life of Sir Frederick Weld*, London, 1914.

LOW, H., *Sarawak, its Inhabitants and Productions*, London, 1848.

McNAIR, J. F. A., *Perak and the Malays: Sarong and Kris*, London, 1878.

MAHAJANI, U., *The Role of Indian Minorities in Burma and Malaya*, Bombay, 1960.

MAKEPEACE, W., BROOKE, G. E. and BRADDELL, R. ST. J. (eds.), *One Hundred Years of Singapore*, London, 1921, 2 vols.

MARJORIBANKS, N. E. and MARAKAYYAR, A. T., *Report on Indian Labour Emigration to Ceylon and Malaya*, Madras, 1917.

MAXWELL, W. E., *Straits Settlements: Present and Future Land Systems*, Rangoon, 1883.

—— *Memorandum on the Introduction of a Land Code in the Native States in the Malay Peninsula*, Singapore, 1894.

MAXWELL, W. G. and GIBSON, W. S. (eds.), *Treaties and Engagements Affecting the Malay States and Borneo*, London, 1924.

MILLS, L. A., *British Rule in Eastern Asia*, London, 1942.

—— *British Malaya, 1824–1867*, with an introduction by D. K. Bassett and bibliography by C. M. Turnbull, Kuala Lumpur, 1966; first published as a monograph in *JMBRAS*, Vol. III, Part 2, 1925, and reprinted in *JMBRAS*, Vol. XXXIII, Part 3, 1960.

MEILINK-ROELOFSZ, M. A. P., *Asian Trade and European Influence in the Indonesian Archipelago between 1500 and about 1630*, The Hague, 1962.

MOUBRAY, G. A. DE, *Matriarchy in the Malay Peninsula*, London, 1931.

NAGLE, J. S., *Educational Needs of the Straits Settlements and Federated Malay States*, Baltimore, 1928.

NANJUNDAN, S., *Indians in the Malayan Economy*, New Delhi, 1950.

NEWBOLD, T. J., *Political and Statistical Account of the British Settlements in the Straits of Malacca, viz. Penang, Malacca, and Singapore, with a History of the Malayan States of the Peninsula of Malaya*, London, 1839; reprinted Kuala Lumpur, 1971, 2 vols.

NILAKANTA-SASTRI, A. N., *The Colas*, Madras, 1955.

OOI JIN BEE, *Land, People and Economy in Malaya*, London, 1963.

PARKINSON, C. N., *British Intervention in Malaya, 1867–1877*, Singapore, 1960.

PARMER, J. N., *Colonial Labor Policy and Administration: A History of Labor in the Rubber Plantation Industry in Malaya c. 1910–1941*, New York, 1960.

PURCELL, V., *The Chinese in Malaya*, London, 1948; reprinted Kuala Lumpur, 1967.

RAFFLES, T. S., *Memoir of the Life and Public Services of Sir Thomas Stamford Raffles . . .*, London, 1830.

RAJA ALI AL-HAJI RIAU, *Tuhfat al-Nafis*, Singapore, 1965.

RAJA CHULAN BIN RAJA HAMID, *Misa Melayu*, (ed.) R. O. Winstedt, Singapore, 1919.

RATHBONE, A. B., *Camping and Tramping in Malaya*, London, 1898.

READ, W. H., *Play and Politics, Recollections of Malaya by an Old Resident*, London, 1901.

14A

212   BIBLIOGRAPHY

ROBINSON, R. and GALLAGHER, J. with DENNY, A., *Africa and the Victorians, the Official Mind of Imperialism*, London, 1961.

ROBSON, J. H. M., *Records and Recollections, 1889–1934*, Kuala Lumpur, 1934.

ROFF, W. R., *The Origins of Malay Nationalism*, Yale, 1967.

—— (ed.), *Stories by Sir Hugh Clifford*, Kuala Lumpur, 1966.

SADKA, E., *The Protected Malay States, 1874–1895*, Kuala Lumpur, 1968; reprinted Kuala Lumpur, 1970.

SANDHU, K. S., *Indians in Malaya*, London, 1969.

SIDNEY, R. J. H., *In British Malaya Today*, London, n.d.

SMITH, T. E., *Population Growth in Malaya: A Survey of Recent Trends*, London, 1951.

SONG ONG SIANG, *One Hundred Years of the Chinese in Singapore*, London, 1922; reprinted Kuala Lumpur, 1967.

SWETTENHAM, F. A., *About Perak*, Singapore, 1893.

—— *The Real Malay*, London, 1900.

—— *Malay Sketches*, London, 1913.

—— *British Malaya, an Account of the Origin and Progress of British Influence in Malaya*, London, 1906; rev. ed., London, 1948.

—— *Footprints in Malaya*, London, 1942.

TARLING, N., *Piracy and Politics in the Malay World*, Melbourne, 1963.

THIO, E., *British Policy in the Malay Peninsula 1880–1910*, Kuala Lumpur, 1968.

TOMÉ-PIRES, *Suma Oriental*, trans. by Armando Cortesão, London, 1944, 2 vols.

TREACHER, W. H., *Notes of Visits to Districts in Selangor, 1894*, Kuala Lumpur, n.d.

TREGONNING, K. G., *Under Chartered Company Rule*, Singapore, 1958.

—— (ed.), *Malaysian Historical Sources*, Singapore, 1962.

—— (ed.), *Papers on Malayan History*, Singapore, 1962.

—— *A History of Modern Malaya*, Singapore, 1964.

—— *The British in Malaya*, Tucson, 1965.

TURNBULL, C. M., *The Straits Settlements 1826–1867: Indian Presidency to Crown Colony*, London, 1972.

TYLER, J. E., *The Struggle for Imperial Unity, 1868–1895*, London, 1938.

VETCH, R. H., *The Life of General Sir Andrew Clarke*, London, 1905.

WANG GUNGWU (ed.), *Malaysia, A Survey*, London, 1964.

WHEARE, K. C., *Federal Government*, London, 1953.

WHEATLEY, P., *The Golden Khersonese*, Kuala Lumpur, 1961.

WIJEYSINGHE, E., *A History of the Raffles Institution*, Singapore, 1963.

WILKINSON, R. J., *A History of the Peninsular Malays*, Singapore, 1923 (3rd ed., rev.).

—— *A Malay–English Dictionary*, Mytilene, 1932.

—— *Malay Beliefs*, Singapore, 1960.

—— (ed.), *Papers on Malay Subjects*, introduced by P. L. Burns, Kuala Lumpur, 1971.

WINSTEDT, R. O., *The Constitution of the Colony of the Straits Settlements and of the Federated and Unfederated Malay States*, London, 1939.

—— *The Malays, A Cultural History*, London, 1953.

—— *A History of Malaya*, London, 1962.

—— *Malaya and its History*, London, n.d.

WONG LIN KEN, *The Malayan Tin Industry to 1914*, Tucson, 1965.

WRIGHT, A. and CARTWRIGHT, H. A. (eds.), *Twentieth Century Impressions of British Malaya*, London, 1908.

WRIGHT, A. and READ, H., *The Malay Peninsula—A Record of British Progress in the Middle East*, London, 1912.

WYNNE, M. L., *Triad and Tabut: A Survey of the Origins and Diffusion of Chinese and Mohammedan Secret Societies in the Malay Peninsula, A.D. 1800–1935*, Singapore, 1941.

ZAINAL ABIDIN BIN ABDUL WAHID (ed.), *Glimpses of Malaysian History*, Kuala Lumpur, 1970.

(ii) *Articles and Pamphlets*

ALLEN, J. DE V., 'Two Imperialists', *JMBRAS*, Vol. XXXVIII, Part 1, 1964, pp. 41–73.

—— 'The Malayan Civil Service, 1874–1941: Colonial Bureaucracy/ Malayan Elite', *Comparative Studies in Society and History*, Vol. 12, No. 2, 1970, pp. 149–78.

ANON., 'Railways', in A. Wright and H. A. Cartwright (eds.), *Twentieth Century Impressions of British Malaya*, London, 1908, pp. 303–13.

ANON., 'Railway, Road and Shipping facilities in the Malay Peninsula', British Empire Exhibition, *Malayan Series Pamphlets*, No. XIX, London, 1924.

ANON., 'Early Days in Pahang', *British Malaya*, November 1929, p. 219.

ANON., 'Report of the Committee on the Constitution of the Federal Council', *British Malaya*, February 1927, pp. 4–7.

ARASARATNAM, S., 'Some Notes on the Dutch in Malacca and the Indo-Malayan Trade, 1641–70', *JSEAH*, Vol. 10, No. 3, 1969, pp. 480–90.

BANNER, H. C., 'The Growth of Education in Malaya', *The Asiatic Review*, Vol. XXVIII, No. 93, January 1932, pp. 103–7.

BASSETT, D. K., 'European Influence in the Malay Peninsula, 1511–1786', *JMBRAS*, Vol. XXXIII, Part 2, 1961, pp. 9–35.

―― 'The Historical Background', in Wang Gungwu (ed.), *Malaysia: A Survey*, London, 1964, pp. 113–27.

BASTIN, J. S., 'Sir Richard Winstedt and His Writings', in J. S. Bastin and R. Roolvink (eds.), *Malayan and Indonesian Studies*, Oxford, 1964, pp. 1–23.

―― 'Problems of Personality in the Reinterpretation of Modern Malayan History', in J. S. Bastin and R. Roolvink (eds.), *Malayan and Indonesian Studies*, Oxford, 1964, pp. 141–53.

BIRCH, E. W., 'Election and Installation of Tunku Muhammad as Yang di-Pertuan Besar', *JSBRAS*, No. 46, August 1906, pp. 6–22.

―― 'The Federated Malay States', *United Empire*, Vol. 3, 1912, pp. 376–87 and 444–52.

BLYTHE, W. L., 'Historical Sketch of Chinese Labour in Malaya', *JMBRAS*, Vol. XX, Part 1, June 1947, pp. 64–114.

BOGAARS, G., 'The Tanjong Pagar Dock Company', *Memoirs of the Raffles Museum*, No. 3, December 1956, pp. 1–274.

BOTTOMS, J. C., 'Malay Sources', in K. G. Tregonning (ed.), *Malaysian Historical Sources*, Singapore, 1962, pp. 36–62.

BOWEN, C. D., 'British Malaya As It Was', *Asiatic Review*, January 1950, pp. 896–910.

BROWN, C. C. (ed.), 'The Malay Annals', *JMBRAS*, Vol. XXV, Parts 2 and 3, 1952, pp. 1–276.

CALDECOTT, A., 'Jelebu, its History and Constitution', *PMS* II, No. 1, 1912, pp. 1–58.

•―― 'An Essay on Adat Perpateh in Negri Sembilan', *University of Ceylon Review*, Vol. 1, No. 1, April 1943, pp. 1–8.

CHEESEMAN, H. R., 'Education in Malaya, 1900–1941', *The Malaysian Historical Journal*, Vol. 2, No. 1, July 1955, pp. 30–47.

―― 'Education in Malaya', *Oversea Education*, Vol. VII, No. 4, July 1946, pp. 346–54; and Vol. VIII, No. 1, October 1946, pp. 391–400.

CLIFFORD, H., 'Life in the Malay Peninsula', *Proceedings of the Royal Colonial Institute*, Vol. 30, 1898–9, pp. 369–401.

—— 'British and Siamese Malaya', *Proceedings of the Royal Colonial Institute*, Vol. 34, 1902–3, pp. 45–75.

—— 'Miscellaneous Essays: Rival Systems and the Malayan Peoples', *North American Review*, Vol. 177, 1903, pp. 399–409.

COWAN, C. D. (ed.), 'Sir Frank Swettenham's Perak Journal', *JMBRAS*, Vol. XXIV, Part 4, 1951, pp. 1–148.

COWGILL, J. V., 'The System of Land Tenure in the Federated Malay States', *Malayan Agricultural Journal*, Vol. 16, 1928, pp. 181–93.

DRENNAN, H., 'A Short History of the Malay College', *Malay College Magazine*, Vol. 2, No. 5, 1955, pp. 8–15.

ELCUM, J. B., 'Education', in A. Wright and H. A. Cartwright (eds.), *Twentieth Century Impressions of British Malaya*, London, 1908, pp. 267–80.

GIBSON-HILL, C. A., 'Notes on the Series "Papers on Malay Subjects" ', *JMBRAS*, Vol. XXV, Part 1, 1952, pp. 194–9.

GULLICK, J. M., 'Sungei Ujong', *JMBRAS*, Vol. XXII, Part 2, 1949, pp. 1–69.

—— 'The Negri Sembilan Economy of the 1890s', *JMBRAS*, Vol. XXIV, Part 1, 1951, pp. 38–55.

—— 'A Careless Heathen Philosopher?', *JMBRAS*, Vol. XXVI, Part 1, 1953, pp. 86–103.

—— 'Captain Speedy of Larut', *JMBRAS*, Vol. XXVI, Part 2, 1953, pp. 4–103.

—— 'Kuala Lumpur, 1880–95', *JMBRAS*, Vol. XXVIII, Part 4, 1955, pp. 5–172.

—— 'The Malay Administrator', *The New Malayan*, Vol. 1, 1957, pp. 69–83.

HALE, A., 'On Mines and Miners in Kinta Perak', *JMBRAS*, No. 16, 1885, pp. 303–20.

HANDS, J., 'Malay Agricultural Settlement Kuala Lumpur', *The Malayan Historical Journal*, Vol. 2, No. 2, December 1955, pp. 146–61.

HARRISON, C. W. (ed.), 'Council Minutes; Perak 1877–1879', in R. O. Wilkinson (ed.), *Papers on Malay Subjects*, Kuala Lumpur, 1971, pp. 155–214.

INNES, J. R., 'The Malayan Civil Service as a Career', *National Review*, Vol. 77, March 1921, pp. 102–7.

—— 'The Protectorate System in the Malay States', *National Review*, Vol. 78, November 1921, pp. 398–406.

KHOO KAY KIM, 'Nineteenth Century Malay Peninsula—1', in Zainal Abidin bin Abdul Wahid (ed.), *Glimpses of Malaysian History*, Kuala Lumpur, 1970, pp. 50–6.

LAMB, A., 'Miscellaneous Papers on Early Hindu and Buddhist Settlement in Northern Malaya and South Thailand', *FMJ*, Vol. VI, New Series, 1961, pp. 1–90.

LINEHAN, W., 'A History of Pahang', *JMBRAS*, Vol. XIV, Part 2, 1936, pp. 1–257.

LOW, J., 'An Account of the Origin and Progress of the British Colonies in the Straits of Malacca', *JIA*, Vol. III, 1849, pp. 559–617.

—— 'On the Ancient Connections between Kedah and Siam', *JIA*, Vol. V, 1851, pp. 498–527.

MACGREGOR, I. A., 'Notes on the Portuguese in Malaya', *JMBRAS*, Vol. XXVIII, Part 2, 1955, pp. 5–47.

MACHIN, G. I. T., 'Colonial Post Mortem: a Survey of the Historical Controversy', *JSEAH*, Vol. 3, No. 2, 1962, pp. 129–38.

MAXWELL, G., 'The "New Policy" for the FMS', *British Malaya*, August 1926, pp. 101–10.

—— 'Sir John Anderson and Decentralisation', *British Malaya*, September 1926, pp. 133–6.

—— 'The Position of the High Commissioner in the Federated Malay States', *British Malaya*, October 1926, pp. 161–6.

—— 'Some Problems of Education and Public Health in Malaya', *United Empire*, Vol. XVIII, 1927, pp. 206–19.

—— 'The Constitutional Problems of Malaya', *Crown Colonist*, Vol. 2, August 1932, pp. 73–8.

—— 'The Malays and the Malayans', *The Nineteenth Century and After*, Vol. CXXXVII, No. 820, 1945, pp. 276–85.

MAXWELL, W. E., 'The Malay Peninsula: Its Resources and Prospects', *Proceedings of the Royal Colonial Institute*, Vol. XXIII, 1892–3, pp. 3–46.

—— 'Law Relating to Slavery among Malays', *JSBRAS*, No. 12, 1883, pp. 247–97.

—— 'The Law and Customs of Malaya with reference to the Tenure of Land', *JSBRAS*, No. 13, 1884, pp. 75–220.

MIDDLEBROOK, S. M., 'Yap Ah Loy', *JMBRAS*, Vol. XXIV, Part 2, 1951, pp. 1–127.

NG SIEW YONG, 'The Chinese Protectorate in Singapore', *JSEAH*, Vol. 2, No. 1, 1961, pp. 76–97.

PARR, C. W. C. and MACKRAY, W. H., 'History of Rembau', No. 56, 1910, pp. 1–157.

QUARITCH-WALES, H. G., 'Archaeological Researches in Ancient Indian Colonisation', *JMBRAS*, Vol. XVIII, No. 1, 1940, pp. 1–85.

RIGBY, J. 'The Ninety-nine Laws of Perak', *PMS* I, 1908.

SADKA, E., 'The Journal of Sir Hugh Low, Perak, 1877', *JMBRAS*, Vol. XXVII, Part 4, 1954, pp. 1–108.

——'The State Councils in Perak and Selangor', in K. G. Tregonning (ed.), *Papers on Malayan History*, Singapore, 1962, pp. 89–119.

SIDHU, J. S., 'Railways in Selangor, 1882–86', *JMBRAS*, Vol. XXXVIII, 1965, pp. 6–22.

SINGHAL, D. P., 'Some Comments on the Western Element in Modern Southeast Asian History', *JSEAH*, Vol. 1, No. 2, 1960, pp. 118–23.

SMAIL, J. W. R., 'On the Possibility of an Autonomous History of Modern Southeast Asia', *JSEAH*, Vol. 2, No. 2, 1961, pp. 72–102.

STONEY, B. O., 'The Malays of British Malaya', in A. Wright and H. A. Cartwright (eds.), *Twentieth Century Impressions of British Malaya*, London, 1908, pp. 222–8.

SWETTENHAM, F. A., 'Some Account of the Independent Native States of the Malay Peninsula', *JSBRAS*, No. 6, 1881, pp. 161–202.

—— 'Journal Kept during a Journey across the Malay Peninsula', *JSBRAS*, No. 15, 1885, pp. 1–38.

—— 'On the Native Races of the Straits Settlements and the Malay States', *Journal of the Royal Anthropological Institute*, Vol. XVI, 1886, pp. 221–9.

—— 'British Rule in Malaya', *Proceedings of the Royal Colonial Institute*, Vol. XXVII, 1895–6, pp. 273–312.

—— 'Malay Problems', *British Malaya*, May 1926, pp. 7–14.

—— 'The Legal Status of the Malay States. A Critical Analysis of Mr. Roland Braddell's Pamphlet', *British Malaya*, January 1932, pp. 243–7.

TARLING, N., 'British Policy in the Malay Peninsula and Archipelago, 1824–71', *JMBRAS*, Vol. XXX, Part 3, 1957, pp. 1–236.

THIO, E., 'The Extension of British Control to Pahang', *JMBRAS*, Vol. XXX, Part 1, 1957, pp. 46–74.

TREACHER, W. H., 'British Malaya', *Journal of the Society of Arts*, Vol. 55, No. 2, 1907, pp. 493–512.

TURNBULL, C. M., 'The Nineteenth Century', in Wang Gungwu (ed.), *Malaysia: A Survey*, London, 1964, pp. 128–37.

WHEARE, K. C., 'What Federal Government Is', *Federal Tracts*, No. 4, London, 1941.

WILKINSON, R. J., 'Literature: History', *PMS* I, 1907.

—— 'Law: Introductory Sketch', *PMS* I, 1908.

—— 'Council Minutes: Perak 1880–1882', *PMS* I, 1909.

—— 'Notes on Negri Sembilan', *PMS* I, 1911.

—— 'Sri Menanti', *PMS* II, 1914.

—— 'Some Malay Studies', *JMBRAS*, Vol. X, Part 1, 1932, pp. 67–137.

WINSTEDT, R. O., 'Education in Malaya', British Empire Exhibition, *Malayan Series Pamphlets*, No. XIV, London, 1924.

—— 'Negri Sembilan: The History, Polity and Beliefs of the Nine States', *JMBRAS*, Vol. XII, Part 3, 1934, pp. 41–111.

—— 'A History of Selangor', *JMBRAS*, Vol. XII, Part 3, 1934, pp. 1–34 and 112–14.

—— 'A History of Malay Literature', *JMBRAS*, Vol. XVII, Part 3, 1939, pp. 1–181; rev. ed., *JMBRAS*, Vol. XXXI, June 1958.

—— 'Kingship and Enthronement in Malaya', *JMBRAS*, Vol. XX, Part 1, 1947, pp. 134–42.

—— 'Richard James Wilkinson (1867—5 December 1941)', *JMBRAS*, Vol. XX, Part 1, 1947, pp. 143–4.

WINSTEDT, R. O. and WILKINSON, R. J., 'A History of Perak', *JMBRAS*, Vol. XII, Part 1, 1934, pp. 1–181.

ZAINAL ABIDIN BIN ABDUL WAHID, 'Glimpses of the Malaccan Empire—I and II', in Zainal Abidin bin Abdul Wahid (ed.), *Glimpses of Malaysian History*, Kuala Lumpur, 1970, pp. 18–26.

UNPUBLISHED WORKS

BURNS, P. L., 'The Constitutional History of Malaya with Special Reference to the States of Perak, Selangor, Negri Sembilan and Pahang, 1874–1914', Ph.D. thesis, University of London, 1966.

KANAGASABAPATHY, T. K., 'The Federal Council in Malayan Affairs', B.A. Hons. Academic Exercise, University of Singapore, 1961.

MALLAL, M. A., 'J. W. W. BIRCH: Causes of his Assassination', M.A. thesis, University of Malaya, 1952.

INDEX